D0338356

SHAM

◊◊◊◊

SHAM

How the Self-Help Movement
Made America Helpless

STEVE SALERNO

CROWN PUBLISHERS

Published in the United States by Crown Publishers, an imprint of the Crown Publishing Group, a division of Random House, Inc., New York.
www.crownpublishing.com

Crown is a trademark and the Crown colophon is a registered trademark of Random House, Inc.

Library of Congress Cataloging-in-Publication Data
Salerno, Steve.
SHAM : how the self-help movement made America helpless / Steve Salerno.—1st ed.
Includes bibliographical references and index.
1. Self-help groups. 2. Self-actualization (Psychology) 3. Recovery movement.
I. Title.
HV547.S23 2005
155.2—dc22 2004030951

ISBN 1-4000-5409-5

Printed in the United States of America

Design by Joseph Rutt

10 9 8 7 6 5 4 3 2 1

First Edition

To Mom and Dad—and the other members of their generation who, thank God, were codependent enough to put their kids first.

CONTENTS

SHAM

Introduction

HOPELESSLY HOOKED ON HELP

It's okay to eat meatloaf.

—*Sample inspirational thought from*
It's Okay to Be Happy, *by J. F. Mulholland*

Compared to the possibilities in life, the impossibilities are vastly more numerous. What I don't like to hear adults tell people your age is that you can be president or anything else you want to be. That's not even remotely true. The truth is that you can run for president, and that's all. . . . In our wonderfully free society, you can try to be just about anything, but your chances of success are another thing entirely.

—*Marilyn vos Savant,*
recognized by the Guinness Book of World Records
for Highest IQ, responding to a young person's letter
in her Parade *column, March 2, 2003*

In twenty-four years as a business writer and an investigative journalist, I have covered all kinds of "money stories." I have written about boondoggles on bankers' row and sleight of hand at Seventh Avenue fashion houses. I've written about the gyrations of the stock market as well as the myriad forces that surround, yet never quite explain, investing itself. I've written about money as it relates to sales, money as it relates to sports, money as it relates to music, money as it relates to love. It's safe to say that if it involves money, combined with some form of human aspiration, I've probably written about it.

Never, during all that time and reporting, have I encountered an industry whose story reads quite like the one at the heart of this book. It's a story that represents the *ultimate* marriage of money and aspiration (although the money invested so exceeds the fulfillment of the aspirations that the marriage probably should be annulled). Never have I covered a phenomenon where American consumers invested so much capital in every sense of the word—financial, intellectual, spiritual, temporal—based on so little proof of efficacy. And where they got such spotty, if not nonexistent, returns.

For more than a generation, the Self-Help and Actualization Movement—felicitously enough, the words form the acronym SHAM—has been talking out of both sides of its mouth: promising relief from all that ails you while at the same time promoting nostrums that almost guarantee nothing will change (unless it gets worse). Along the way, SHAM has filled the bank accounts of a slickly packaged breed of false prophets, including, but by no means limited to, high-profile authors and motivational speakers, self-styled group counselors and workshop leaders, miscellaneous "life coaches," and any number of lesser wisemen-without-portfolio who have hung out shingles promising to deliver unto others some level of enhanced contentment. For a nice, fat, nonrefundable fee.

Self-help is an enterprise wherein people holding the thinnest of credentials diagnose in basically normal people symptoms of inflated or invented maladies, so that they may then implement remedies that have never been shown to work. An entire generation of baby boomers searching desperately for answers to the riddle of midlife has entrusted itself to a select set of dubious healers who are profiting handsomely, if not always sincerely, from that desperation.

The self-help movement has not been a wholesale failure. Surely it provides some help to some people (albeit no more so than sugar pills provide help to some patients in controlled studies of investigational drugs). Here and there a marriage is saved, a parenting dilemma solved, a mental-health problem identified and eventually corrected as a result of advice imparted in a self-help product. Here and there. But for the most part, SHAM does not do what it promises. It is the emperor's new life plan.

That's actually being charitable about it. To describe SHAM as a waste of time and money vastly understates its collateral damage. To date, the industry has escaped intense scrutiny because even those who doubt its effectiveness regard self-help as a silly but benign pursuit, an innocuous vice that plays to the Jerry Springer set, and even then is taken to heart by only a small number of perpetual victims and defenseless dupes. Self-help's best-known critics—like Wendy Kaminer, author of *I'm Dysfunctional, You're Dysfunctional*—have mostly played it for laughs, offering up their barbs with a wink and a smile.

That is, in fact, SHAM's stealth weapon, the sinister secret of its success: Everyone underestimates it. You may think Dr. Phil is the greatest thing since sliced bread, or you may chortle at his braggadocio and his sagebrush sagacity. But almost no one *worries* about Dr. Phil. Like the rest of SHAM, he slips under the radar.

Self-help is everywhere and yet it's nowhere, seldom recognized for what it is: a contributing factor (at a minimum) to many of the problems now plaguing our society. It is almost impossible to reckon the full magnitude of what SHAM has done to America besides take its money—though this book will try. Whether you follow self-help's teachings or not, you have been touched by it, because SHAM's effects extend well beyond the millions of individual consumers who preorder Phil McGraw's latest book or attend Marianne Williamson's seminar-style love-ins. The alleged philosophies at the core of the movement have bled over into virtually every area of American social conduct and day-to-day living: the home, the workplace, the educational system, the mating dance, and elsewhere. Corporations spend billions of dollars each year on SHAM speakers, boot camps, wilderness outings, and any number of similar programs; increasingly they incorporate SHAM's beliefs into office protocols, mandating "enlightened" policies that add cost, offer no documented benefit, and may even work as *dis*incentives for quality, productivity, and morale. SHAM rhetoric has recently infected health care, too, spawning an aggressive new wing of alternative medicine that shoos people away from proven mainstream treatments by persuading them that they can cure themselves through sheer application of will.

In the most macro, cultural sense, the ongoing struggle between

SHAM's two polar camps—both of which this book will analyze in detail—has parsed the meanings of right and wrong, good and bad, winning and losing, while attaching entirely foreign connotations to once commonly understood terms like *family, love, discipline, blame, excellence*, and *self-esteem*. The implications of this for legislation, the judicial system, and public policy are about what you'd expect. One camp, *Victimization*, has eroded time-honored notions of personal responsibility to a probably irrecoverable degree, convincing its believers that they're simply pawns in a hostile universe, that they can never really escape their pasts (or their biological makeup). The other camp, *Empowerment*, has weaned a generation of young people on the belief that simply aspiring to something is the same as achieving it, that a sense of "positive self-worth" is more valuable than developing the talents or skills that normally win recognition from others. Those in this second category tend to approach life as if it were an endless succession of New Year's resolutions: It's always what they're *going* to do. Meanwhile, the months and years pass.

And the self-help onslaught continues. As the *New York Times* has reported, SHAM gurus aim to be in their followers' "kitchen cupboards, medicine chests, and gym bags, as well as their heads, coaching them to peak performance, 24/7."

It somewhat embarrasses me to admit that for a long time self-help slipped under my radar as well. For decades I have been tracking the self-help movement without fully realizing its place in the zeitgeist, even though I've written often about its component parts. My first book, in 1985, described the "mainstreaming" of veteran sales and motivational trainers like Tom Hopkins and Zig Ziglar, both of whom were then beginning to expand their brands; they were subtly turning their antennae away from hard-core salesmanship to the much airier patter of mass-market training, with its exponentially greater target audience. Their efforts signaled the beginning of what we now call "success training" or, in its more intensive, small-group settings, "life coaching."

During the late 1980s and 1990s I wrote separate magazine pieces about:

TONY ROBBINS. Today he's the Eighty Million Dollar Man (per year). Back at the beginning of his career, customers were paying as little as $50 apiece to learn how to "focus" enough to be able to walk over hot coals pain free (a bit of gimmickry that the debunker James Randi tells us has nothing to do with mental preparation and everything to do with the principles of heat conduction).

TOMMY LASORDA. By the mid-1990s the former Los Angeles Dodgers manager had become a huge draw on the banquet circuit, commanding at least $30,000 an hour for imparting such philosophical gems as "Ya gotta want it!"

THE PECOS RIVER LEARNING CENTER. At Pecos River, otherwise rational corporate citizens fully expected to buttress their self-confidence and negotiating skills by falling backward off walls and sliding down the side of a mountain on a tether.

PETER LOWE. In 1998 I covered one of the barnstorming impresario's weekend-long success-fests for the *Wall Street Journal*. I guesstimated the two-day take at $1.4 million, plus ancillaries. We'll get to the ancillaries in a moment.

In reporting these and other stories, I never quite recognized all those trees as a forest. I also watched, but didn't quite apprehend, as scholarship and complex thought fell to the wayside amid the influx of simple answers delivered via bullet points, as logic and common sense took a backseat to sheer enthusiasm and even something akin to mass hysteria.

What brought everything into focus for me was a career move of my own in mid-2000. For the ensuing sixteen months, I served as editor of the books program associated with *Men's Health* magazine, the glamour property in the vast better-living empire that is Rodale. In addition to publishing such magazines as *Prevention, Organic Gardening*, and *Runner's World*, Rodale had become the premier independent book publisher in the United States largely through its aggressive and ingenious mail-order books program. The company conceived, wrote, printed, and sold millions of self-help or other advice books each year. Thus, my experience there gave me a bird's-eye view of the inner workings of the self-help industry. Rodale's professed mission statement, as featured on its corporate Web site at the time of my arrival, was simple: "To show people how they can use the power of their bodies and minds to make their lives better."

At considerable expense, Rodale undertook extensive market surveys, the results of which dictated each business unit's editorial decisions. In the case of self-help books specifically, the surveys identified the customers' worst fears and chronic problems, which we were then supposed to target in our editorial content. One piece of information to emerge from those market surveys stood out above all others and guided our entire approach: *The most likely customer for a book on any given topic was someone who had bought a similar book within the preceding eighteen months.* In a way that finding should not have surprised me. People read what interests them; a devoted Civil War buff is going to buy every hot new book that comes out on the Civil War. Pet lovers read endlessly about pets.

But the Eighteen-Month Rule struck me as counterintuitive—and discomfiting—in a self-help setting. Here, the topic was not the Civil War or shih tzus; the topic was showing people "how they can use the power of their bodies and minds to make their lives better." Many of our books proposed to solve, or at least ameliorate, a problem. If what we sold worked, one would expect lives to improve. One would not expect people to need further help from us—at least not in that same problem area, and certainly not time and time again. At some point, people would make the suggested changes, and those changes would "take." I discovered that my cynicism was even built into the Rodale system, in the concept of *repurposing*—reusing chunks of our copyrighted material in product after product under different names, sometimes even by different authors.

Worse yet, our marketing meetings made clear that we counted on our faithful core of malcontents. (Another important lesson in self-help theology: SHAM's answer when its methods fail? You need more of it. You *always* need more of it.) One of my Rodale mentors illustrated the concept by citing our then all-time best-selling book, *Sex: A Man's Guide*. This individual theorized that the primary audience for *Man's Guide* did *not* consist of accomplished Casanovas determined to polish their already enviable bedroom skills. Our buyers were more likely to be losers at love—hapless fumblers for whom our books conjured a fantasy world in which they could imagine themselves as ladies' men, smoothly making use of the romantic approaches and sexual techniques we described. Failure and stagnation, thus, were central to our ongoing business model.

Failure and stagnation are central to all of SHAM. The self-help guru has a compelling interest in *not* helping people. Put bluntly, he has a potent incentive to play his most loyal customers for suckers.

Yet it's even worse than *that*. Much of SHAM actively fans the fires of discontent, making people feel impaired or somehow deficient as a prelude to (supposedly) curing them. One striking example comes from no less an insider than Myrna Blyth, a former *Ladies' Home Journal* editor. In her 2004 book, *Spin Sisters: How the Women of the Media Sell Unhappiness—and Liberalism—to the Women of America*, Blyth repents for her own role in an industry that was supposed to help women grow but instead wreaked incalculable harm on the psyches of its devoted followers. What women's magazines mostly have done, argues Blyth, is create and implant worry, guilt, insecurity, inadequacy, and narcissism that did not exist in women before the magazines came along.

PAYING THE (PIED) PIPERS

The American love affair with self-help is unmistakable in the sheer size of the SHAM fiscal empire. Granted, the movement's total cash footprint defies down-to-the-penny measurement. There's just too much of it out there, perpetrated to an increasing degree by independent life coaches or poor-man's Tony Robbinses giving small-ticket motivational speeches at the local Ramada Inn. But just what we know for sure is staggering. According to Marketdata Enterprises, which has been putting a numerical face on major cultural trends since 1979, the market for self-improvement grew an astonishing 50 percent between 2000 and 2004. This substantially exceeds the already robust annual growth figures Marketdata forecast in 2000. Today, self-improvement in all its forms constitutes an $8.56 billion business, up from $5.7 billion in 2000. Marketdata now expects the industry to be perched at the $12 billion threshold by 2008.

Remember—this is only what we can document. And it does not include the broader social and political costs, which we'll discuss separately.

Between thirty-five hundred and four thousand new self-help books appeared in 2003, depending on whose figures you use and precisely how you define the genre. The higher figure represents more than double the number of new SHAM titles that debuted in 1998, when wide-eyed social commentators were remarking at self-help mania and what it signified about the decline of premillennial Western civilization. Together with evergreens like *Codependent No More*, Melody Beattie's seminal 1987 tract on overcoming self-destructive behaviors, these books accounted for about $650 million in sales, according to Simba Information, which tracks publishing trends.

Self-help was well represented on best-seller lists in 2004, anchored by a spate of musings from the Family McGraw (Dr. Phil and son Jay); Rick Warren's *The Purpose Driven Life*; Joel Osteen's spiritually tinged *Your Best Life Now: 7 Steps to Living at Your Full Potential*; Greg Behrendt's cold shower for lovelorn women, *He's Just Not That into You*; and actualization demigod Stephen R. Covey's *The 8th Habit: From Effectiveness to Greatness*. The last is a sequel to Covey's blockbuster work, *The 7 Habits of Highly Effective People*, which remains a postmodern classic, as do Tony Robbins's various tomes about that giant who slumbers within you and the six dozen separate *Chicken Soup* books now in print. Stephen Covey, too, has a son, Sean, and Sean Covey has his very own best seller, *The 7 Habits of Highly Effective Teens*. Freshly minted guru-authors appear like clockwork each year.

They almost have to, if the demand is to be met. In fact, by 1983, so substantial were sales figures for books of this genre that the lofty *New York Times Book Review*, which for decades fought the good fight on behalf of books written by actual writers, threw in the towel and added another category, "Advice Books," to its distinguished best-seller list. In an accompanying announcement, *Times* editors explained that without this new category even the most compelling works of authentic nonfiction—memoirs, exposés, biographies, think pieces, and the like—might never appear on their own best-seller list. They were being swept aside by this massive wave of self-improvement. Ten years later, a study quoted in *American Health* magazine said that self-help addicts—and *addict*, evidence suggests, is the right word—continue to buy books "long after their shelves are stocked." *Publishers Weekly* put it this way in October 2004: "Self-help books are a Teflon category for many booksellers. No matter the economy or current events, the demand is constant."

Another cultural signpost: A fair percentage of these book-buying transactions take place at the five thousand New Age bookstores now spread throughout the United States. (Industry sources thought the New Age trend had peaked a few years ago, when the number of stores hit four thousand.) Thus it should come as no surprise that the fastest-growing self-help sectors are also the softest and least utilitarian. Sales of inspirational, spiritual, and relationship-oriented programs and materials constitute a third of overall SHAM dollar volume and are tracking upward. The more brass-tacks stuff—business and financial materials, tactical training—constitute 21 percent and are tracking down. Americans seem to think it's more important to get along than to get ahead.

For today's budding self-help star, the usual progression is to parlay one's pseudoliterary success into a thriving adjunct career on TV or radio, on the lecture circuit, or at those intensive multimedia seminars known to the industry as "total immersion experiences." According to Nationwide Speakers Bureau founder Marc Reede, whose specialty is booking engagements for sports celebrities, "personal-improvement experts" account for no small part of the *9,000 percent* increase in membership in the National Speakers Association since 1975. Just the top dozen speakers grossed $303 million in 2003; their fees generally ran between $30,000 and $150,000 per speech. More than a decade after her ethereal book *A Return to Love* dominated best-seller lists, Marianne Williamson's personal appearances still sell out as quickly as Springsteen concerts. Mass-market single-day presentations by Tony Robbins must be held in basketball arenas and convention centers. He attracts upwards of ten thousand fans at $49 a head—still a bargain-basement price for salvation when compared to his weeklong Life Mastery seminar at $6,995. "You have to have something for all the market segments," Robbins once told me. "You can't ignore the folks who can only afford a quick dose of inspiration." By 1999, more than a decade of having something for all market segments had paid off big-time for Robbins; *Business Week* pegged his annual income at $80 million.

It was the lure of such lucre that sparked the mainstreaming phenomenon among Hopkins, Ziglar, and other training specialists from fields closely allied to sales and motivation. Ziglar, the author of arguably the most successful "crossover" book ever written, *See You at the Top*, now preaches to thousands of eager disciples at his sky's-the-limit tent revivals. (Herewith a free sample of the indispensable advice Ziglar offers to husbands: "Open your wife's car door for her." And, as an added bonus, a bit of all-purpose wisdom: "You have to *be* before you can *do*, and you have to *do* before you can *have*.") Suze Orman followed Ziglar's lead as well as his advice and soared to the top: Starting with a background in institutional finance, she mastered the art of talking about money in a way that sounded as if she was really talking about "something more meaningful." She then threw in a dollop of spirituality for good measure and became a touchstone for millions of women who'd always felt unwelcome at the financial party.

A truly hot SHAM artist may franchise himself. Relationships guru John Gray presides over just a handful of the estimated five hundred monthly "Mars and Venus" seminars that bear his imprimatur. The rest he entrusts to a cadre of handpicked stand-ins who can parrot his kitschy trademark material. And then there are the barnstormers, like the aforementioned Peter Lowe, who took the seminar industry to another level by packaging a number of speakers into themed motivational road shows. His evangelical tours teamed an improbable rotating cast of eclectic presenters, ranging from former United Nations ambassador Jeane Kirkpatrick to actor Edward Asner to professional football coach Mike Shanahan. They also featured a formidable, at times almost overwhelming, menu of ancillary products.

Ah, the ancillaries. All major seminarists reap a substantial added windfall from their so-called ancillary products: the $10 workbooks, the $19 videos and DVDs, the $49 series of CDs and cassettes for the car, to give you that all-important motivational jolt during the commute to work. To keep the good vibes flowing once you're ensconced at your desk with your misanthropic boss hovering over you, there are the inspirational trinkets, like those $29 paperweights engraved with uplifting slogans. Robbins occasionally takes time out from his usual seminar patter to hawk unrelated products—like QLink, a pendant that, he says, will protect you from cell-phone radiation, electromagnetic pulse, and other types of harmful ambient energy. The pendant costs anywhere from $129 for the bare-bones model to $839 for a version finished in brushed gold—the perfect complement for one's newly gilded self-image. Tom Hopkins, at one time the unquestioned dean of trainers in the field of real-estate sales, now depends on his low-cost success seminars to generate sales of his ancillary goods. The modest fee for the seminar is Hopkins's loss leader for an array of high-margin products.

Topping it all off are the miscellaneous do-it-yourself "personal-enhancement" products and "revolutionary new technologies!" sold via infomercial. Dale Beyerstein, a philosophy professor who has written extensively on pseudoscience, argues that the customary formula calls for taking a modicum of legitimate research and "piggybacking" onto it—that is, extending and misapplying its conclusions in a way that's just plausible enough to skirt criminal sanctions by the Federal Trade Commission or the U.S. Postal Service. The hubris of some of these pitches—not to mention the contempt for the consumer—almost defies description. For a while during the 1980s, a company called Potentials Unlimited was selling subliminal audiotapes to cure deafness.

Which begs the question: What has America gotten in return for its $8.56 billion investment?

The answer: There is no way of knowing. So much money, so few documented results.

Yes, SHAM gurus have no trouble producing the obligatory testimonial letters, the heartrending anecdotal stories of women who found the courage to leave abusive men or men who found the courage to face up to the demons within. But in any meaningful empirical sense, there is almost no evidence—at all—for the utility of self-help, either in theory or in practice. There's only one group of people we can prove benefit from the books: the authors themselves.[1]

For example, as Martin Seligman, a past president of the American Psychological Association, told *Forbes* in 2003, though some of Tony Robbins's preachments may be worth listening to, they remain altogether untested—despite the unambiguously rosy claims made for Robbins's material and the quasi-scientific pretense of the material itself.

Actually, that's not quite true. A growing body of evidence *challenges* SHAM's ability to do what it says. For one thing, despite all the talk of personal empowerment, limitless potential, and a world in which glasses are always at least half full, Americans have become ever more dependent on chemical modification. Almost four decades after Thomas A. Harris's landmark self-help tract *I'm OK—You're OK*, we live in a culture in which some of the most profitable products made are named Prozac, Paxil, and Xanax. Evidently a great many Americans don't think they're all that "OK." In the final analysis, it's not the thousands of seminars or millions of books with their billions of uplifting words that Americans seem to count on to get them through the day. *It's the drugs.*

That's no great shock to Archie Brodsky, a senior research associate for the Program in Psychiatry and the Law at Harvard Medical School. "Psychotherapy has a chancy success rate even in a one-on-one setting over a period of years," observes Brodsky, who coauthored (with Stanton Peele) *Love and Addiction*. "How can you expect to break a lifetime of bad behavioral habits through a couple of banquet-hall seminars or by sitting down with some book?"

Brodsky alludes to twelve-step recovery meetings, which don't often feature celebrity speakers or hordes of pricey ancillary products but do have a strong and loyal following nonetheless. The twelve-step movement developed as an outgrowth of Alcoholics Anonymous and now encompasses programs for a staggering range of problems, whether compulsive shopping, or loving too easily or too much, or overeating. These days, if it's a problem for someone, somewhere, it's a treatable disorder. And a support group likely exists for it. At the apex of the Recovery phenomenon, in 1992, *American Demographics* reported that twelve million Americans belonged to at least one of the nation's five hundred thousand support-group chapters.

Americans for some reason assume that Recovery groups work, when in fact there is little or no hard evidence of their ability to help people recover from anything, as this book will document. Consider, for the time being, this one fact: The results of a 1995 study conducted by Harvard Medical School indicated that alcoholics have a better chance of quitting drinking if they *don't* attend AA than if they *do*. Americans seldom hear about such results, in part because AA and its sister organizations have actively opposed independent research that could test their programs' effectiveness.

The dearth of good science can be recognized throughout SHAM. In her revealing book *PC, M.D.: How Political Correctness Is Corrupting Medicine*, psychiatrist Sally Satel complains bitterly about the faulty (or nonexistent) research underlying the nostrums and home remedies that contemporary SHAM artists preach. "We have a generation of healers who unflinchingly profess to know everything that's good for everybody," Satel told me in an interview. "They make no distinctions between science, pseudoscience, and pure fantasy. They liberally dispense their dubious prescriptives as if they'd been blessed by an NIH double-blind study." Tony Robbins, for example, contends that diet is an integral part of a successful lifestyle—not an eyebrow-raising notion, except that he goes on to counsel his audiences on the "energy frequency" of popular foods. The energy frequency of Kentucky Fried Chicken, for example, is "3 megahertz." Satel knows of no such food term and has no idea what it could possibly mean in any case. I checked with Yale University's Dr. Kelly Brownell, one of the nation's foremost experts on diet and nutrition. He was similarly mystified.

This is not to say that all SHAM rhetoric is patently false. In fact, there are whole categories of self-help precepts that can't possibly be disputed. That's because they're *circular*—the guru who espouses them is saying the same thing in different ways at the beginning and end of a sentence. The conclusion merely restates the premise.

Here's a perfect illustration, from Phil McGraw's *New York Times* number one best seller *Self Matters*: "I started this process by getting you to look at your past life, because I believe that the best predictor of future behavior is past behavior. That being true, the links in the chain of your history predict your future." The "that being true" makes it sound as if McGraw is rousing to some profound conclusion. But he isn't. The part after "that being true" merely repeats what he said in the first sentence, with slightly altered wording. It's not a conclusion at all. It's what logicians call a tautology. I am reminded of Larry Bird's priceless response to an interviewer who besieged the Indiana Pacers executive with statistics. The reporter demanded to know what Bird made of them and what they implied about the Pacers' chances in an upcoming play-off series. "All I know," Bird replied wearily, "is that we win 100 percent of the games where we finish with more points than the other guy."

Other SHAM kingpins, or ambitious pretenders, achieve a certain contrived plausibility by using puffed-up, esoteric-sounding jargon. In August 2004, Dan Neuharth, PhD, the author of *Secrets You Keep from Yourself: How to Stop Sabotaging Your Happiness*, told the readers of the magazine *First for Women* that "avoidance is a knee-jerk response to a core fear that threatens your ego." Translation: We avoid things we're really afraid of.

Far too often, the SHAM leaders delivering these pompous philosophies of life and living have no rightful standing to be doing any such thing. "There's a tendency on the reader's part to think these people are unimpeachable authorities speaking gospel truth," says Steven Wolin, a professor of psychiatry at George Washington University. "That's hardly the case." In truth, writes Wendy Kaminer in *I'm Dysfunctional, You're Dysfunctional*, the only difference between a self-help reader and a self-help writer may be "that the writer can write well enough to get a book deal." In Kaminer's view, the end result is that consumers make sweeping changes in their lives based on "something their aunt or auto mechanic could have told them."

By the time the most powerful woman in American media plucked him from obscurity and conferred the Oprah Touch, Phil McGraw had given up on clinical psychology, in part because, he later said, he was "the worst marital therapist in the history of the world." But McGraw, at least, holds a degree to practice what he now preaches. As we'll see, others of similar SHAM stature hail from far less convincing backgrounds; they proclaim themselves "relationship therapists" or "dating coaches," made-up specialties that require no particular licensing yet *sound* credible, thus duping unsuspecting patrons by the millions. At meetings of Alcoholics Anonymous and other support groups, the leader's sole credential may consist of his being in recovery from whatever the specific addiction is. Society, again, seems to think this makes good sense. I would ask two questions: Isn't it possible that fellow sufferers are a bit too close to the problem to lead effectively and impartially? And if your problem was, say, that the electrical fixtures in your house were acting funky, would you really want a workshop taught by some other homeowner who couldn't get his lights to work right (and who, by his own admission, still *had the problem*)? Or would you want a trained electrician?

In today's SHAM marketplace, individuals who stumbled into celebrity sans talent, or who managed to "conquer adversity" entirely by accident, now collect hefty fees for talking up their experiences as if they'd planned the whole thing out as an inspirational crucible. Get stuck on a mountain for a while, lose some body parts, and *presto!*—instant motivational icon. I refer to Beck Weathers, the Texas pathologist who lost his nose, his right hand and part of his left hand, and nearly his life in the notorious May 1996 Mount Everest disaster that was chronicled in Jon Krakauer's *Into Thin Air*. Weathers, now in his late fifties, travels the lecture circuit, expounding on the theme of "surviving against all odds." You wonder, though: How many people live in situations that are truly analogous to what Beck faced up on the mountain? For that matter, what role did any of Weathers's own actions play in his survival? According to Krakauer, Weathers was like a hapless pinball bounced around the mountaintop for sixteen hours, and he almost surely would have died if others hadn't helped him down the treacherous slopes at significant risk to themselves, and if his wife had not arranged for a dangerous helicopter rescue. (To be blunt about it, Weathers probably had no business being up on that mountain in the first place, as Krakauer himself strongly implies.) So what do we learn from a Beck Weathers? Tellingly, he informs his admiring audiences that "Everest, in many ways, was one of the best things to happen to me." At $15,000 per speech, he's not kidding. Even pathologists don't make that kind of money.

The bizarre case of Beck Weathers boldfaces the huge question mark that punctuates so much of SHAM doctrine and its myriad applications. The sitcom *Seinfeld*, in the famous words of its creator and title character, was a "show about nothing." Much the same could be said of SHAM. To a disconcerting degree, it is an $8.56 billion social crusade about nothing. It is a religion whose clerics get very, very rich by stating the obvious in a laughably pontifical fashion. As Anne Wilson Schaef, best known for her book *Co-Dependence: Misunderstood—Mistreated*, informs us in a later work, *Living in Process*, "Life is a process. We are a process. The Universe is a process."

To which a cynic might add: Making airy, asinine statements meant to impress or hoodwink gullible people is also a process.

NO WAY OUT

In the summer of 1993 the *Los Angeles Times Magazine* sent me to Santa Fe, New Mexico, to do a story on the Pecos River Learning Center. Now a part of the vast Aon Consulting network, Pecos River was the brainchild of former NFL cornerback, car dealer, and motivational superstar Larry Wilson; it was the most well regarded of the faddish boot camps then surreally popular among the Fortune 500. Even leading software companies were sending their befuddled, sunshine-averse developers to Santa Fe to climb trees and fall backward off walls into their comrades' waiting arms—all for about $4,000 a head. Wilson promised that such activities would pay off in esprit de corps, consensus building, and self-reliance. (And how did Wilson reconcile *self-reliance* and *consensus building*, two core goals that would seem to be at least potentially incompatible? I asked and got a rambling, obfuscatory 650-word reply that was not usable in my story.)

The climax of the Pecos River program came with its infamous zip line, a sharp half-mile descent from a rocky cliff to ground level via cable, which participants executed one by one, dangling and sliding like runaway human ski lifts. I stood at the bottom of the line and interviewed the shrieking, hyperventilating outdoor adventurers as they reached terra firma. My most memorable exchange took place with a real-estate salesman I'll call Eric.

"You look pretty stoked," I told him.

"Oh man," Eric replied. "That was something."

"Pretty exhilarating stuff?"

"Definitely."

"You think it's gonna help you sell more homes?"

"Oh yeah."

"How?"

This time he had no ready answer. He just looked at me, his breath settling back to normal, his smile giving way to a grimace. I stood there holding my mini cassette recorder aloft in the New Mexico air, which seemed to have chilled considerably. He didn't want to have to think too hard about the experience. I was raining on his parade. This impromptu interview occurred toward the end of my visit to Pecos River, by which time I recognized Eric's reaction as a knee-jerk proclivity among participants and staffers alike. Wilson himself, earlier in the week, had characterized the dividends of his program as "largely inexpressible. You sense that something inside you has clicked over. You can't articulate it. You just have to go with it."

Minutes seemed to pass before Eric finally stammered, "I don't know how, but I'm sure it will." And he turned and walked away.

I don't know how, but I'm sure it will.

To its credit, Pecos River, in contrast to most of SHAM, has tried to measure the effectiveness of its programs. Its follow-up studies do appear to show improvement, particularly among larger sales outfits. But most of the quoted results reflect "soft" improvements: "People are willing to make mistakes in order to get where we want to go"; "There's a greater sense of the big picture"; "The alignment to total operational objectives is focused and condensed and the effectiveness and mood of the team has risen exponentially."

You don't see "hard," balance-sheet testimonials, such as "Sales jumped 92 percent!" Almost any motivational effort pays short-term dividends in morale. This is common in sales organizations. But the euphoria doesn't last, and it seldom shows up demonstrably in the bottom line, because the motivational effort *hasn't changed anything specific about the manner in which people go about their jobs*. Perhaps workers do feel more inclined to produce when their employers pay attention to them. Perhaps these efforts do cheer people up for a while, and cheery people tend to work harder and longer. So what? The same effect might be achieved by taking the staff out for dinner and drinks once a month. A top sales trainer I knew, Danielle Kennedy, used to argue precisely that. "Don't blow the budget on high-priced boot camps," Kennedy liked to say. "Just do little nice things for your people on a more frequent basis. It's cheaper, and you don't have to worry about ticks."

Clearly many criticisms can be lodged against the organized, entrepreneurial SHAM juggernaut. We'll be discussing them in detail in the course of this book. But if the movement has a most egregious, overarching sin, it's the climate of false hope it has unflaggingly promoted and sold to a nation desperate for answers—a nation made vulnerable by that very desperation. *I don't know how, but I'm sure it will.* At this moment, across America, millions of hopeful Erics and Ericas are repeating those words in various forms, dutifully droning their affirmations each morning, telling themselves that what they're saying and doing is bound to make life better, richer, fuller, less scary. And how, exactly, will this wondrous transformation happen? What is the mechanism, the link between their self-talk and the course their lives may take? (And while we're on the subject, what if the folks they hope to beat out for that promotion are also home repeating affirmations of their own?) Never mind! Those are the questions SHAM artists teach you never to ask, because to even entertain such doubts reveals a negative attitude, and lord knows you can't achieve *anything* in this life without your positive mental attitude. Unless, that is, you've entrusted yourself to a guru who's selling Victimization. In that case, you're *supposed* to think ill of yourself. And somehow, by accepting the fact of your powerlessness, you'll gain the upper hand in life. Got it?

So stop asking. Just keep repeating and affirming, and buying those books, and watching those shows, and writing those checks for all those seminars—and when you get there, by gosh, remember to buy that gold-plated pendant!—and one day we'll all meet in the Kingdom of Happy. Over meatloaf, if you like.

PART ONE

◇◇◇◇

THE CULPRITS

1

◇◇◇◇

HOW WE GOT HERE—WHEREVER *HERE* IS

If you're reading it in a book, folks, it ain't *self*-help. It's *help.*

—*Comedian George Carlin*

As a concept, self-help is no Tony-come-lately.

The term *self-help* was not coined as a synonym for psychobabble. It has a long and rich tradition of usage in connection with far more reputable practices in the realm of law. Legal self-help refers to a raft of situation-specific remedies available to a complainant directly—that is, without involving lawyers or even courts. This facet of American jurisprudence, in marked contrast to the type of self-help this book mostly tackles, has always been about *action*, not words. Remedies of this nature are formal step-by-step procedures designed to bring about lawful satisfaction for the individual. Properly handled, they enjoy full courtroom standing, should they later be challenged by those on the receiving end. Some of America's most familiar legal instruments include self-help provisions. Depending on the state in which you live, your auto loan may contain a clause that stipulates your banker's right to simply come out to your driveway and retrieve your car the minute you fall into arrears on payments.[1] That is legal self-help.

Some of the earliest self-help books were written in this vein. In "300 Years of Self-Help Law Books," a fascinating piece for the Web site of the legal publisher Nolo, Mort Rieber tells us that as early as 1784 the book *Every Man His Own Lawyer* was already in its ninth edition here in America, after original publication in London. *Every Man*, writes Rieber, was touted as "a complete guide in all matters of law and business negotiations for every State of the Union. With legal forms for drawing the necessary papers, and full instructions for proceeding, without legal assistance, in suits and business transactions of every description." The book may have been one of the self-help industry's first best sellers. According to Rieber, *Every Man*'s author, John Wells, states in his introduction that the first edition "was prepared and presented to the public many years ago and was received with great favor, attaining a larger scale, it is believed, than any work published within its time." So-called layman's law was a hot publishing genre. Rieber reports that from 1687 to 1788, every law book published in America was intended for use by laypeople, not lawyers.

Even in psychiatric settings, *self-help* didn't, and doesn't, always refer to the softer, frothier stuff of Drs. Phil and Laura. Serious-minded clinicians use the term to describe efforts by mentally or emotionally impaired patients to live independent, productive lives. A sizable contingent of the psychiatric industry is engaged in this cause, and legitimate practitioners bristle at the pejorative ring the term *self-help* has acquired in recent decades.

In a sense, the currently popular conception of self-help also dates back to colonial times. It's not far-fetched to propose that Benjamin Franklin wrote the first American SHAM book—1732's *Poor Richard's Almanack*, with its bounty of homespun witticisms. Advice columnists and others offering "tips for better living" have been with us more or less continuously ever since. Two genuinely historic works flowered from the spiritual dust bowl of the Depression, and in the same year, no less: 1937 saw the publication of Napoleon Hill's *Think and Grow Rich* as well as Dale Carnegie's *How to Win Friends and Influence People*, which many still consider *the* quintessential self-help book. For sheer longevity, it's hard to argue. On a September day some sixty-six years after its publication, *How to Win Friends* still came in at number ninety-nine in Amazon.com's sales rankings. Sales haven't been hurt by the book's prominence in Dale Carnegie Courses taught by an army of twenty-seven hundred facilitators worldwide. Corporate trainers will tell you that the book is as relevant today as it was in 1937. Another landmark self-help tract in the Carnegie mold was Norman Vincent Peale's *The Power of Positive Thinking*, published in 1952.

Significantly, though, until the advent of modern self-help, and with the handful of exceptions just noted, writers usually saw themselves as mere conduits of information, not experts in their own right. When she started her column in the 1950s, even the supremely opinionated "Dear Abby," Abigail Van Buren (given name: Pauline Friedman Phillips), would invoke recognized authorities in addressing readers' questions. "Abby's" real-life sister, Ann Landers, also relied on outside experts; Landers "had a Rolodex to kill for," according to Carol Felsenthal, one of her biographers. M. Scott Peck, the psychiatrist whom some rank with Carnegie as a seminal force in modern self-help, felt compelled to source and footnote his signature 1978 work, *The Road Less Traveled.* Peck credited many of his key concepts to such "name" forebears as Jung and Freud, and he bulwarked his opinions with ample excerpts from scholarly journals.

Then, in 1967, came the revolution that Carnegie's book had foreshadowed: the rise of the guru, the transformation from simple advice giver to cultural and motivational soothsayer. That year witnessed the publication of psychiatrist Thomas A. Harris's smash hit *I'm OK—You're OK*, which transformed self-help in three critical respects. First, it answered any remaining questions about the viability of self-help publishing as an ongoing genre. Second, it refocused psychology's lens: Harris sought less to make sense of the individual per se than to make sense of the way that individual functioned in, and was shaped by, relationships—a pursuit that has occupied virtually all of self-help, as well as a good deal of standard psychology, ever since.[2] Third and most important, although Harris strained for an upbeat tone and always insisted that he intended his book as a blueprint for happier living, the overriding inflection was that most people *aren't* OK. The author explicitly posited that the average person is damaged early in childhood and walks around thereafter in a paranoid, self-pitying state Harris called "I'm *not* OK, you're OK." (Harris's other three basic states of relational being were "I'm not OK, you're not OK"; "I'm OK, you're not OK"; and—hallelujah—"I'm OK, you're OK.")

It would be unfair to hold Harris personally responsible for all that happened in his book's wake. But this much is certain: The melancholic view of people and personality set forth in *I'm OK—You're OK* succinctly captured the sense of Victimization that dominated self-help—and, to no small degree, American culture—for the next quarter century.

A WORLD OF VICTIMS

Victimization.

Some readers, especially recent arrivals to the self-help arena, might be surprised to see that term associated with the movement. The most visible and successful proponents of today's self-help are not out of the Thomas Harris mold. Dr. Phil McGraw, Tony Robbins, and their various imitators spend little time wringing their hands over the childhood traumas that leave one ill equipped for coping with life. They more closely resemble Dale Carnegie and Norman Vincent Peale, who, long before it became an army recruiting slogan, were essentially screaming, "Be all that you can be!"

But, in fact, the self-help movement still divides, roughly, into two camps.

There is *Empowerment*—broadly speaking, the idea that you are *fully* responsible for *all* you do, good and bad.

And, in contrast, there is *Victimization*, which sells the idea that you are *not* responsible for what you do (at least not the bad things).

Victimization and Empowerment represent the yin and the yang of the self-help movement. It is likely that this schism will always exist, no matter which guru or message becomes the flavor of the day. Further, it's important to realize that *visibility* is not the same as *influence*; though one or the other side may seem to go underground at any given time, its effects continue to be felt, sometimes in seismic fashion.

While nothing as wide-ranging and multifaceted as SHAM follows a neat time line, clearly after Thomas Harris's success and the rise of self-help publishing, Victimization held sway for more than twenty years, from the late 1960s through the 1980s. The earlier of those two end points, of course, represents more than a date. The 1960s were and are an *ethos*, a time conjured in words and phrases that remain freighted with personal disillusionment and cultural discord to this day: Vietnam. Integration. The Sexual Revolution. Turn On, Tune In, Drop Out. In a society that seemed to be losing its bearings, the narrative of Victimization, with its backstory writ of excuses and alibis, appealed to growing numbers of Americans.[3] Whether the climate of rising social unrest fueled the culture of blame or the culture of blame helped fuel the unrest, the two currencies undoubtedly catalyzed each other, with an explosive effect on the average person's understanding, or misunderstanding, of his relationship to the outside world.

This is not to say that all of the Americans who began flocking to self-help during the late 1960s embraced Victimization. Just a few years after Thomas Harris encouraged people to dwell on their child hood traumas, Werner Erhard touted a regimen known as "est," in which trainers would literally scream obscenities at followers in an effort to bully them past their hang-ups to a higher, more tough-minded plane of "beingness."[4] But est remained on the fringe. It was too quirky, and its chief architect too flaky, to capture the popular imagination. Besides, like other upstart regimens that sold unabridged Empowerment, it depended on a worldview that was out of sync with what most people could plainly see happening around them. (Arguing for full control of one's destiny was not easy in the era of the draft.) On the contrary, Victimization's success—then as now—was that it appealed to, and indeed legitimized, the human tendency to feel sorry for one's self.

But above all, Victimization thrived because there existed a ready-made template for reaching out to—and inside of—people. It was a template that already enjoyed some respect, one that, the movement's leaders soon realized, could be cloned and applied to almost any problem. It offered not just explanations but also the precious hope of recovery from whatever ailed or troubled you. That template was the twelve-step program of Alcoholics Anonymous (AA).

The twelve-step approach spawned an entire submovement—*Recovery*—that has profoundly influenced not just SHAM but society as a whole. The specific twelve steps are generally credited to Bill Wilson (the much-mythologized "Bill W."), a salesman and contemporary of

Dale Carnegie who in 1935 cofounded AA with a proctologist/surgeon, Robert ("Dr. Bob") Smith. Wilson was an interesting character—among other things, an inveterate spiritualist who fancied Ouija boards and regularly conversed with the dead. After starting AA, Wilson and some of the organization's early members codified the steps of Recovery in the book *Alcoholics Anonymous*. With minor variations in nuance as well as some adaptations to fit changing mores, the twelve steps have remained pretty much the same ever since, regardless of the specific problem being "treated."

All members of Recovery groups have engaged in the following twelve steps:

1. Admitted they were powerless over their addiction—that their lives had become unmanageable.

2. Came to believe that a Power greater than themselves could restore them to sanity.

3. Made a decision to turn their will and their lives over to the care of God as they understood God.

4. Made a searching and fearless moral inventory of themselves.

5. Admitted to God, to themselves, and to another human being the exact nature of their wrongs.

6. Were entirely ready to have God remove all these defects of character.

7. Humbly asked God to remove their shortcomings.

8. Made a list of all persons they had harmed, and became willing to make amends to them all.

9. Made direct amends to such people wherever possible, except when to do so would injure them or others.

10. Continued to take personal inventory and when they were wrong promptly admitted it.

11. Sought through prayer and meditation to improve their conscious contact with God as they understood God, praying only for knowledge of God's will for them and the power to carry that out.

12. Having had a spiritual awakening as the result of these steps, they tried to carry this message to other addicts, and to practice these principles in all their affairs.

If you've had little exposure to the twelve steps, you may be surprised at the religiosity of the foregoing. In truth, through the years, while the steps have remained fairly constant, Recovery's "tone" has grown more secular, featuring greater emphasis on a generic "Power" and less overt mention of God per se. This is particularly true of twelve-step programs that originated in the antiestablishment 1960s, as God fell out of fashion and twelve-step impresarios understood that by hewing so closely to the old spiritual line, they risked alienating their target audiences. Some of today's most "progressive" twelve-steps fudge the issue by arguing that the higher power is something that resides in a person's untapped "spiritual consciousness."

But no matter who or what the "Power" is, kneeling before it is integral to the twelve steps. "'The overriding message is that your own will is basically what got you into this mess in the first place, which is why you have to surrender it," Steven Wolin, a professor at George Washington University and a practicing psychiatrist, told me. "In a sense, the argument is that in order to salvage yourself, you have to surrender yourself."

Bill W. and his twelve-step program symbolized a revolutionary outlook on a problem—alcoholism—that had long been treated as a character flaw or moral failing. Since a character flaw or moral failing wasn't normally seen as something you'd "recover" from, like chicken pox, AA's twelve-step method represented a landmark moment in America's appraisal of addictions. Despite the twelve steps' discussion of "defects of character," the unmistakable implication was that alcoholics had *a disease*. By the late 1960s, that new way of looking at alcoholism had gained institutional support from both the American

Psychiatric Association and the American Medical Association. At this point, all it took to pave the way for the SHAM juggernaut was someone to expand the validity of those assumptions and treatment concepts beyond alcoholics.

Enter Thomas Harris. Pre-Harris, the tendency to excuse one's own faults or blame them on others was seen as a character flaw in itself. The particular genius of *I'm OK—You're OK* and the books it inspired was that such works broadened the context: Suddenly it wasn't just alcoholics who were dogged by self-destructive tendencies they could not control or even fully explain. Victimization became socially permissible, if not almost fashionable in certain circles. (If you didn't confess to being haunted by the demons of your past, you were "in denial.") If Harris could be believed, almost *all* of us had something we needed to "recover from." Thomas Harris took Victimization mainstream.

Its moorings sunk in notions of Recovery, Victimization theory was embraced by a loose coalition of pop psychologists, social scientists, and academics. Often citing Harris, as well as his mentor, Eric Berne, they sought to explain every human frailty as a function of some hardwired predisposition or inescapable social root: You were basically trapped by your makeup and/or environment and thus had a ready alibi for any and all of your failings. As Wendy Kaminer observes in *I'm Dysfunctional, You're Dysfunctional*, Victimization encouraged people to find fatalistic patterns—and the rationalizations they afforded—everywhere: "Grandfather was an alcoholic, mother is a compulsive rescuer, Uncle Murray weighs 270 pounds. Father is a sex addict, your sister is anorexic . . ." Within the movement, a teapot tempest raged over whether the real culprit was nature or nurture, or what degree of each. But both camps arrived at the same philosophical end point: You were helpless against the forces that made you what you were.

Consequently, Victimization told people to stop beating themselves up: No one wants to make hurtful mistakes, but we're human, and as Alexander Pope told us, humans err. *You gotta let go of all that guilt!* You didn't make yourself this way, so *it's not your fault*. After all, wasn't the very first step out of twelve an admission of *powerlessness*? Victimization framed guilt as a bad thing, which, by implication if not definition, also framed conscience as a bad thing.

By extension, the message became *Your needs are paramount here. It's all about you.* Recovering a healthy sense of self entailed forsaking your excessive or unhealthy concern for others—for in the twelve-step universe, such excessive concern came to constitute the pitiable emotional quagmire of *codependency*. (As we will see later in the book, by the concept's heyday in the late 1980s, the term would be applied to just about every interpersonal relationship that fell short of sheer bliss.)

In their eagerness to provide additional mechanisms for overcoming guilt and self-loathing, the Victimization movement's spiritual leaders made an important discovery: They could help a constituent better cope with the burden of his failings by *redefining* them. This insight led to clever semantic distinctions that either made the untoward behaviors sound tamer or, following Bill W.'s example, framed those shortcomings as actual medical or psychological conditions. Such artful use of language became a hallmark of the self-help movement and had dramatic repercussions far beyond the world of SHAM. Under this guiding principle, which became known as the "disease model" of bad or unproductive behavior, the roster of newfound conditions naturally mushroomed. Drug abuse, sex addiction, compulsive eating, compulsive lying, compulsive shopping, compulsive gambling—eventually these problems and many others were deemed diseases.

With Victimization's momentum thus established, and new books and gurus debuting as fast as publishers could sign the deals, it hardly seemed to matter that this widespread application of the disease model struck some knowledgeable observers as offhand and implausible. In *PC, M.D.*, Dr. Sally Satel indicts the American Psychiatric Association, factions of the American Medical Association, and allied interests for scrapping hard science in favor of political correctness. "They arbitrarily devised convenient syndromes and talked about them as if they were uncontested medical fact," Satel told me. "It didn't matter whether there was any clinical evidence for it. It fit the behavioral model they had adopted." Further, according to Satel, as the feminist movement picked up steam, premenstrual syndrome and postpartum depression, once the punch lines of male-chauvinist jokes, became fodder for earnest debate, then viable defenses in homicide trials. It wasn't long, she says, before women as a class were conditioned to think of themselves as slaves to this hormonal governance.

Politicians and their operatives also saw the possibilities here. They stirred the pot, adding to the sense of disenfranchisement among already disgruntled factions while reinforcing their feelings of oppression and entitlement. *The government owes you. Society owes you. They made you this way.* Again: *It's not your fault.* Inexorably, such notions began to undermine clear-cut judgments about morality, since blame was being shifted from the people who transgressed to the people who (allegedly) *caused* the transgression. Even murderers sometimes ceased to be murderers and instead became *victims* of the conditions that made them murder. After a Jamaican immigrant, Colin Ferguson, shot twenty-five Long Island Railroad commuters, killing six, on December 7, 1993, Ferguson's attorneys broached a novel "black-rage" defense, claiming that years of white oppression had driven him to the edge of insanity. Ferguson ultimately rejected the defense, decided to represent himself, and was convicted—but the case sparked ongoing discussions of black rage and its sociological effects, with the Reverend Al Sharpton and others insisting on the legitimacy of the concept.

THE EMPOWERERS STRIKE BACK

The black-rage defense represented the mentality "Dr. Laura" Schlessinger had in mind when, long before George W. Bush, she ignited controversy by observing, "There is evil in the world, and giving it a different name doesn't make it less evil." Notions of good and evil, right and wrong, have grown steadily more difficult to apply, even define, since SHAM got involved.

Schlessinger emerged as part of the early backlash against Victimization, and surely became its most strident voice. But while members of the nascent Empowerment movement claimed they were promoting a more liberating and responsible view of human nature, they had difficulty getting people to relinquish the moral relief that Victimization afforded. The gospel of Victimization gave its followers easy outs for ugly behavior; it also made questions of guilt or innocence eye-of-the-beholder judgments—and in the end made such judgments largely irrelevant anyway. If individuals were driven by dark circumstances and barely remembered (but irresistible) forces from childhood, how could they be blamed for whatever stupid or immoral acts they committed along the way?

This was an extraordinarily appealing message that critics of Victimization found impossible to overcome with half measures. The Empowerment camp had to create a form of sloganism that was as seductive as Victimization's. "We are a very *doing* society," Dr. Michael Hurd, the author of *Effective Therapy* and one of psychology's canniest observers, told me. "People buy self-help books because they're looking for answers. The extreme views tend to produce books with bullet points and catchy titles that sell. . . . In general, people in our culture don't want to think through complex issues. They want to know, 'What do I *do*?'" And when that's the need you're trying to meet, says Hurd, "There's going to be a tendency to oversimplify."

Thus, Empowerment developed a new message: "You're not powerless—you're omnipotent!" Under the rules of Empowerment, you were the sovereign master of your fate and could defeat any and all obstacles in life.

So were these second-stage gurus knowingly disingenuous? Promising more than they knew they could deliver? Here Hurd treads delicately. "It's possible that some of them have been disingenuous," he told me, "but you don't like to think that it's all about making money." He concedes that the developing self-help industry was "a real test of integrity for the psychiatric profession." Whatever their degree of sincerity, the fathers of Empowerment—soon joined by the keepers of political correctness and by opportunistic (if barely credentialed) SHAM gurus—trotted out their own clever semantics, in this case designed to make people feel unconstrained by anything. The handicapped or disabled became "special" or "differently abled." Homes wracked by divorce and other domestic upsets became "nontraditional households."

The tenor could not have differed more from that of Victimization, but the goal was the same: eradicate the problem by couching it in destigmatizing language.

Far from merely affecting how America spoke, these semantic shifts inevitably determined how America thought and felt about the circumstances they described. David Blankenhorn, founder and president of the Institute for American Values and the author of *Fatherless America*, told me, "There's no question that one subtle change in terminology—replacing *unwed* with *single* before the word *mother*—altered the way society perceived the condition itself. It made out-of-wedlock pregnancy so much more palatable to a generation of women, and the nation."

Ultimately, despite its own excesses, Empowerment would not do away with Victimization or even stunt its growth very much. As we'll see in more detail in chapter 8, even today, if you can't stop smoking or snorting or stealing or gambling or having sex with people who are wearing a ring you didn't give them, it's probably not because you're weak, venal, or decadent. It's because you *can't help yourself*. The stalker who knifed tennis great Monica Seles during a match avoided jail time because the judge was moved by his confession of his obsessive love for Seles's rival Steffi Graf.

Though the Empowerment camp now gets most of the coverage (and profits), Empowerment and Victimization represent a pair of formidable estuaries flowing from the same river. They exist side by side on bookshelves, and sometimes exist side by side in the same self-help expert. Joseph Jennings, a former gangbanger who has fashioned a thriving speaking career out of his squalid past, tells his inner-city scholastic assemblies "you can be anything you want"—but that if they fail, "it's the legacy of slavery."

Two generations after *West Side Story*'s "Gee, Officer Krupke" poked fun at psychiatric cop-outs, that same core principle—what ails you is beyond your control—remains alive and (un)well. But paradoxically, it's been joined by a second belief: There's not a *thing* wrong with you, and you can have it all, if you just go for it with gusto!

SHAM LAND

In his brilliant book *Fat Land*, Greg Critser points out that more than a generation's worth of faddish weight-loss programs have served only to produce the fattest generation of Americans on record. (Not insignificantly, weight-loss programs have become, in essence, self-help programs, especially now that both Phil McGraw and John Gray are actively involved.) So, too, almost four decades after *I'm OK—You're OK*, one wonders what happened to all the self-improvement this mountain of help was supposed to bring about.

Certainly SHAM's debut in the 1960s coincided with a period wherein the nation began to make great strides in race relations, the glass ceiling, and other barometers of overall social health. America today "feels like" a more enlightened place in which to live than America in 1960: We conduct ourselves with greater sensitivity to the feelings of those around us. We communicate more openly and productively with our spouses and friends. We're better at raising our children—or, at least, we give a whole lot more thought to it than did our parents and particularly their parents, who raised kids by the seat of their pants, seldom sparing the rod.

But anyone who watches the news knows that not all of the changes in American society have been positive, and that even some of the "positive changes" may have more to do with redefining the bad things than with actually making them better. When you get away from the pleasant-sounding spin, the statistics are far less encouraging.

Divorce in 1960 claimed about a quarter of all marriages. Today it claims about half. Although thankfully that statistic is trending back down, American marriages have the highest known failure rate in the world. It can be argued, and has been by feminists, that increased divorce isn't necessarily a bad thing. People in general, and women in particular, no longer feel compelled to suffer dismal unions in silence. The rising tide of women's rights and opportunities, combined with other societal support factors, has given restless wives the initiative and optimism to leave the kinds of marriages with which their counterparts from prior generations "made do."

But how many Americans walk out the door because they no longer feel compelled to suffer *so-so* marriages in silence? Worse, how many Americans has SHAM conditioned to *think* their marriages are so-so, when in reality they're pretty normal?

Nowadays, young marrieds of both genders may be a tad *too* focused on their own fulfillment, with catastrophic effects for domestic tranquillity. I first interviewed David Blankenhorn for a magazine assignment in 1988, and he told me, "I think people today are less forgiving in relationships, and more inclined to walk at the drop of a hat." He made an interesting point about the famous JFK quote "Ask not what your country can do for you . . ." and its relevance to a wholesale change in society's perspective on the institution of marriage. "In years past," Blankenhorn told me, "getting married was more of a selfless act. You did it in order to build something bigger than you—a family—and to be able to give what you could to the children of that union." That's all changed, he said: "People today go into a marriage expecting to a far greater degree to have their own needs met. Instead of giving *to* the marriage, they want much more *from* the marriage. And often what they want is unrealistic." It's hard to see such mental turnabouts as anything other than a consequence of SHAM-bred "insights." Indeed, it may not be coincidence that the greatest jump in American divorce, postwar, came between 1975 and 1990, a fifteen-year period that roughly corresponds to the most feverish SHAM activity. (At the same time, more and more Americans are turning to SHAM gurus for advice on matters of the heart, which makes relationships one of the largest segments of the self-help movement, as we will see later in the book.)

Whatever the ultimate truth here, there's one group of Americans who don't have the luxury of considering the matter with academic detachment: children. As a direct result of all this coupling and uncoupling, 45 percent of American children today live in "nontraditional households." One child in three is born to an unmarried mother. The figure in 1960 was one child in *twenty*, adding credence to Blankenhorn's observation about the semantics of unwed parenthood. An alarming number of those mothers are teenagers. To understand the larger consequences of divorce and illegitimacy, consider just this one statistic: According to the Bureau of Justice Statistics, 72 percent of incarcerated juveniles come from single-parent households.

Standardized test scores tell us that when kids from "nontraditional households" go to school, they do not learn as much as they should—but neither do their peers from intact families. Here, we may be seeing more bitter fruit from another SHAM tree: self-esteem-based education (a topic we'll explore in detail in chapter 10). For these and related reasons, school discipline is not what it once was, and school violence is a national embarrassment. To be sure, pernicious forces besides SHAM are at work, but events like the Columbine massacre would've been "unthinkable" back in the days before schools lost their way, as Christina Hoff Sommers wrote in a 2000 issue of the *American Enterprise*. Before school administrators began worrying about everything except their mission of helping to raise technically competent, morally centered students.

Speaking of attitudes and behaviors that once were unthinkable: In 1960, would a man who got drunk, broke into an electrical substation, and grabbed hold of a transformer that filled him with thirteen thousand volts have even considered suing the power company? That's exactly what Ed O'Rourke of Tampa, Florida, did in March 2000. O'Rourke also sued the six bars and liquor stores that sold him booze on the fateful night. His lawsuit claimed that he was "unable to control his urge to drink alcoholic beverages."

O'Rourke's case was no anomaly. On May 3, 2000, Seong Sil Kim threw herself in front of a speeding Manhattan subway car. She later collected $9.9 million from the city because the train, instead of killing her, merely amputated her right hand and inflicted assorted other injuries. And, of course, there is the now-infamous McDonald's coffee spill. While riding in her son's sports car in February 1992, Stella Liebeck of Albuquerque, New Mexico, spilled the coffee in her lap. She sued the fast-food giant, claiming the coffee was too hot. When a jury initially awarded her $2.9 million, many commentators pointed to the case as a fitting symbol of wasteful litigation and what one writer called the "death of common sense." In fact, the case was more complicated than it was sometimes made to appear, and the award was later reduced to "only" $640,000. Still, the reasoning of jurors like Betty Farnham is compelling: Explaining why McDonald's was at fault, Farnham told the *Wall Street Journal*, "They were not taking care of their customers." As if people aren't responsible for realizing on their own that hot coffee is hot.

As a highly regarded trial lawyer told me, "These cases would've been laughed out of court during the fifties, if anyone even had the balls to bring the suit." While such lawsuits may be extreme examples, they do indicate that for all the recent talk about "empowerment," America in 1960 was a more *genuinely* self-reliant place than America today.

Further testimony: In her tell-all book *Spin Sisters*, Myrna Blyth, a former editor of *Ladies' Home Journal*, admits that far from empowering women, the nominally feminist industry in which she worked has eroded women's confidence by sending negative message after negative message. Blyth describes her experience of thumbing through women's magazines of the "June Cleaver" era and being shocked at how "tough and resilient" those magazines assumed women to be. Whatever 1950s American women lacked in education and financial independence, Blyth argues, they more than made up for it in their ability "to cope with whatever hardship they had to face." Yet today, after decades of nonstop exposure to an editorial mentality that makes them feel fat, out of style, sexually inadequate, and prone to every new psychic malady or invented disease that comes down the pike, women feel far less power over their domains, Blyth argues.

If America of 1960 was a more self-reliant place, it was also, evidence suggests, a safer, more harmonious place. The U.S. homicide rate has declined in very recent years, but at 5.6 murders for every 100,000 members of the population in 2002, it loitered about 10 percent above where it stood throughout the mid-1960s—an era we then lamented as the height of urban unrest. Not just that, but when today's perpetrators are brought to trial, they're more likely to be acquitted because of the introduction of evidence that once would have been considered extraneous. Even Alan Dershowitz, a defense lawyer par excellence, conceded in his book *The Best Defense* that "almost all criminal defendants are, in fact, guilty." Nonetheless, Paul Pfingst, a former prosecutor and San

Diego district attorney, told me, "Guilt often gets obscured nowadays by all sorts of issues about *how* they turned out that way and *why* they did what they did."

All of which begs two questions:

(1) If self-help is so effective at what it's supposed to do, then why is there so much evidence that Americans, and the society they inhabit, are so screwed up?

Some have argued that things would be even *worse* without self-help; no doubt they imagine a nightmarish world in which *every* marriage ends in divorce, and crime sprees claim the lives of *all* teens in any given city on any Friday night. This is not to say that the self-help movement is directly responsible for all the problems around us: Any number of variables have conspired to tear at the social fabric over the past generation. But as we will see in Part Two of this book, SHAM exacerbated some of those variables. And in any case, the self-help movement, if it works, should have been able to make some major areas of human interaction measurably better than they used to be. Wasn't that SHAM's founding covenant with individuals and society? Didn't it promise to make things better? Make America happier? Make life more rewarding and stress-free? That simply hasn't happened. Which leads to the next question:

(2) What if it's actually SHAM that's screwing people up?

If SHAM simply induced individuals to waste their money on self-help books and seminars that don't dramatically change their lives for the better, we as a society wouldn't really have that much of a problem. Granted, many SHAM artists bear a closer resemblance to con artists; and worse, sources that millions of Americans trust—think Oprah Winfrey and the *Today* show—lend legitimacy to gurus' self-help programs. But a close investigation of the self-help movement leads to even more troubling questions about its larger consequences. While social trends arise from a complex set of circumstances, SHAM doctrine has so pervaded our culture—from our schools to our offices to our homes and even to our hospitals—that we have to confront the role it has played in what's happened in our society since SHAM took root.

Does it not make sense that a society in which everyone seeks personal fulfillment might have a hard time holding together? That such a society would lose its sense of community and collective purpose? That the self-centered individuals who compose that society would find it difficult to relate to, let alone make sincere concessions to, other self-centered individuals?

Yet SHAM artists and their apologists refuse to accept responsibility for the collateral damage self-help does to society. That's no surprise, really, given that they refuse to be held accountable even when they harm the very individual consumers whom they lure in with grand promises of transformation, happiness, and success. Invariably, in fact, they project the blame back *on* the individual. For example, Zig Ziglar, a seminarist extraordinaire, will tell his audiences, "There's no immunity to the disease of self-doubt. It's always in there, waiting to flare up again!"

Therein lies the beauty of it all, from the guru's point of view. If SHAM doesn't transform your life, it's not because the program is ineffective. It's because *you're unworthy.* Victimization-based formats make this point unflinchingly, telling participants whose lives remain stagnant that they are slaves to their dysfunctions, that they'll have to invest more effort if they hope to rise above their innate handicaps. And so you go away thinking, *Well, maybe the next book or seminar will do the trick. Or the next after that . . .*

Surprisingly, Empowerment subscribers are no better off in this regard. Empowerment preaches that you can achieve whatever you set out to achieve, that success is a function of desire and/or commitment. But there is an inescapable converse: that failure is a function of a *lack* of desire and/or commitment. In its purest form, Empowerment admits no circumstances that are unresponsive to the human will. Every shortfall in achievement must be accounted for somehow. And if it's not the program's fault, or the guru's fault . . . then whose?

Whether you're plagued by inner demons you can never quite exorcise (as Victimization intones) or by your demonstrated inability to "conquer all" (as Empowerment insists you must), you arrive without fail at the same despairing place: the dismal state of woe-is-me-ism.

2

◇◇◇◇

FALSE PROPHETS, FALSE PROFITS

Titans in the field may preach self-reliance, but the self-help industry thrives on repeat business.

—New York Times

In a highly entrepreneurial industry that grosses $8.56 billion annually, a comprehensive listing of all the practitioners and pretenders, and their assorted channels of delivery, would be impossible. Consider that trailblazing figures like Dale Carnegie, Napoleon Hill, Norman Vincent Peale, and Thomas A. Harris still play a role in today's SHAM marketplace, even posthumously. Other significant figures include the seminarist Jim Rohn and the late, great super-salesman Og Mandino, who generate little buzz nowadays except among cliques of true believers but who had as much to do with SHAM's core rhetoric as Tony Robbins. Mandino's *The Greatest Salesman in the World* (1968), despite its parochial-sounding title, examined the whole landscape of human motivation and is another of publishing's great "crossover" success stories. One also thinks of quirky L. Ron Hubbard and his *Dianetics*, which posited that all human failure and frustration stemmed from the so-called reactive mind, in which agglomerated pain was stored and then "used against you" later. Despite its shaky scientific foundations, Hubbard's work spawned not just a New Age movement but also a quasi-religion: the Church of Scientology, conspicuously embraced by A-list entertainment celebrities including John Travolta and Tom Cruise.

Some SHAM artists enjoyed flashes of brilliance hot enough to rate a mention in the movement's epidemiological history, though they've lost greater or lesser amounts of their luster since they emerged on the scene.

RICHARD CARLSON. Today, all but the most avid Carlson fans probably wouldn't know the name, but there's no forgetting his signature book: 1997's *Don't Sweat the Small Stuff . . . and It's All Small Stuff.* It wasn't the first time anyone said it, but Carlson elevated the bumper-sticker banality to a cultural rallying cry. The holder of a PhD in psychology, Carlson had written more than a dozen modestly performing self-help books before he scored big with *Small Stuff*, which enjoyed a stunning two-year run on best-seller lists. No dummy, he followed it up with *Don't Sweat the Small Stuff for Women, Don't Sweat the Small Stuff at Work, Don't Sweat the Small Stuff for Teens, The Don't Sweat Affirmations*, and *The Don't Sweat Guide for Couples*. In 2003 he tried something different: *What About the Big Stuff?*

DEEPAK CHOPRA. A decade ago, Chopra's beatific face was everywhere. An endocrinologist by trade, Chopra has been a key figure in the New Age movement since the mid-1980s, but he launched himself to the top of the heap with his 1994 SHAM classic, *The Seven Spiritual Laws of Success*. Over the next few years the uncommonly versatile guru weighed in on everything from astrology to preventive medicine to spiritually enriching golf. He also sold teas and spices, soothing music, and assorted wellness products, and ran a pricey health spa in California. A powerful literary agent told me that Chopra simply spread himself too thin and "burned out his audience." Still, his books continue to sell rather well, if not at the level of *The Seven Spiritual Laws of Success*.

JACK CANFIELD. Together with his coauthor/editor Mark Victor Hansen, Canfield, a motivational speaker and self-styled godfather of self-esteem, conceived what *Time* magazine eventually would label "the publishing phenomenon of the decade" for the 1990s: the endlessly segmented *Chicken Soup for the Soul* book series, now with seventy-two books in print in English alone. Notable recent entries include *Chicken Soup for the Horse Lover's Soul, Chicken Soup for the Prisoner's Soul*, and *Chicken Soup for the NASCAR Soul*.[1] The original book's manuscript was famously rejected by thirty-three publishers during its first month of circulation alone before tiny Health Communications picked it up. Sales of *Chicken Soup* books have leveled off somewhat from their initial peaks, but the brand has become an industry in its own right.

ROBERT FULGHUM. Fulghum is the one-hit-wonder author of *All I Really Need to Know I Learned in Kindergarten* (1988), a sweet but forgettable paean to minimalism about which the brilliant social critic Wendy Kaminer wrote, "Only people who die very young learn all they need to know in kindergarten." For a time the book made Fulghum a superstar on the SHAM circuit; he got deals for several subsequent books, none of which quite matched the success of the first.

A handful of SHAM luminaries, however, have achieved such eye-popping success that they have affected not just the course of the movement but American culture itself. Accordingly, their careers tell us as much about ourselves as they do about them. Two of these megastars, Tony Robbins and Phil McGraw, merit their own chapters in this book. Four others who gained prominence in the 1990s and retained their lofty position into the twenty-first century include radio host and author Dr. Laura Schlessinger, relationship adviser John Gray, author and lecturer Marianne Williamson, and personal financial expert Suze Orman.

One other observation must be made here. It's no coincidence that three of the four shot to the top of the heap after being blessed by the person who, though not formally part of the self-help movement, is as responsible as anyone for its ascendancy: Oprah Winfrey. Winfrey's ability to single-handedly make or break a book (or a perfume, or a hotel, or a vacation destination, or a car line, or a diet, or beef) by now is common knowledge. But few observers have given her appropriate credit (if that's the right term) for legitimizing self-help in American society. Those whom Oprah smiles upon get the full force of her billion-dollar corporation, Harpo Productions, behind them. They're granted repeat guest spots on her show, where they can schmooze her 22 million viewers. They're offered guest columns if not regular bylines in her magazine, where they can put their names and faces and expertise in front of her 2.7 million readers. They get priceless value-added PR when she mentions them in casual conversation with an interviewer or gives them an outright endorsement during the course of a show. They may become adjuncts to her Personal Growth Summit, a Winfrey-sponsored barnstorming spectacular.

The trajectories of Gray, Williamson, and Orman offer unmistakable evidence of why *Time* anointed Winfrey one of the most influential people of the twentieth century.

DR. LAURA—HER WAY

What to make of a doctor who isn't a doctor . . . an Orthodox Jew who isn't an Orthodox Jew . . . a crusader against pornography whose naked come-hither image is splashed all over the Internet . . . a critic of premarital and extramarital sex who's indulged in both . . . a champion of family values who was so far removed from her own mother's life that she didn't even know it had ended till months later?

All of this self-contradiction exists in one person, the nonpareil "Dr. Laura" Schlessinger.

Schlessinger rose to fame on a platform of moral clarity, vowing to undo the damage wreaked by SHAM's Victimization wing, which gave followers an endless supply of self-serving rationalizations to use in excusing dissolute behavior. She told her listeners to take responsibility for what they did and to accept the consequences of their mistakes. She favored adoption, not abortion. She wanted couples to actually marry before having kids, or even having sex, and expected American mothers to assign a higher priority to caring for their children than ensuring they had just the right shoes to wear to work with that new Donna Karan outfit. Introducing herself each day, she would say her name, followed by "and I am my kid's mom," an in-your-face reproach to feminism and its contempt for domesticity. Millions embraced her message, which seemed long overdue in postmodern America. And if Schlessinger frequently went overboard in reproving her callers, branding them *bums* and *sluts* and *pigs* and *shack jobs*—well, who phoned whom?

But Schlessinger also has become a striking and, in some ways, tragicomic poster girl for everything that's wrong with SHAM: how its practitioners play fast and loose with the truth, ignore rules they mandate for others, put entertainment value before true helpfulness, and prize their own careers above all else. Moreover, the rise and not quite fall of Dr. Laura Schlessinger underscores how people desperate for solutions—or just a "higher power" to entrust themselves to—overlook untidy loose ends in order to allow themselves to go right on believing.

Schlessinger's holier-than-thou persona has taken some serious hits since the spring of 1998, when *Talkers* magazine, a trade publication covering talk radio, ranked *The Dr. Laura Show* number one on the airwaves, surpassing even the mighty Rush Limbaugh. In those days an estimated 250,000 listeners tried to get through on her show each week, while another 20 million tuned in to shake their heads over the woes of those who did. Schlessinger's clout and cachet were such that in 1997, when she opted to sell the ownership of her three-year-old syndicated show, Jacor Communications ponied up a staggering $71.5 million.

Schlessinger's books, too, flew off the shelves. At the apex of her popularity she was Amazon.com's most "preordered" author, thanks to her canny, highly accessible "10 Stupid Things _____ Do to Mess Up Their _____" formula. She followed up 1994's *10 Stupid Things Women Do to Mess Up Their Lives* with *10 Stupid Things Men Do to Mess Up Their Lives, 10 Stupid Things Couples Do to Mess Up Their Relationships*, and *Stupid Things Parents Do to Mess Up Their Kids* (released originally as *Parenthood by Proxy: Don't Have Them If You Won't Raise Them*, the latter a patented Schlessingerism that has won her no friends at the National Organization for Women). Having exhausted the "stupid things" motif, she began writing books more forthrightly linked to her growing absorption in Judaism: *How Could You Do That?! The Abdication of Character, Courage, and Conscience* and *The Ten Commandments: The Significance of God's Laws in Everyday Life*. Then came the children's books: *But I Waaant It! Why Do You Love Me? Growing Up Is Hard*, and *Where's God?*

By the time the last few titles saw print, however, America's most unabashed pop moralist had been humbled by a succession of scandals. The worst was the Internet publication of the nude photos in the fall of 1998, courtesy of radio personality Bill Ballance, the ex-mentor and -lover who gave Schlessinger her start. As harmful as the photos were Schlessinger's coy efforts at damage control; in a temporary injunction she simultaneously claimed that (a) the woman in the pictures wasn't her and (b) she owned the copyright to the photos. Barely had that firestorm begun to abate when Schlessinger made a series of on-air comments about homosexuals that left even some opponents of gay rights shifting in their seats. She told one gay caller that her lifestyle was "unholy," and during later remarks intended to quell the mounting controversy, she described homosexuals as a "biological error."

Then came the family tragedy. At the end of a Friday show on December 20, 2002, stunned listeners heard Schlessinger announce that her mother had been found murdered. According to police reports, the seventy-seven-year-old woman, who lived alone in a Beverly Hills condo, had been dead a long time. Granted, Schlessinger had made no secret of their estrangement, which she blamed on her mother's aloofness. Yet her oft-given admonition to "honor thy father and mother" seemed gruesomely out of sync with the image of Yolanda Schlessinger lying dead for months and her celebrity daughter not even missing her.

For not a few, the scandals changed the perception of Schlessinger's over-the-top behavior toward callers, making her sound less like a zealous apostle of good and more like a mean-spirited hypocrite. This would take its toll among the faithful. At this writing her show is syndicated to 300 stations, down from a peak of 471. The unpleasantness also helped derail her TV show for Paramount, which appeared and disappeared in the span of a year. But beyond that, people began to look more closely at Dr. Laura herself. What they discovered has implications for anyone who feels himself falling under the spell of a SHAM guru.

Among other things, Dr. Laura's critics learned that she wasn't even a psychologist. This no doubt came as a shock to the 75 percent of Schlessinger's audience who, according to a survey reported by the *Washington Post* in December 1997, "think she is a psychologist, psychiatrist or therapist." Schlessinger does hold a PhD from Columbia University—in physiology.[2] The California Board of Behavioral Science Examiners reserves the title "doctor" for medical doctors and professors in the field of clinical psychology, and the use of a doctorate from one field to convey credibility in another is considered unethical in most professional disciplines. Schlessinger received a certification in Marriage, Family, and Child Counseling (MFCC) from the University of Southern California and set up a practice in 1981, but she has not kept that credential active.

Schlessinger also turned out to be a woman with a morally undisciplined history. She had a habit of stealing the hearts of older authority figures, not all of whose hearts, and other physical paraphernalia, were technically or legally available. While in college in New York she met a dentist, Michael Rudolph, who became her first husband. A few years later she left Rudolph to answer the siren call of Los Angeles. One day in 1974 she phoned Bill Ballance's radio show and got on the air. A zesty bit of byplay on the relative merits of divorce and widowhood, which Ballance allowed to go on for an unheard-of twenty minutes, led to a weekly slot on his show. It also led the still-married Schlessinger to his bed. (Decades later, at the height of the flap over the nude photos, Ballance gibed that his pet name for her should have been Ku Klux, since she was "a wizard in the sheets.") Still later, while teaching at USC, Schlessinger met the very married Lew Bishop, who had three dependent children at home. Exit Ballance, enter Bishop. By some accounts their affair was messy; when USC did not renew Schlessinger's contract, Bishop walked away from his tenured professorship in neurophysiology. He walked away from his wife as well, and he and Schlessinger lived together without benefit of matrimony for at least eight years before making it official in 1985. Bishop became Schlessinger's business manager, though he showed less enthusiasm for tending to his erstwhile family's business: His former wife had to go to court to extract child support from him. Further, his relationship with his children deteriorated after his marriage to Schlessinger, who, associates say, sought a clean break from Bishop's past life, and thus his kids.

Schlessinger has reinvented herself whenever she deemed it expedient. This is most noticeable in her outlook on religion, or the lack of same. Brought up in what she describes as an "inter-faithless" marriage, she admits to living her early life in "secular" fashion. Schlessinger and her son Deryk, her only child with Bishop,[3] embraced Judaism in 1996.

Two years later the family converted to Orthodox Judaism, aspects of which she cited freely in rendering her moral pronouncements. Jewish organizations, including the National Council of Young Israel, honored her for her religious stances. But on August 5, 2003, Schlessinger opened her show by announcing that she would practice Judaism no more. In a series of introspective descants over the ensuing month, she explained that she felt frustrated by the effort she'd invested in following the Jewish faith, and openly chafed at her shabby treatment at the hands of fellow Jews. She even hinted at increasingly warm feelings toward Christianity, a move that—some insiders say—might enable her to reverse the attrition in listener base she's suffered in recent years.

Schlessinger will say that she "made mistakes," but some think she's made perhaps a few too many to be taken seriously as an oracle of probity and righteousness. "You suspect after a while that maybe she's not so much about helping people as using them to elevate her own standing and have a forum for thoughts she just wants to get 'out there,'" Michael Hurd, PhD, a psychologist and the author of *Effective Therapy*, told me. "And sometimes I've wondered if she's trying to heal herself." Schlessinger's unauthorized biographer, Vickie Bane, similarly paints her as an obsessive-compulsive narcissist whose concern for others is limited to what they can do for her, and whose will to win can be almost frightening.

There was, for instance, her mostly one-sided feud with Barbara De Angelis, a fellow talk-therapist. After De Angelis beat out Schlessinger for a coveted time slot, Schlessinger apparently embarked on a sub-rosa campaign to undo her. Derogatory information on De Angelis somehow found its way to the desks of personnel at the radio station that employed them both. Companies who interacted with De Angelis began receiving anonymous calls informing them that De Angelis wasn't actually a doctor and therefore should not be described as one on the air. Even years after De Angelis left the station and Schlessinger inherited her time slot, the bad blood reportedly continued, at least on Dr. Laura's part.

Notwithstanding all these doubts about Schlessinger's character, a much more basic question emerges: Does radio therapy even work? Surprisingly, some in psychiatric circles vote yes. They voice qualified support for the idea that radio shows can provide value to people who are already 98 percent of the way toward a momentous decision and just need that final pat on the back—or kick in the butt—from someone they respect. Also, a radio shrink like Dr. Laura may represent a worthwhile form of shock therapy for a caller who does, in fact, inhabit a world of alibis and denial. Hurd concedes, "She has a bullshit detector unlike anything I've ever seen. That's a very useful quality for a psychotherapist. She pays very close attention to contradictions in what people are saying, and confronts them on it."

Unfortunately, says Hurd, there's a huge difference between recognizing a problem and fixing a problem. He believes that in her rush to reduce even the most complex behavioral issues to words like *slut*, Schlessinger "does her callers a disservice." Hurd adds, "I would never say, 'Kick your husband out.' I would say, 'What would happen if you kicked your husband out? What would happen in the short run, and what would happen in the long run?' A therapist's job is to help people think." Making matters worse is that many people who call radio shows are nowhere near that defining moment described above. On the contrary, they're in obvious distress, struggling with major complicated dilemmas that seem insoluble to them. The radio format seldom allows for long-form calls, and Schlessinger is historically impatient with callers who don't cut to the chase, at times to the extent of chiding her screener for giving a forum to callers whose questions were too vague or multifaceted. If Schlessinger tolerates such calls at all, she'll generally seize on a subjective vision of the caller's distress and bulldoze forward with her verdict regardless of any added context or embellished character studies that emerge as the call proceeds. She'll interrupt callers at will, bullying them until they commit to positions that, surely in some cases, do not represent their true reasons for calling. "Not everything can be so easily resolved to black and white," says Hurd. "Even the law recognizes shades of guilt and mitigating circumstances." Rarely, halfway through a call, the caller will blurt something that manages to bring Schlessinger up short, forcing her to begin anew. But for every caller in that category, how many others are there who never quite get to the remark that broadens the good doctor's perspective?

The worst treatment is reserved for callers and others who touch on Schlessinger's pet peeves. At those times her determination to climb on her soapbox and trumpet her ideals may result in the merciless character assassination of innocents. She berated a Connecticut eighth-grader—by name—for writing an award-winning essay on free speech that disagreed with Schlessinger's very public call for restrictions on Internet usage in libraries.

"If she was my daughter," said Schlessinger, "I'd probably put her up for adoption."

Lastly, following Dr. Laura's advice sometimes has put callers in the position of needing even more advice from her, on more desperate or sensitive matters. During Schlessinger's show of July 30, 2004, a young female caller complained about her husband of one year, who, as this woman described him, was turning out to be a sexual pervert. Among other things, he displayed a fondness for "facials," which disgusted the caller (and, seemingly, the host). For this reason, as well as others that surfaced during the call, Schlessinger advised the woman to leave her new husband. Now, it's reasonable to assume that if this woman had learned more about her mate's proclivities earlier in the courtship, she might have avoided disaster. But because she was trying to follow Dr. Laura's staple script about "saving yourself for marriage," she did not discover her husband's sexual tastes until after she'd already said "I do." So back she came to Schlessinger for advice on extricating herself from this unsavory mess. Note, also, that Schlessinger did not tell the woman she might be overreacting, or that finding a comfortable sexual style often requires great patience and understanding—especially when couples have had no intimate exposure to each other before the wedding. Such are the catch-22's that can result when people (a) entrust their outlooks on life to a self-styled guru and (b) make momentous decisions based on the simplistic patter of call-in shows.

NOTABLE FOR:

Her explanation after nude pictures of her appeared online in 1998. Schlessinger said, simply, "In my twenties, I was my own moral authority."

Some things never change.

MEN ARE FROM MARS, JOHN GRAY IS FROM PLUTO

"Once upon a time," reads the signature line of the Web site for John Gray Counseling Centers Inc., "men lived on Mars and women lived on Venus. They met, fell in love and lived happily together, entranced by and accepting their differences. And then everything changed when they came to Earth and forgot they were from different worlds."

A different world is where Gray himself came from, some would argue. There are also nagging questions about where his credentials came from. But we're getting ahead of ourselves.

Gray's 1992 book, *Men Are from Mars, Women Are from Venus*, was the best-selling book of the 1990s, excepting only the various versions of the Bible, collectively. His publisher, HarperCollins, which publishes more than a few SHAM authors, proclaims Gray "the best-selling relationship author of all time." It's hard to argue. *Men Are from Mars* has sold some fifteen million copies in forty-three languages—it reportedly hit the best-seller lists in Bosnia—as well as two million audiocassettes and three hundred thousand videos. It also created a new linguistic and social currency revolving around that whole Mars/Venus dichotomy.

At a time when many women were pushing for a gender-blind society, Gray emerged with a message that was politically incorrect and culturally anachronistic. He preached that men and women *really are* fundamentally different, and he reduced male-female communication problems to those hoary stereotypes that feminists hated: Mars was more logical and analytical, Venus was more given to emotionalism and flights of fancy.

But it worked. Today, Gray's annual income exceeds $10 million. Spin-off books have included *Mars and Venus Together Forever, Mars and*

Venus in the Bedroom, Mars and Venus in Love, and, my own nomination for hokiest self-help title, *What You Feel You Can Heal*. Like Dr. Phil and others in the movement, Gray increasingly has taken a the-world-is-my-oyster approach to brand extension. In 1999 he wrote a parenting book, *Children Are from Heaven*. In 2003 he published *The Mars and Venus Diet and Exercise Solution*.

At the height of the Mars/Venus craze, Gray became a frequent guest on *The Oprah Winfrey Show, Good Morning America*, and *The Today Show*. He sat for interviews with Barbara Walters and Larry King. *Time, Newsweek, People*, and *Forbes* profiled him. For a while, Gray had a TV show hosted by Cybill Shepherd. *Men Are from Mars, Women Are from Venus* even inspired a board game, an exclusive deal with Club Med for Mars/Venus-themed getaways, and a musical. That's right. *Men Are from Mars, Women Are from Venus*, the musical, opened at the storied Flamingo Hotel in Las Vegas in 2000 and ran for a year. Memorable line: "I think my libido has gone incognito."

All the while Gray continued dispensing his unique brand of relationship advice. His syndicated column still reaches thirty million readers through two hundred papers, among them the *Los Angeles Times*, the *Chicago Sun-Times*, and the *New York Daily News*. He gets $50,000 per speech. Ongoing, too, is a gamut of large seminars, smaller workshops, and personal-coaching sessions conducted in eighteen states and Mexico by thirty-six counselors, all of whom "have been personally trained by Dr. John Gray in the principles presented in his books, tapes, videos, and seminars," according to Gray's literature. For those who can't wait for a seminar, Gray offers real-time Mars/Venus relationship coaching via telephone. For $1.99 per minute, another set of trained counselors will address such timeless topics as "Are you attracting the wrong people?" "Are you wasting your time?" and "Why doesn't he call?"

And what sort of advice are his readers and clients getting? In his advice column for *Redbook* magazine, he offers this banal insight to a married couple trying to resolve a series of arguments: "The outcome you want is one that works for both of you." In *Mars and Venus in the Bedroom*, Gray tells women who want to talk during sex to "make little noises and not use complete sentences," because a woman using complete sentences in bed "can be a turnoff." He pontificates on the meaning of women's underwear, explaining that when "she wears silky pink or lace, she is ready to surrender to sex as a romantic expression of loving vulnerability" and that a "cotton T-shirt with matching panties . . . may mean she doesn't need a lot of foreplay." According to Gray, such boudoir attire suggests that the woman whom it adorns "may not be in the mood for an orgasm" but rather might be "happy and satisfied" by feeling her partner's "orgasm inside her."

Clearly such precise knowledge of the most minute aspects of human sexual behavior and etiquette can only result from a significant track record of academic study and clinical research. Or so one would think.

First of all, "Dr." John Gray is not a medical doctor but a PhD—and a questionable one at that. In recent years multiple sources and reports have challenged Gray's credentials. He received his doctorate in 1982 from Columbia Pacific University, a nonaccredited correspondence college that California's attorney general once described as a diploma mill. The state later fined the school and ordered it to shut down. The professional therapist societies to which Gray belongs, the American Counseling Association and the International Association of Marriage and Family Counselors, both require PhD's—real ones—for membership. They've avoided comment on the Gray situation.

This makes Gray's counseling centers a particular matter of concern to some of his credentialed colleagues, one of whom likens the vast counseling network to a house of cards. "To talk about his 'certification procedure' "—a short course designed to produce entrepreneurial John Gray clones—"seems a little odd when the head guy himself isn't certified," the psychiatrist told me.

Gray's master's and bachelor's degrees aren't from conventional institutions of higher education, either. They're from the Maharishi European Research University in Switzerland. It's not often that experts on human sexuality spend the better part of a decade as celibate monks, but that's what Gray did, as secretary to the Maharishi Mahesh Yogi, who achieved his greatest fame as a spiritual adviser to the Beatles. The Maharishi's various schools of higher learning are best known for their emphasis on levitation. Maharishi University came to Iowa during the 1970s, and the largest structure on campus, its "Golden Dome," is reserved for practice in that Eastern art.

Revelations about Gray's academic past have not dulled his hubris in the least. "You can measure that school by the quality of the students they put out," he has said of Columbia Pacific. "Myself for example." Lack of professional licenses notwithstanding, Gray continues to identify himself in his official bio as "an internationally recognized expert in the fields of communication and relationships." In a realm that's rife with fraud and scandal, the "credential gap" of some of SHAM's exalted leadership is one of the great underreported stories.

A final, interesting Gray tidbit: He was once married to the irrepressible Barbara De Angelis, the same radio host who became involved in a feud with Laura Schlessinger. De Angelis is another self-proclaimed sexologist; she came to the field after being, among other things, a magician's assistant to Doug Henning. She was wife number one for Gray; he was husband number three (of five, to date, including Henning) for her. De Angelis's contributions to the SHAM oeuvre include the optimistically titled *How to Make Love All the Time* and *Are You the One for Me?* Perhaps Gray and De Angelis found their own answers to the latter question during some function at Columbia Pacific University, where De Angelis received her doctorate as well.

NOTABLE FOR:

Telling *Inside Edition* in 2003, "I don't need to put PhD by my name. I'm the most famous author in the world."

MARIANNE WILLIAMSON: A RETURN TO GIBBERISH?

The ex–cabaret songstress Marianne Williamson has been a key figure in SHAM's Spiritual Division ever since Oprah, the éminence grise of self-help, embraced Williamson's 1992 book, *A Return to Love: Reflections on the Principles of A Course in Miracles*. For thirty-nine weeks the book sat atop the *New York Times* best-seller list, and three of her next eight books reached that same lofty perch. At the height of her appeal, Williamson acquired the nickname "Mother Teresa for the '90s," joining Deepak Chopra and unreconstituted psychic Sylvia Browne as the anointed leadership of the New Age.

In explaining the spiritual underpinnings of secular life, Williamson looks back to Christianity's misunderstood (she would argue) origins. Her books, tapes, lectures, and usual proliferation of other materials provide a unique vision of spirituality, one that offers salvation without sacrifice, satisfaction without sin. Lots of gain, no pain. The New Age movement as a whole, says Robert Ellwood, a professor of religion at the University of Southern California and the author of *The Sixties Spiritual Awakening*, represents "a sort of build-your-own-religion kit, a way to pick and choose the rules, keeping the convenient precepts while discarding the cumbersome ones."

Above all, the cheery thought that one could have a self-improvement program anchored in miracles or angels is a manifestation of the force Williamson has exerted on the culture over the past decade. She made it sound credible.

Williamson's formative influences are interesting. She was born in Houston to Jewish lawyers, and to say her parents indoctrinated her in liberalism understates the case: In 1965, when she was just thirteen, her father took her to Vietnam to see the reviled "military-industrial complex" at work. She later majored in philosophy and theater at suburban Los Angeles's Pomona College, and supported herself for a time as a nightclub act, at one point sharing an apartment with budding actress Laura Dern. Williamson has been honest about the drug abuse and heavy drinking that preceded her spiritual rebirth.

She first won note in 1983 when her Los Angeles–area talks on the link between spirituality and life began drawing dozens, then hundreds, then thousands. (Her striking, if vaguely haunted, looks didn't hurt.) Williamson chose as her topic "A Course in Miracles," which she described as a "self-study program of spiritual psychotherapy." The lecture was really her spin on a theology expressed in a three-book series of the same name by psychologist Helen Schucman, who claimed she was channeling Jesus when she compiled it. According to Schucman, Jesus said to her, "This is a course in miracles; please take notes." She did, and the resulting volumes, published in 1975 by the Foundation for Inner Peace, represent "Christianity lite": more love, forgiveness, and unity; less suffering, sacrifice, and ceremony. One million copies of the original course were in print by the time Williamson's lectures had graduated from coffeehouses to amphitheaters, attracting some powerful admirers en route. Liz Taylor asked her to preside over her 1991 wedding to Larry Fortensky at Michael Jackson's now-infamous Neverland Ranch. Hillary Clinton had her to the White House for a chat.

After *A Return to Love*, the books all but tumbled out of her: *A Woman's Worth* (spirituality as it relates to women), *Illuminata* (spirituality as it relates to prayer), *Enchanted Love* (spirituality as it relates to relationships), *Healing the Soul of America* (spirituality as it relates to politics), *Emma and Mommy Talk to God* (spirituality as it relates to children), *Everyday Grace* (spirituality as it relates to daily living, which essentially brought her publishing career full circle to *A Return to Love*), and so on. Through all this, Williamson continued her barnstorming lectures at an impressive pace; for someone who preaches that "enlightenment is not a weekend seminar," she certainly does enough of them. These, too, have been recycled as audiotapes and CDs, like 2004's *Letting Go and Becoming*, and a series of *Marianne Williamson on . . .* any number of touchy-feely topics.

Williamson must realize that for a fair segment of today's marketplace, fiscal well-being outshines sheer spirituality. As she has broadened her outreach, she has incorporated material designed to target more conventionally success-minded readers—albeit still couched in a New Agey patois (no doubt so that her core followers won't feel she "sold out"). Thus, a new $69.95 video series promises to help buyers "develop a prosperity consciousness," unlock their "capacity for personal and professional success," and "view every new experience as an opportunity for growth."

Even for some industry insiders, the unswerving fidelity of Williamson's sizable base constituency can be puzzling, since her books are so repetitive, and she spends so much time blithely stating the obvious: "A sense of separateness dissolves in the presence of real intimacy," Williamson tells audiences. Or, "The reason we feel powerless is simply because we're not expressing our power." Or, "The challenge is to create on Earth as it is in Heaven."[4] Now and then she'll burst forth with poesy that reduces to far less than meets the eye: "The rest we seek we will not find from sleeping, but only from waking." There's this, on money: "Money is energy, and energy is infinite in the universe." And on the unity of all being: "We think that because we dwell inside our bodies that we are separate from other people who dwell inside theirs. Because our consciousness is tied to the physical manifestation of reality, we are tied to the belief in separation. When we begin to see each other through what the metaphysician calls the third eye, we begin to know each other on a level that is beyond what our physical eyes can see." Of course, once you open the door to realities the eye cannot see—well, what possibilities, if any, does that exclude? Such lines, like so much of SHAM, have that whiff of contrived profundity that obscure modern poets often employ to mask the odor of dubious sense. Here's another: "An idea doesn't leave its source. So what I think about you, I will not be able to escape thinking about myself, and what I do to you, I will not be able to escape experiencing myself."

But the final, fatal flaw in Williamson's dialectic is its attempt simultaneously to sell idyllic notions of community and unconstrained personal development. Plainly, these cannot coexist unless all of the individual members of any given society just happen to aspire to the very same goals. And lest we forget, Williamson is a staunch one-world cheerleader, so this accidental brotherhood of men and women would have to apply among individuals not just in America but also across international borders. "Each and every person knows what the next step is for them," she says, acknowledging that each of us wants something different out of life, sometimes radically so. And yet how does she expect all of those "next steps *for them*" to resolve neatly into the level of global harmony she extols? One supposes that is where the miracles and angels come in.

Or perhaps Williamson is well aware that her ideas break down in the end, but she's just having such a jolly time on her way to the bank. As long ago as *A Return to Love* she wrote, "Don't go to work to make money; go to work to spread joy. Seek ye first the kingdom of Heaven and the Maserati will get here when it's supposed to." For Williamson, the Maserati got there and then some.

NOTABLE FOR:

Her homeland-security program: On her Web site, Williamson advises followers to "pray for angels to surround the country" and form a "mystical shield" around "every airplane, every nuclear facility, the Golden Gate Bridge, etc."

SUZE ORMAN: THE GENDER OF MONEY?

At first blush, Suze Orman might seem out of place in this crowd—and even unjustly miscast as a SHAM cleric. Whereas others mentioned here are mostly teaching you to feel better about you, Orman imparts specific skills having to do with a less airy concern: money. And that's precisely what makes her so interesting. Orman epitomizes the new breed of self-helpers who aim to enhance legitimacy and distance themselves from their SHAM lineage by focusing at least in part on something external to the psyche itself. This is what Andrew Weil—author of *8 Weeks to Optimum Health* and *The Healthy Kitchen*, among many other books—has done so successfully with health and medicine. Orman has sold more than six million books, two of which, *The 9 Steps to Financial Freedom* and *The Courage to Be Rich*, were *New York Times* number one best sellers. The latter book still holds the all-time QVC record for most books sold in an hour, at a jaw-dropping 35,000. She hosts an eponymous personal-finance show on CNBC that 113,000 American households regard as staple viewing. She's a financial adviser to *The Oprah Winfrey Show* as well as a columnist for *O, The Oprah Magazine*. She has the obligatory Web site, and even if the links don't always work, it's comprehensive and helpful—to Orman as well as her fans. Not unlike some other SHAM artists, she uses her site to collect data for possible future ventures. At this writing, a box on the site's main page solicits feedback from "those of you who are 25 to 35 years old" regarding what Orman's next book should cover; in today's fickle consumer climate, it never hurts to be able to go directly to the market and ask it what it wants to be sold. Orman also features the usual spin-offs to her core products, in this case step-by-step guidebooks, day planners, calendars, and financial "kits" that include pro forma wills, trusts, and miscellaneous other do-it-yourself (or at least start-it-yourself) forms.

In sum, the onetime $400-a-week waitress has built an empire, the Suze Orman Financial Co., that generates $40 million a year—$4 million of which, Orman admits, is pure profit. She estimates her personal net worth at $20 million. As the writer Maria Halkias declared in the *Dallas Morning News*, "Suze Orman is a brand." For the promotional tour for Orman's latest book, her publisher chartered the same forty-five-foot MCI Renaissance bus normally reserved for rock stars like Ozzy Osbourne, done up in a glossy red that would've served Revlon well as a billboard announcing some hot new lipstick shade.

Orman's unique "trade dress" resides in her holistic blending of financial wisdom with an appeal to a "higher level" of consciousness and emotion. At seminars, she'll hold up a dollar bill and, referring to the eye in the pyramid engraved on its back, she'll say, "The eye represents spirituality, the third eye, and there's an aspect of money that is very emotional and spiritual. It's on a one-dollar bill because we need to be one with our money."

People didn't tend to say things like that where Suze Orman grew up, on Chicago's "Bad, Bad Leroy Brown" South Side. As a child, she hardly seemed destined to become the head of a multimillion-dollar financial empire. (Nor did she seem likely to be a regular on the lecture circuit, particularly given the serious speech impediment she had as a child.) Her father was a small-business owner whose entrepreneurial track record reads like the answer to "What's the opposite of the Midas touch?" Morry Orman ran a takeout chicken shack that burned down when Suze—or, in those days, Susie—was fourteen. His subsequent try at a boardinghouse fell to earth along with a tenant who'd slipped on a broken staircase. The man filed suit, and Morry lost his shirt.

Left with little of a material nature, Orman focused on her spiritual side. In her first brokerage job, at Merrill Lynch, she supplemented the usual stock charts and corporate financials by using a crystal to help her assess a given stock's prospects. (She now says she realizes that *she* was the crystal.) After she founded her own financial-planning firm, she had clients deposit their checks under a statue of Ganesh, a Hindu deity and Remover of All Obstacles.

Orman took herself national in 1990, joining forces with the writer James Jorgensen (*It's Never Too Late to Get Rich*) to create a 900 number for dispensing financial advice over the phone. Orman's solo breakout began with the 1995 book *You've Earned It, Don't Lose It*, which showcased her ability to speak a fiscal language friendly to women. But it was her 1998 follow-up, *The 9 Steps to Financial Freedom*, that made Orman a SHAM superstar. The book remained on the *New York Times* best-seller list for almost a full year, and was the number one nonfiction best seller on *Publishers Weekly*'s 1998 hardcover list.

Orman has never married—a bit odd for a woman who spends so much time talking about balance in life. She does show balance in other areas. When touring to promote a book or some other business cause, sometimes she'll take the bus, sometimes she'll just hop on the Learjet. She has an unusual ability to (convincingly) play rich and poor at the same time, and is one of the few ultrarich SHAM figures who can talk about her fondness for eating at McDonald's without provoking cynical groans among her listeners.

Orman gets a great deal of mileage out of her seminars, workshops, and speeches (at $35,000 an hour). Personawise, she's been called a "fiscal Dr. Laura," and for sheer messianic, in-your-face intensity, it's hard to think of someone more deserving of the label. There is the famous Orman Death Stare, which moved one member of a Suze chat group to note that Orman's face looks "like someone highlighted it and selected bold print."[5] But her intensity is leavened by an irrepressible perkiness and a sometimes-maddening optimism, as when she'll tell interviewers, seeming honestly to mean it, "I love getting stuck in traffic!"

Orman's rhetorical flourish can have her sounding vaguely like a political candidate making stump speeches—a candidate with a hell of a sense of self. "Having talked to literally tens of thousands of people," she will declaim during an interview, "I can say that what is good for America—and not just what is good theoretically, or for some financial wizards, but what is good literally—is not having credit card debt, not leasing a car, and not having mortgage debt." She will urge other "ivory tower" investment advisers to "get out there and talk to people, like I do. People don't have any money to invest. Invest *what*?" She can also sound pretty proletarian for someone whose livelihood is so directly linked to the fruits of the capitalist system. "It was not 9/11 that killed this economy," she was saying during sold-out speeches the following year. "The ones doing it are Enron, Merrill Lynch, Arthur Andersen, Kmart . . ."

From a marketing standpoint, Orman's genius is her ability to examine money from an intensely female perspective that conceives financial issues in emotional terms. She uses much the same language to talk about financial vigilance that one might use to talk about raising kids ("Your money will work for you when you give it energy, time, and understanding") or sustaining an important intimate relationship ("Money will respond when you treat it as a cherished friend—never fearing it, pushing it away, pretending it doesn't exist or turning away from its needs, never clutching so hard it hurts"). Some of her patter is so derivative of SHAM boilerplate that you can easily imagine almost any other guru using it in almost any other setting merely by substituting a key word here and there: "Financial freedom is when you have power over your fears and anxieties instead of the other way around," says Orman. The basic line works equally well if you replace *financial freedom* with such words as *happiness, security, a good marriage*, or any other number of subjects. Or you could replace *financial freedom* with *succesful parenting*, and *fears and anxieties* with *anger and frustration*, and . . . voilà! Instant child-rearing formula!

To her credit, Orman recognized that a less hard-boiled approach to money would be more comfortable and less intimidating to an audience that so often had felt left out of financial planning. "Nobody was really talking to women about that," says Christina Diekman, a financial planner with New England Financial Services. "And the people who *were* talking to them were talking down to them." Orman, through the years, has solidified her grip on her core audience (which does include some men) by connecting money matters to the larger scheme of things. There was nothing haphazard about the second clause in the title of Orman's sixth straight best-selling book, 2003's *The Laws of Money, the Lessons of Life*.

And the advice itself? A fair amount of it tends to be oversimplified feel-good patter. Consider Law 1 in *The Laws of Money, the Lessons of Life*: "Truth creates money, lies destroy it." Sometimes yes, sometimes no. Like it or not, many people have made a pile of money by lying—some of them in Orman's own movement—while many people (like, presumably, Orman's own hardworking father) have gone honestly, ethically broke.

But the line *sounds* so good. It's something people *want* to be true, *hope* to be true. So it resonates with her buyers.

In the mold of such predecessors as the financial writer Jane Bryant Quinn and the beauty-queen-cum-consumer-advocate Bess Myerson, Orman does give honest-to-goodness financial tips: Cut expenses. Pay off credit-card and mortgage debt. Don't obsess over your 401(k) (an offering she cynically describes as "a very nice thing for the corporations to get out of funding their employee retirement plans"). Accumulate an eight-month emergency war chest before you even think of other investments. When you do invest, pick the known (e.g., your house) before the unknown (e.g., that hot new company you've been hearing about, which Martha Stewart and everyone else of any status or savvy had already crossed off the list six months ago). She says she keeps almost all her money in municipal bonds and money-market funds.

Suze Orman has achieved extraordinary influence by positioning herself as an objective observer dispensing unbiased millennial advice on money management. By simultaneously putting out the vibe that she's "one of us," she has ingratiated herself with millions of women around the world. This gives her a gilt-edged platform for selling product—and in Orman's case, it's not just the usual books and tapes and coffee mugs: It's her very own financial instruments.

"Suze's Choice" long-term-care insurance is issued through GE Financial and sold on her Web site and QVC. Orman gets a commission for each plan that's sold. She has shrugged off questions about a possible conflict of interest, explaining that she's been warning her fans for years of the need to protect themselves against sudden, catastrophic medical costs. She has been issuing such warnings, but one may wonder: How long were the plans for the insurance in the works? How far ahead was Orman thinking when she began giving the advice? A more basic question is: Does her plan really offer the most bang for the buck? Not necessarily, according to the National Advisory Council for Long Term Care Insurance. The council says the "one company for all" approach is not a smart move in the long-term-care insurance game, certainly not for all comers.

Suze's Choice embodies a worrisome trend wherein some of SHAM's most influential leaders exploit their accrued credibility via products that supposedly are the answers to the problems the gurus have been building up in people's minds. Now that Orman is so deeply invested in her product, would she be more apt to spin it in a favorable light, regardless of any changes in the financial marketplace that occur as time goes by?

Time will tell. It'll be interesting to see whether Orman herself does.

NOTABLE FOR:

Boasting that "people love me 'cause I tell it like it is. You get financial advisers who tell you to keep your stocks, but they can't tell you the truth because they own those damn companies." See above remarks about her Suze's Choice insurance.

3

◇◇◇◇

DR. PHIL MCGRAW: ABSOLUTE POWER

Sometimes it's hard to see your face without a mirror.

—Dr. Phil McGraw

And now Dr. Phil's latest book, *Here's Some More Advice I Pulled Out of My Ass.*

—David Letterman

You probably know the script already, but it goes something like this: On April 16, 1996, at the height of the first mad-cow scare, a talk-show diva says the threat of disease "has just stopped [her] cold from eating another burger." Millions of grossed-out housewives rethink their dinner menus, and the price of ground beef plummets.[1] Down on the range, a billionaire Texas cattleman persuades his buddies that the smart-mouthed celebrity has run afoul of his state's novel "food disparagement" law. There follows a $12 million lawsuit, which requires the woman's presence in Amarillo, Texas. Looking for every advantage in unfamiliar territory, she reaches out to a company with a national reputation in jury analysis and witness preparation, Irving, Texas–based Courtroom Sciences Inc. (CSI), whose clients include most major airlines, three major television networks, and about half of the Fortune 100. One of CSI's cofounders is a burly, six-foot-four-inch lapsed psychologist who, a decade earlier, walked away from a successful private practice because, as he told it, "I had no patience for my patients." The talk-show host and the burned-out shrink hit it off immediately, and he spends much of the next year working with her one-on-one, "helping her be who she is on the witness stand." In February 1998 she wins the six-week trial and gives the shrink a Texas-sized chunk of the credit.

Through such bizarre serendipity do fortunes (in every sense of the word) turn.

Had Oprah Winfrey not dissed burgers, an otherwise ordinary PhD named Phillip C. McGraw would not have been catapulted to the pinnacle of American gurudom. Today, 6.5 million Americans, mostly female, tune in Dr. Phil's syndicated television show (which is never scheduled against that of his mentor) for life-changing advice on the sublime, the ridiculous, and all points between—everything from whether they should get a divorce to whether they really need that second helping of rosemary potatoes. He has built a reputation as someone who "tells it like it is," dispensing homespun one-liners and put-downs to advice-seeking guests who, in his estimation, are evading the real issue or making excuses for their behavior. Among his greatest hits: "Get real." "And how's that workin' out for ya?" "Is that the truth or a lie?" "This is gonna be a changing day in your life." "Are you avoiding reality?" "Don't think, just start talkin'." "Are you nuts?" "You can't change what you don't acknowledge." "Quit takin' yourself so damn seriously." "Now lemme just be honest here." "Now lemme tell ya something." "*Rea*lly" (said with an appropriately incredulous, mocking tone).

America first met Phil McGraw during Oprah's regular "Tuesdays with Dr. Phil" sessions, wildly popular weekly gabfests that showcased McGraw's unforgiving style. (Oprah's ratings, always enviable, rose another 25 percent when Dr. Phil was a guest.) McGraw spent the rest of his week writing a succession of books that reveal a rare gift for sequelization, even in a derivative, self-cannibalizing genre like SHAM. *Life Strategies: Doing What Works, Doing What Matters* (January 1999) sold a half-million copies within three months of its release, and later begat *The Life Strategies Workbook: Exercises and Self-Tests to Help You Change Your Life* (January 2000) as well as *The Life Strategies Self-Discovery Journal: Finding What Matters Most for You* (October 2001). For those who made it through the journal without finding out what really matters, McGraw soon provided the answer: *Self Matters: Creating Your Life from the Inside Out* (November 2001). That, in turn, spawned a series of *Self Matters* daily calendars and *The Self Matters Companion: Helping You Create Your Life from the Inside Out*. In between those two series Dr. Phil whipped up *Relationship Rescue: A 7-Step Strategy for Reconnecting with Your Partner* (February 2000), which led to *The Relationship Rescue Workbook* (October 2000). September 2003 saw McGraw's first true brand extension, *The Ultimate Weight Solution: The 7 Keys to Weight Loss Freedom*. The book debuted at number one on the *New York Times* best-seller list, with 2.5 million copies in print by the end of its first month in stores. In December came *The Ultimate Weight Solution Food Guide*. Then in 2004 he brought out *Family First: Your Step-by-Step Plan for Creating a Phenomenal Family*, beneficiary of a 2.3-million-copy first printing.

In perhaps the ultimate sequel, Dr. Phil also has spun off his son. At age twenty-three, Jay McGraw, whose chief qualification rests on being the progeny of Phil and Robin McGraw, had a best-selling book in his own right, *Life Strategies for Teens*. In addition, Jay McGraw is listed as the author of *Closing the Gap: A Strategy for Bringing Parents and Teens Together* and *The Ultimate Weight Solution for Teens: The 7 Keys to Weight Freedom*. (The McGraws, clearly, are fond of strategies, keys, and anything that has seven steps.) Can a book by Dr. Phil's teenage son, Jason McGraw, be far behind? Probably not—Phil McGraw has made a point of turning the SHAM game into a family affair, at one stage teaming with *his* dad to rake in $1 million per year putting on success seminars.

All told, McGraw stands at the heart of a multimillion-dollar brand that evokes Martha Stewart/Omnimedia before the fall; he is a one-man corporation, quite literally, having incorporated himself in 2000. The advertising agency he hired in August 2003 to help build his brand, Michigan-based powerhouse Campbell-Ewald, has numbered among its clients such corporate icons as Pier 1, Borders, and Chevrolet.

McGraw needs no help in the promotion department. His own skills are unquestioned, even when ranked against those of other members of the breed. Much like his mentor, Winfrey, McGraw stages themed episodes for his shows in a way that's guaranteed to create buzz while also underscoring his central significance to the goings-on. The TV show thus gives him what marketers call "golden visibility," as well as an ideal platform for selling his wares. To help promote *The Ultimate Weight Solution*, he sequestered thirteen obese volunteers in a Beverly Hills mansion, gave them a weeklong crash course in the relatively complex program at the heart of the book, then made their trials, tribulations, and degrees of "ultimate" success a part of his show for the next year. (A master of holistic, across-the-brand promotion, McGraw also created interactive Web logs and other ingenious wrinkles to allow viewers to share in the experience, either as interested observers or at-home participants in the weight-loss challenge.) As reported in *Business Week*, when McGraw was asked how to solve America's thorny obesity problem, he replied simply, "Everyone needs to read my book." He also writes a newsletter, *Dr. Phil: The Next Level*, available at $24.95 for twelve issues. On DrPhil.com, he sells videotapes and transcripts of his shows at $29.95 and $7, respectively. At Dr. Phil's Online Store, a fan can buy a Dr. Phil baseball hat, a weight-loss "Booty Camp" T-shirt, an "I Love Dr. Phil" nightshirt, or a coffee mug dominated by a photo of the maestro's own mug in that trademark hand-on-chin pose. Industry sources estimate that McGraw pockets $20 million a year. It's the mark of his success that he recently sold his 50 percent stake in CSI—by all accounts an enormously profitable venture with day rates exceeding $25,000—because he no longer has time to devote to the company.

It was not always thus. Growing up in Oklahoma and Kansas City, Phil McGraw and his three sisters moved at the whim of a nomadic father. When Phil was twelve, his father quit his job to go back to school, and the family income came courtesy of a daily fifty-two-mile paper route. The elder McGraw earned a degree in his late thirties and became a psychologist, but in the meantime young Phil had become a restless, temperamental slacker. One semester at the University of Tulsa, which he attended on a football scholarship, McGraw managed a GPA "like .6 on a four-point scale," he later told CNN. "But I could catch a football and knock you down and so that was kind of my identity." It was a time of boozing and bar fights for McGraw, who once admitted that he'd "fight a buzz saw" if he had the chance. He finally earned a PhD in neuropsychology from the University of North Texas, but by 1988, he would later say, he had grown fed up with whiny patients who sought coddling he was unprepared to provide. He gave up his practice, and he and a fellow burnout, trial lawyer Gary Dobbs, created CSI. A decade later came the mad cows, and Oprah.

The same contentious demeanor that made Dr. Phil, by his own admission, the world's "worst marital therapist" somehow made him the perfect guru in a culture drowning in the moral ambiguity and projected blame of the Victimization movement. Today's viewers get frequent glimpses of this when McGraw berates guests for being lousy husbands or parents, being "too fat," or otherwise not facing up to their self-made foibles. "A lot of people do have tragic childhoods," he said in one interview. "But you know what? Get over it. . . . Do something and get back in charge of your life."

On the other hand, McGraw isn't above exploiting Victimization when it suits his purposes. An announcement on his Web site in the summer of 2004 sought adults who are "scarred for life by strict parents," an unambiguous rendering of the so-called disease model of hapless behavior. This victim-based thinking turns up again in his preface to his son's book *Closing the Gap*, in which he writes, "If you're a parent, grandparent or teenager, you are infected with a very serious disease. It is not a disease of biological origin, it does not attack the tissues of your body, but it *is* a disease—an acute social disease which attacks the fiber of your family. The danger is *real*; it is *right now* and it spans the physical, mental, emotional and spiritual realms." Straddling the fence between Victimization and Empowerment, McGraw describes obesity as a "disease of choice" that "can't be cured, only managed." Such reasoning encourages his overweight followers to buy his book, but it also gives him an ironclad excuse should his weight-loss plan fail to deliver the hoped-for results.

OVERREACH?

Many of Phil McGraw's professional peers take issue with the manner in which he delivers his advice. Though Dr. Michael Hurd generally likes the way McGraw engages his guests and "draws them out," he recoils from McGraw's abrasive way of rousing to a finish. "You have to realize, it's about showmanship," Hurd told me, "but therapy shouldn't take a backseat to showmanship. People shouldn't get beat up in the process."

Hurd and other critics wonder whether those moments—which, indisputably, make for great television—send McGraw's guests home with a profound sense of shame and embarrassment rather than lay the foundation for progress on whatever issues they had to begin with.

Criticism in this vein may be somewhat naive, in that shows like McGraw's, notwithstanding the patina of professional integrity, are more about theater than therapy; they provide viewers with a slightly elevated, SHAM-inspired twist on the likes of Jerry Springer. Accordingly, there are accusations that where McGraw's TV show is concerned, his own trademark mantra "Get Real" takes a backseat to "Get Ratings." In September 2004 McGraw outraged working mental-health professionals and children's advocates when, during the course of a prime-time special, *Family First*, he came dangerously close to predicting that a nine-year-old boy was destined to become a serial killer. "There are fourteen characteristics of a serial killer," McGraw told little Eric's somber parents on the air. "Your son has nine. Jeffrey Dahmer had seven." To drive the point home, McGraw then treated the show's thirteen million viewers to a split-screen image of Dahmer's face next to Eric's. Michael Fitzpatrick, executive director of the National Alliance for the Mentally Ill, denounced McGraw's stunt as "unethical" and later told the *Washington Post*, "You don't do that for ratings. This is a human being."

Similar accusations come from a pair of spokeswomen for the obese—374-pound Sally Smith, editor of *Big Beautiful Woman* magazine, and 400-pound Maryanne Bodolay, executive administrator of the National Association to Advance Fat Acceptance. Longtime fans of Dr. Phil, the women were thrilled to be invited to appear on his show, though they did plan to challenge McGraw on his belief that obesity is, in essence, a bad habit. To set up the on-air segment, McGraw's producers sent Smith and Bodolay on an undercover mission in Las Vegas. A hidden camera followed them to a mall, a fitness center, and a buffet restaurant, with the producers hoping to preserve for posterity (and especially for the viewing pleasure of McGraw's audience) instances when strangers harassed the women. Except, the women would later allege, something went horribly wrong: No such harassment occurred. Nobody bothered Smith and Bodolay as they went through their paces. Not a single caustic remark was picked up via covert taping.

That would have made for lousy television, so—the women contend—McGraw's producers primed the pump. Smith says she knows for a fact that one man was paid to "make a rude comment." In any case, when the footage aired in November 2003, viewers saw onlookers snickering at the women and making snide remarks as they went by. Onstage, McGraw identified Smith and Bodolay simply as a pair of obese women, "Sally" and "Maryanne," withholding their professional credentials to speak on behalf of their constituencies. To their dismay, the segment deteriorated into a freak show at their expense, with their former idol refusing to engage them on serious issues, instead using them as convenient props for his bracing, opinionated repartee. A few weeks after the show aired, producers invited Smith and Bodolay to make a return appearance; ratings had been terrific. (The two women, needless to say, declined the second invitation.) McGraw later denied that the show was a setup, and members of his staff declined comment. (I had hoped to discuss this and many other topics with McGraw himself, but he declined to be interviewed for this book.)

On the other hand, it's clear that many among McGraw's legions of fans take him *very* seriously. To them, he is The Unimpeachable Dr. Phil, an authentic oracle of modern living. They'll compare notes on how they're applying *Self Matters* in their own lives, or share a moment of laughter at the day-care center or watercooler over some memorable, instructive moment from the previous day's show. They'll fill the message boards on DrPhil.com with their personal epiphanies, earnest pleas for help, and snappy one-line put-downs of one another in the parroted voice of their mentor. This growing discipledom becomes an added problem, say McGraw's critics, now that his manic pursuit of brand extension has led him to stray far beyond his core competencies. His 2003 diet book is the most notable illustration, but others include his sermons on talking to kids about the gruesome events in Iraq and his down-home financial advice in the March 2004 issue of *Good Housekeeping*. The *Good Housekeeping* piece came three months before McGraw reassured an interviewer from Business Week Online, who had inquired about his growing reach, "I'm not going to tell you what to do with your 401(k). That's not my long suit."

"It's not clear he's staying within the limits of his expertise," Peter M. Barach, a psychiatry instructor at Case Western Reserve University, told *Business Week*. When I interviewed Barach, he told me, "A mental-health expert who cultivates this degree of following has a responsibility to ensure that he's always on solid ground." In 2004 Neal David Sutz, an Arizona mental-health activist, petitioned the Federal Communications Commission (FCC) to rein McGraw in by mandating a more prominent disclaimer than what is presently displayed during the show's closing credits. Noting that guests are required to sign a waiver form in which they acknowledge that Dr. Phil's advice is not to be construed as "therapy or a substitute for therapy," Sutz sought to have McGraw more forthrightly describe his show as entertainment rather than counseling. This, of course, is not the impression one gathers by observing the heavy-handed way in which Dr. Phil dispenses his advice to frazzled, often helpless guests. As of this writing, the FCC has taken no action on Sutz's complaint. Questioned on the point by *Time* magazine—"Do you consider the show therapy or entertainment?"—McGraw hedged. "I consider it to be education," he replied, in part. "It's very different from therapy and much more than entertainment."

McGraw may be overreaching in an entrepreneurial sense, too. Some of his more serious-minded peers questioned the marketing program for nutritional supplements bearing Dr. Phil's name, timed to coincide with the launch of *The Ultimate Weight Solution*. McGraw had given his stamp of approval to Shape Up!, a line of weight-loss supplements, bars, and shakes created by his former CSI colleague Gary Dobbs. A class-action suit later filed against McGraw and Shape Up! alleged that the ads for the products made dubious nutritional claims. As Gregg Easterbrook pointed out in an October 2003 column for the New Republic Online, "Dr. Phil's Shape Up! Chocolate Peanut Butter bar contains 3.5 grams of saturated fat and 340 milligrams of sodium. A Milky Way contains 5 grams of saturated fat, and 95 milligrams of sodium. . . . Adjusting for its smaller size, the Milky Way Lite bar has the same calories per gram as Dr. Phil's Shape Up! Chocolate Peanut Butter bar." Easterbrook drew the logical conclusion that "Dr. Phil's Shape Up! Chocolate Peanut Butter bar is a *candy bar.*" In an interview with the *Chicago Tribune,* Dawn Jackson, a registered dietitian and spokesperson for the American Diabetes Association, voiced concerns that McGraw was "preying on the vulnerability of people trying to lose weight. We all know there is no quick fix or magic pill, and this could give them false hope."

Though McGraw has expended considerable effort defending the product line, by some reports he quietly ended his endorsement deal with Shape Up! in mid-2004. Repeated calls to his office for confirmation went nowhere.

All of this hints at the most intriguing and potentially troubling aspect of Dr. Phil McGraw: his megalomania. "McGraw is a harsh, charismatic man of high intelligence and higher self-regard," one of his (unauthorized) biographers, Sophia Dembling, wrote in a July 2004 column for the publishing-industry Web site Mediabistro. His seldom-mentioned first wife, Debbie Higgins McCall, agrees. She told me that during their marriage, which lasted from 1970 to 1973, McGraw insisted on being informed of her every move, even requiring her to phone him before she left the house—this, while McGraw himself was leaving the house to see other women, she alleges. As recounted by Debbie, McGraw's response at being confronted about his infidelities is particularly intriguing, as it represents an ironic harbinger of what would become, decades later, one of Dr. Phil's signature lines. "I told him I knew he was fooling around on me," Debbie told me, "and instead of denying it, he basically told me that's how things are, and I needed to just *get over it.*" (McGraw has publicly sidestepped the question of adultery but not explicitly denied it.)

This notion—that rules are made for others—forms a pattern in McGraw's life. Early in his clinical career, the Texas State Board of Examiners of Psychologists reprimanded him for giving an office job to a female patient who later accused him of similarly intimidating behavior, as well as sexual harassment. He was ordered to retake his licensing exams, undergo counseling on professional ethics, and submit to a physical and psychological exam. McGraw's critics also have observed that

CSI was an amoral enterprise at heart; it was not the firm's job to find "the truth," but rather to help clients put their best foot forward in court and, in a very real sense, to manipulate juries. Members of McGraw's own production staff complained to Dembling and coauthor Lisa Gutierrez about their boss's brusque, bullying manner around the set.

McGraw does not deny that he "loves a good fight," but his ex-wife goes a step further. "He takes a difference of opinion personally," Debbie told me. "And especially, anything anybody points out that's a negative about him, he interprets as jealousy. Whatever's wrong is *your* problem, not his."

Dembling's experience in writing *The Making of Dr. Phil: The Straight-Talking True Story of Everyone's Favorite Therapist* underscores McGraw's enormous sense of personal sovereignty, as well as his reach. In Dembling's telling, the authors embarked on their research hopeful that McGraw would talk to them, but his lawyer fielded their request, brusquely informing the writers that McGraw would not cooperate. In the Mediabistro piece, she described an admonishing phone call from the attorney, who had tried to dissuade her from completing the project: "You people just want to dig up dirt and bring people down" was a phrase that stuck in Dembling's mind. McGraw's friends and associates also closed ranks around him, refusing to speak ill—or even good—of their powerful acquaintance. *The Making of Dr. Phil* caused hardly a ripple on publication, even though Dembling and Gutierrez had managed to dig up a fair amount of new information and believed their timing to be impeccable. They couldn't get booked on the shows where authors of such a book might be expected to appear. They couldn't generate buzz in the places where high-profile biographies normally generate buzz. The book developed no media traction.

Though no proof of any conspiracy against Dembling's book exists, it would not be the first time powerful media celebrities conspired to undo their detractors, and such a sub-rosa campaign hardly seems beyond the realm of possibility here. McGraw has evolved into a major media player in his own right, and of course he continues to have the backing of Oprah and the Harpo Productions monolith.

Indeed, in the history of broadcasting, it's doubtful that such an alliance of omnipotents—prima donna and protégé—has existed quite the way it exists between Winfrey and McGraw.

MANIPULATION

And so, in the end, one must ask: Is Dr. Phil really about helping people engineer "a changing day" in their lives? Or does he simply get off on being in charge and enforcing his will over his gullible subjects? It's a question McGraw's legions of loyal fans would do well to ask themselves. As one wag wrote in a column on McGraw-mania for the entertainment magazine *The Wave*, "The only thing that's changed is that instead of manipulating 12 jurors, Dr. Phil now manipulates 6.5 million television viewers."

Or as his ex-wife, Debbie, puts it, "It's always about him. No matter what the supposed subject is or how he comes across, it's always about him."

4

◇◇◇◇

TONY ROBBINS: LEAPS (AND BOUNDS) OF FAITH

The people who are there, the ones who made a sizable investment to go, they're going to be excited and get into it. But when you're talking about the people who don't go, well, it's hard to say how they feel.

—Niurka Turner, a former salesperson for Tony Robbins Enterprises, explaining why people who attend Robbins's seminars probably have more faith in his methods than those who don't

It's hard to capture the full impact Tony Robbins has had on American culture over the past few decades. He is, to begin with, a man of near-mythological proportions: a broad six-foot-seven with a bestubbled jaw worthy of Mount Rushmore. It would not be stretching things to say that he has become a metaphor for himself and his ideas of personal greatness. Robbins understands as well as anyone the special advantage his physical size gives him in an industry whose whole point is about feeling larger than life. Allusions to size and potency are everywhere in his public image, from the titles of his best-selling books, *Unlimited Power* (1986) and *Awaken the Giant Within* (1991), to the none-too-subtle hints of mythological sexual endowment in that memorable elevator scene from the film *Shallow Hal*, in which the title character, played by the comic Jack Black, remarks with wide-eyed awe at the size of Robbins's feet. *Shallow Hal* is one of two high-profile Hollywood products in which Robbins makes key cameo appearances; the other was *Men in Black*, which also riffed on Robbins's aura of unreality by suggesting that he is not of this earth.

A figure shrouded in such mystery could only have the most mysterious of all possible birthdays: leap day, February 29. The year was 1960.

Otherworldly is as good a word as any for his success. Robbins likes to talk about how he once worked as a janitor and lived in quarters so cramped that he stored his dishes in the bathtub. He now stands at the helm of a motivational empire that *Business Week* has estimated provides him with $80 million per year. His books, most of them originally published in the 1990s, became major best sellers and still sell today. He pioneered and perfected the art of the late-night infomercial, which eventually, with the emergence of cable TV, became the all-day infomercial: Robbins claimed a few years ago that there had never been a thirty-minute interval since April 1989 when one of his spots wasn't on TV somewhere. He boasts that he has "directly impacted the lives of 50 million people from 80 countries," and his one-on-one clients have included Nelson Mandela, Mikhail Gorbachev, Margaret Thatcher, François Mitterrand, Princess Diana, and Mother Teresa. President Clinton beckoned him to Camp David for a chat (perhaps having a particular need for Robbins's expertise in the artful use of persuasive language). Because Robbins was among the first to take a "holistic" approach to motivation by arguing that all human activities figured in one's odds of success, he's ideally positioned to claim market share in nutrition and wellness. Though he may be eclipsed at any given time by the motivational flavor of the week, in the end, there is always Tony Robbins.

It helps that many insiders rank him as SHAM's most convincing motivational theorist, treading as he does that perfect line between brilliance (or at least pseudobrilliance) and accessibility. Even though his theories owe a great deal to others', Robbins has put it all together in a way that few have managed. Yes, he sells the usual actualization liturgy, which vastly oversimplifies the mechanism of success. "The only limit to your impact is your imagination and commitment," he will say, or "Using the power of decision gives you the capacity to get past any excuse to change any and every part of your life in an instant." But for someone out of the Empowerment camp—indeed, one of its founding voices—Robbins has also talked quite a lot about pain. And that resonates with people. To wit: "All personal breakthroughs begin with a change in beliefs. So how do we change? The most effective way is to get your brain to associate massive pain to the old belief. You must feel deep in your gut that not only has this belief cost you pain in the past, but it's costing you in the present and, ultimately, can only bring you pain in the future. Then you must associate tremendous pleasure to the idea of adopting a new, empowering belief." And: "The secret of success is learning how to use pain and pleasure instead of having pain and pleasure *use you*. If you do that, you're in control of your life. If you don't, life controls you." He has also said, now and then, things with clear practical implications: "Successful people ask better questions. As a result, they get better answers."

Nor has it hurt Robbins that, like all of the seminarists, he uses the dozens of seminars he puts on each year as extended sales pitches for his books, other products, and further seminars. But that still doesn't give the man enough credit for being the sui generis force he is in modern-day SHAM culture. Let's put it this way: If motivation were a religion, Tony Robbins would almost certainly be its pope.

But is it a religion you'd want to belong to?

THE EVENT

A Tony Robbins seminar is a multiday event, a Happening. For starters, there are the venues: Robbins's seminars, like others of the breed, take place in large hotels and resorts—but he often holds his in San Juan, or Palm Springs, or even Fiji, where he maintains a second home. (The first is in coastal Del Mar, California, which isn't exactly slumming it.) The seminars bear evocative, uplifting names, like Life Mastery, Wealth Mastery, Leadership Academy, Date with Destiny, Mastery University, and Unleash the Power Within. Once you get beyond Robbins's entry-level offerings (such as Unleash the Power Within), the appeal is *grand luxe* throughout. Consider this description of a Date with Destiny seminar, from Robbins's promotional literature, which appears under the heading "Awaken to Your Dreams in the Most Spectacular Settings":

> What if you could experience some of the most important moments of your life in some of the most spectacular and breathtakingly beautiful resorts . . . If you could spend a week in the most exclusive company in the world, enjoying Anthony Robbins' most intimate program . . . In the sophisticated surroundings of a world-class getaway for sun worshipers, golf lovers and nature buffs alike . . . You must act now! This opportunity will vanish! [Ellipses in original]

Availing yourself of this particular date with destiny will make $6,995 vanish. And that sum does *not* include the hotel accommodations themselves—a technicality that goes unmentioned in the literature and that, judging by the grumbling in Tony Robbins online discussion groups, doesn't occur to some customers until after they've paid for their seats and received their registration materials. Recognizing that the price of admission may seem daunting to some, Robbins includes top-shelf testimonials, such as this one from Oscar-nominated screenwriter Jeff Arch: "A month after Date with Destiny, I wrote *Sleepless in Seattle*, and sold it for a quarter of a million dollars."

Robbins likes to bundle his seminars, promising maximum bang for the buck. Sign up for the five-and-a-half-day Mastery University and you get Life Mastery, Wealth Mastery, Date with Destiny, and VIP Coaching, all neatly packaged in an "exclusive opportunity to condition every area of your life" by "learning from the finest movers and shakers of our time." The coaching follow-up is spread over three months, in a total of a half-dozen thirty-minute sessions. No, you do not get Tony himself for each session, but rather a Robbins stand-in. All this for the low, low price of $10,995 per person. He also may offer several tiers of admission. The price structure of a 2004 Unleash the Power Within seminar, held in New York City, ran from a general-admission tariff of $795 to "executive" ticketing at $1,095, "VIP" ticketing at $1,395, and "Diamond" ticketing at $1,995. The higher tiers get special seating, perks, and freebies.

The events themselves are state of the art: sound systems worthy of a Sting concert, Hollywood-grade stage lighting, digital-video feeds to JumboTron screens alongside the stage (or in adjacent rooms for the overflow crowd), music, dancers, other performers. Some have compared a Robbins seminar to a nonstop advertisement for success, and in a way the analogy is dead-on, since the senses-filling spectacle features regular promos for Robbins's ancillary materials as well as other products he shamelessly shills. This is hardly unheard-of in the self-help culture, as top SHAM artists routinely cut side deals with people selling "complementary" products. For a time, Laura Schlessinger was regularly touting the literacy program Hooked on Phonics, and her show ran ads for the product starring her son, Deryk. The creator of Hooked on Phonics, John Shanahan, happened to be her partner in Synergy Broadcasting, which then owned her radio show. Gurus make the most of the audience they have in the palm of their hands. Robbins of late has been particularly fond of QLink, a pendant that, he argues, enhances a person's resistance to ambient radiation of the kind that comes from cell phones. (Deepak Chopra endorses QLink, too.) While Robbins includes testimonials and endorsements among his seminar materials and mentions the "double-blind tests" that supposedly validate QLink, seminar attendees have had trouble getting scientific verification, and the Web site to which Robbins's minions direct interested parties www.clarus.com) shows no conclusive studies. The major bit of verification on the actual QLink site comes via a small Australian study that deals only with exposure to "active mobile phones"—and it begins by conceding that "research has failed to find consistent relations between [mobile phones] and human pathology." Later, the authors of the study note that, while they detected certain neural changes in cell-phone users, "it has not been shown that such changes are detrimental."

Whether he's pushing products or not, Robbins likes to jump up and down and from place to place while onstage; he does impromptu jigs and other dexterous physical stunts, and high-fives his accomplices, assistants, and any attendees he plucks from the audience for various demonstrations and favored shticks. "To see this human brand standing up there modeling all these behaviors he's encouraging from you is really something," California real-estate broker James Mencini, a confessed Robbins junkie, told me. "I don't care how much initial skepticism you may have. He's a master."

When he's there. Sometimes the master turns up missing, for not unlike other SHAM superstars, Robbins employs hired hands to lead certain phases or days of his training. Industry-wide, the consternation level seems directly proportional to the fee paid: Though John Gray now farms out the majority of his Mars/Venus seminars, people who paid a few hundred dollars or less are inclined to shrug it off, figuring they got their money's worth. On the other hand, one hears a fair amount of carping from Robbins "newbies" who had assumed that for $1,000 or more, they'd get unlimited helpings of the maestro himself, at least for the duration of the seminar.

"IT'S A CROCK"

It may be symbolic that Tony Robbins got his start teaching his followers to walk over hot coals, since this "fire walk experience" is a bit of gimmickry that appeals to naïfs despite having been so thoroughly debunked as to invite comparisons with snake oil. "In technical, scientific terms, it's a crock," says James Randi, the legendary debunker whose organization, the James Randi Educational Foundation, offers a $1 million prize to "anyone who can show, under proper observing conditions, evidence of any paranormal, supernatural, or occult power or event." In an interview, Randi told me, "Fire walking works, but not for any reasons related to spiritualism or metaphysics. It's the *physics* of the thing, having to do with heat conduction and transfer."

Undeterred, Robbins to this day kicks off some of his ultra-high-tech seminars with this ultra-low-tech mood-setter. "It's really about getting people's attention," he once told me. "The fire walk really embodies the whole of what we try to achieve with mental focus."

When Robbins began the fire walks two decades ago, getting ever-hopeful Californians to pay $50 a pop, he taught his followers to eliminate fear and pain by inducing an altered, self-hypnotic state that could be attained by repeating the phrase "cool moss." The phrase was one of the earliest manifestations of his growing absorption in neurolinguistic programming (NLP), a way of controlling thoughts and reworking basic assumptions about life developed in 1975 by a linguist and a mathematician at the University of California at Santa Cruz. NLP can be slippery to define succinctly, but it rests on the pithy cliché (at least in NLP circles) that "the brain did not come with a user's manual." John Grinder, the linguist, and Richard Bandler, the mathematician,[1] believed that how we define things and explain life to ourselves determines how we relate to those things and react to life in general. It followed that changing those explanations, or the way people subjectively interpret what's happening to and around them, should change the way people operate in the world. A fairly typical NLP tenet, now perceived as groundbreaking, is: "There is no such thing as failure—only feedback." That is, do something that has a bad outcome and you haven't *failed*; you've merely *learned*. NLP has shown up in many settings inside and outside SHAM, but of late it has acquired particular cachet in business circles for its usefulness in negotiations and conflict resolution—which is interesting, because Grinder and Bandler ultimately ended up in court, unable to resolve their own conflict over who owned the licensing rights to NLP. Nonetheless, dozens of firms offer derivative programs today, if not with quite the success Tony Robbins enjoys.

Robbins made NLP his own, refining it and personalizing it into what he christened "neuroassociative conditioning." In 1986 came publication of his *Unlimited Power*, the first formal statement of his thesis. The book took off immediately, as did Robbins, who piloted his own helicopter over buildings where he used to work as a janitor.

As remarkable as Robbins's success is his staying power in the face of adversity. If Ronald Reagan was the Teflon President and John Gotti was the Teflon Don, then Tony Robbins is the Teflon Guru, brushing off sticky situations large and small. In the small category: For someone whose stock in trade is the precise, life-changing use of language, Robbins can be surprisingly careless with it. Promotional materials describing his new line of nutritional products twice refer to one of the key ingredients as *collodials* instead of *colloidals*. (And whatever the spelling, it is debatable how much of a role, if any, these supplements play in proper nutrition.) Perhaps more problematic for Robbins's followers is the explanation of his three-day cancellation policy in his seminar-registration materials: It appears to be a no-day cancellation policy, requiring "a signed and dated written notice postmarked prior to midnight of the business day after the date of this agreement."

Robbins has math issues, too. When I visited his Web site in the summer of 2004, I discovered that both his Date with Destiny and his Life Mastery seminars were listed at $6,995 and that Robbins offered a 28 percent discount for ordering online—which is fine except that in one case (Date) the sale price became $4,995, and in the other case (Mastery) the sale price became $4,495. Perhaps Robbins himself needs a Date with Long Division or a course in Math Mastery.

If those problems seem insignificant, critics have highlighted more troubling aspects of Robbins's approach. Robbins uses science as if it existed solely for his convenience in making the points he wants to make. He'll offer up blithe correlations between technology and disease or caffeine and breast cancer, as if they were unimpeachable medical truths. He condemns meat and milk, strongly implying that you can't reach maximum potential if you're still chained to those vestiges of old-style food consumption. Then there's that whole bit about the energy frequency of foods, which simply does not make sense, because frequency is a measure of oscillation or vibration, not energy. "How," asks Yale University nutrition expert Kelly Brownell, "would that possibly apply to food?"

Despite the quasi-intellectual pretension of much of Robbins's patter, his seminars incorporate routines with a high kitsch factor. Robbins will invite an audience member onstage and easily lift him up off the ground. Then he'll order his subject to "feel centered and grounded. Imagine you are connected firmly to the earth!" Robbins will try to lift the man a second time and won't be able to. No, I am not kidding.

For such reasons, the happy little community of Robbins World occasionally displays signs of unrest. You see it mostly on the discussion boards he provides for dedicated disciples, if you check often enough. Recently people have complained about management censorship: the sudden disappearance of posts and threads that voice displeasure with any of Robbins's materials or the long-term efficacy of his programs. In 2001 some fans were dismayed to learn that Robbins and his wife, Becky, had divorced; after all, many followers had bought his books and tapes on the surefire steps to a lasting marriage.

Worse publicity has stemmed from events that hint at a certain disingenuousness on Robbins's part. In 1995 he agreed to settle Federal Trade Commission (FTC) allegations that his company overstated the profit potential in video franchises for his seminars. According to the FTC, prospective franchisees paid fees between $5,000 and $90,000 for the rights to charge admission to seminars featuring the master on tape. Robbins agreed to reimburse franchisees for a total of $221,260 in basic expenses, and up to $49,875 for any unused "video kits" beyond what was supplied with the original agreement.

But if anything symbolizes the emperor's-new-clothes aura surrounding Robbins, and the dangers attending today's blind faith in SHAM, it's an Internet venture-cum-boondoggle known as Dreamlife.com.[2] The New Age Web site with the mind-blowing multimedia effects was supposed to deliver SHAM content in six categories: mind and spirit, money and finance, relationships and family, health and fitness, career and business, and creativity and fun. Subscribers could avail themselves of "live" chats with such New Age celebrities as Shirley MacLaine, advice for the lovelorn, job-hunting pointers, even tips on selling a screenplay in Hollywood—in short, everything you could want in SHAM evangelism under one colossal digital tent. Robbins had lofty goals for Dreamlife's size and profitability, saying he wanted to build the site into "the eBay of personal and professional empowerment."

Unfortunately—for its average-Joe investors above all—the project never quite made it past beta stage after its launch in the fall of 1999 and is now defunct. More to the point, at no time in its development cycle did Dreamlife have any meaningful revenue stream, proprietary products, or realistic strategies for generating either. This should not have been surprising, given the origins of the deal. Dreamlife was put together by Allen & Co., a Wall Street investment-banking firm long identified with mergers and start-ups marked by imaginative financing. To avoid the usual paperwork and reporting rigors of an initial public offering, Allen & Co. spun off Dreamlife from an obscure medical-services firm, Global Health Systems Inc. Global Health Systems had nothing to do with self-help and no income from online operations. What it did have was a stock already up and running. That stock, however, was listed not on the white-glove New York Stock Exchange or on the sexy NASDAQ, but on the Over-the-Counter Bulletin Board, which Bloomberg's Christopher Byron later described as "the cheesiest, rankest, most volatile sub-basement on Wall Street." Further, though Robbins was to be the marquee player, he already had long-term agreements in place with two publishers, Fawcett and Fireside, and was reluctant to assign any of his seminar revenues to Dreamlife. This effectively left the new venture bereft of anything to sell except "T-shirts and trinkets," wrote Byron, who followed the project closely from its inception.

Under those sketchy circumstances, most savvy investors would have run and hid. What made the difference here was Robbins. In exchange for the use of his name, he got a 57 percent stake in the deal without investing one dime of his own money. Allen & Co. then went out and effected so-called private placements of Dreamlife stock to a who's who of the rich and famous: newsmen Tom Brokaw and Bryant Gumbel, NBC president Bob Wright, sports impresario Wayne Huizenga, tennis great Andre Agassi, and Hollywood producer Jon Peters. All of them queued up for a slice of the Tony Robbins mystique.

The outreach to Brokaw et al. raised $15.1 million in seed money. But more important, as word of this "opportunity" spread, assisted by credulous if not downright fawning media coverage, the stock soared. Once trading at 75 cents per share, it hit $16 by Christmas 1999. With some 40.4 million shares outstanding, Robbins's stake was suddenly worth $368 million. On February 12, 2000, Robbins introduced Larry King and his one million viewers to Dreamlife. With characteristic élan, Robbins described his new portal as a place "where you can take any dream you want and turn it into reality." Too bad Robbins could not do that with the site itself. By the fall of 2000, the Internet bubble was bursting, and Dreamlife—still, really, with nothing to sell—saw its stock price plummet to a year-end low of just 94 cents, according to its SEC filing. There is no hard proof of how many of the big early stakeholders, including Robbins, had dumped their shares by this time. But there's no question that most of the average Joes took their lumps.

After further financial gyrations, notably a deft merger with Discovery Toys, Dreamlife reemerged as EOS International on December 31, 2001. EOS has nothing to do with anyone's dreams, and it still doesn't have any true products of its own to sell, but it does acquire firms that sell them, mostly through product parties, catalogs, and the Internet. The company declared a loss of $16.7 million in 2003. Robbins remains as vice chairman of the board. On a late October day in 2004, EOS stock was selling, on that same OTC Bulletin Board, for 16 cents a share.

The astonishing thing about Robbins is that even skeptical followers don't usually abandon him. They'll post dubious messages on his discussion boards, questioning the usefulness of going to that next seminar . . . but they'll end up going anyway. Michael Roes, who admits to being hooked on Robbins for "some time now," told me, "Tony's got great material, and he's so personally compelling. It's clear that he lives this stuff through and through. We've got some of his nutritional formula, we're working through his CD sets, we're off the meat and dairy." All this, says Roes, even though more than a few elements of the Tony Robbins experience "really bug me and I'd really like some answers."

After attending a seminar in Anaheim in 2003, Roes was particularly bothered by the QLink connection. "It was all very suspicious," he says. "I don't understand Tony's emphasis on it. Nowhere [in the literature] does it say, 'We have this thing, and it works, and we can prove it.'" He concludes, "I guess crowds don't think very well. They just follow." And yet Roes is one of the followers. He and his wife still plan to follow Robbins right to the next Life Mastery Program in Fiji, at a cost of tens of thousands of dollars.

In Michael Roes, we once again see the fundamental paradox of self-help: If it works, people should emerge from their larval state and become the fully evolved individuals SHAM vowed to help them be. But many of them never seem to emerge. And with the self-help gurus dependent on selling a steady stream of products and services to a loyal following, you question the sincerity of the effort to transform all those caterpillars into butterflies.

"Robbins and the others may talk a good game about self-reliance," says James Randi, "but this is an industry that survives on repeat business. If you could go to every seminar or every bookstore, you'd see the same faces over and over and over again."

AND TONY MARCHES (OR FIRE WALKS) ON

Having embedded himself deeply in his disciples' heads, Robbins now has designs on their "kitchen cupboards, medicine chests, and gym bags," as the *New York Times* put it in an August 2003 article. That is to say, he has begun plotting and executing an ambitious assault on the "wellness" marketplace. According to at least one knowledgeable insider, Paul Zane Pilzer, a former Reagan administration economist, the wellness industry pulls in some $200 billion annually, and that figure could hit $1 trillion before 2010, as more and more baby boomers try to fight off the ravages of age. Robbins, in the *New York Times* interview, made no secret of his ambitions when it came to the wellness market. "I want to own it," he declared.

Robbins isn't alone in that goal. Phil McGraw, you will remember, has pursued the same market with his controversial line of energy bars and "nutraceuticals." McGraw also has his diet book and his cookbook. Meanwhile, several high-end resorts nationwide now feature "Chopra Centers," offering the wellness regimens endorsed by the guru whose name they bear. For a fee, cell-phone users can avail themselves of the preachments found in Chopra's book *The Seven Spiritual Laws of Success*, delivered daily.

But no one seems as ideally positioned, with as captive an audience, as Robbins. He is vice chairman of IdeaSphere, which manufactures organic food and other health products sold under the Robbins banner. His Web site and seminar literature promote a wide array of health products, from his Life Balance Pack, which promises to "cleanse and revitalize your system" (and includes a helping of those "collodials"), to his Alkaline Weight Loss Program (which not only promotes "the permanent weight loss you deserve" but also "neutralizes the excess acids in your blood," with the help of still more collodials), to his Ultra Greens method of deriving "pure energy" through a "unique formulation of sprouted grains, organically grown grasses, and fibrous herbs," among other things.

Equally important to Robbins's long-range vision, IdeaSphere's executive offices are stocked with former Amway brass who know the ropes of direct-to-consumer marketing. To help things along, Robbins looks to gobble up companies that can give him an instant presence in health and nutrition markets. In 2004, for example, IdeaSphere announced that it had purchased Twinlab, a once-strong nutraceutical brand weakened in recent years by the ephedra scare. Twinlab gave IdeaSphere a ready-made line of sports drinks, herbal teas, food bars, and other popular products. And Robbins isn't done. He says he's poised to forge a revolutionary alliance with one of America's largest manufacturers of athletic shoes and sports apparel, and has his eye on a major chain of health-food stores—edging him ever closer to his dream of becoming a full-service wellness powerhouse with some degree of influence over almost all of the faithful's choices. As George Carlin opined, thus does self-help become, simply, *help*. And—just maybe—*control*.

As for the real long term? Robbins has said he wouldn't mind taking over for Oprah Winfrey when she's ready to pass the torch. It's a fitting aspiration; those are, after all, shoes that only the inimitable Tony Robbins may be big enough to fill.

5

"YA GOTTA WANT IT!"

He's supremely confident. He knows he's going to do what he wants.

—*Baseball player David Bell, age thirty, explaining what makes former teammate Barry Bonds such a great hitter, in the* Morning Call *(Allentown, Pennsylvania), April 27, 2003*

He has the best batting eye I've ever seen, and probably the quickest hands to the ball as well. And his upper-body strength is almost superhuman.

—*Hall of Famer Mike Schmidt, age fifty-three, explaining what makes Bonds so great, quoted much later in the same* Morning Call *article, almost as an afterthought*

Some years back I sat in attendance as Tommy Lasorda, baseball's reigning ambassador-at-large, delivered an hour-long after-dinner speech to about fifty employees of Staedtler Inc., a manufacturer of precision writing and drafting instruments. The Staedtler personnel were carefully selected for their worthiness to be present on such an august occasion. Before the speech, the firm's marketing vice president, Ted Wheelock, shared his hopes for the evening's festivities. The company had been stingy with its expenditures for training and motivation, but the sales team was mired in a dismal slump. Wheelock felt that Lasorda, motivator extraordinaire, could help the staff "take things to the next level."

I came away spellbound by Lasorda's presentation, albeit not for the reasons one might think. At no time during his $500-a-minute spiel did he impart a single shred of tactical wisdom. Lasorda discussed nothing specifically relevant to Staedtler's business; he might have been talking about pens, he might have been talking about chicken parmigiana. His advice ranged from the merely banal ("There are people who make things happen, and there are people who wonder what happened") to the childishly simpleminded ("Ya gotta want it"); he even spouted nonsense of Yogi Berra proportions ("The thing you notice about losers is, they don't win"). Along the way, he told inspirational stories about athletes who succeeded against all odds; like all self-help gurus, but more than most, sports speakers *love* inspirational stories. For his pièce de résistance, he trotted out the well-worn tale of how a hobbled Kirk Gibson lifted his battered frame off the bench and, through sheer grit, blasted a pinch-hit, game-winning home run in game one of the 1988 World Series. "Kirk just wasn't going to be beaten that day!" Tommy thundered, as if to imply that the losing pitcher, Dennis Eckersley, a notorious competitor in his own right, came to the ballpark that afternoon not especially caring whether he cost his team the series.

What, then, was so spellbinding? The reaction to all this. At the end of his talk, Lasorda was applauded and backslapped as enthusiastically as if he'd just delivered the Sermon on the Mount. A joyous Wheelock opined that he'd gotten his money's worth and then some. "Already?" I asked. "How do you know?" He answered by way of a broad gesture at the smiling faces and general vigor that still simmered in the room as Lasorda made his gracious (but efficient) exit. "The guys are stoked," he said.

A few months later I called Wheelock to find out how things were going. The sales slump continued.

Today, there's just no sating corporate America's appetite for the lessons and putative logic of that very special offspring of SHAM we'll call Sportsthink. Simply stated, if there's a twist on self-actualization that's distinctively, emblematically American in this nation of people whose spirits soar and sag with the latest ESPN ticker, Sportsthink is it.

"Look on any manager's bookshelf today and there's Walsh's books," Karlene Sugarman, a sports-psychology consultant, told me. The Walsh is Bill, coach of the once-dynastic San Francisco 49ers, and the books are

Finding the Winning Edge and *Building a Champion*, both early winners in sports-motivation publishing. Sugarman continues, "Sports becomes the model for how things are done." John K. Mackenzie, a corporate-communications theorist and writer, puts it this way: "Nothing can suppress our compulsion for moving the locker room into the meeting room."

Mackenzie understates the impact—Sportsthink now extends well beyond the meeting room. But corporate America's unbridled enthusiasm for it certainly gives some indication of the magnitude of the phenomenon. Between 1991 and 2002, U.S. corporate-training budgets grew from $43.2 billion to $66 billion per annum. Though the portion of that sum given over to sports-influenced protocols is hard to pin down, the answer clearly runs to ten figures. Insiders peg the domestic banquet circuit alone as a $500 million annual enterprise, with Lasorda and his imitators and successors putting in appearances at not a few of the eight hundred thousand off-site meetings corporate America holds each year, pocketing fees from $5,000 to upward of $100,000. Companies spend additional billions on "after-action"—the books, videos, CDs, workshop tutorials, and other ancillary materials designed, says Mackenzie, to create "a bright shining world where never is heard a discouraging word and everybody is a winner all the time."

LIFE IS A GAME—WIN IT

America's desire to bask in the greatness of its sports heroes is nothing new. The banquet circuit already existed in Babe Ruth's day, and was in fact a concern of some Yankees officials, who worried about the weight the not-exactly-svelte Babe would add during his off-season banquet binges. But in those days, even top-tier athletes often appeared gratis, deeming it an honor just to be invited to speak. Legendary Notre Dame football coach Knute Rockne, of the fabled "Gipper" pregame speech, did a fair amount of speaking in public, though surprisingly it did not come naturally to him, and he never considered himself good at it. Vince "Winning Is the Only Thing" Lombardi emerged as a huge draw during the 1960s, becoming one of the first sports luminaries to be paid decent sums for his motivational appearances. His son now trades on the famous name and an uncanny physical resemblance, delivering after-dinner inspiration at the relatively modest $5,000 to $10,000 level.

One could say that the modern era of sports motivation began on September 1, 1993. That was the publication date of basketball coach Pat Riley's book *The Winner Within*, which formulated what Riley knew of sports motivation into a complete philosophical system—or as his subtitle put it, *A Life Plan for Team Players.* The book became an instant classic and required reading among corporate strategists. It also spawned an entire publishing category of credibly "nichified" alternatives to such blue-suited success books as Kenneth Blanchard and Spencer Johnson's *One Minute Manager* and Stephen Covey's *7 Habits of Highly Effective People.*

In the wake of Riley's smash hit, if you coached basketball at almost any level, corporate America wanted to hear what you had to say about life, work, empowerment, fulfillment, actualization, or [fill in the desired SHAM buzzword]. In 1995 Phil Jackson, then coaching the Michael Jordan–era Chicago Bulls, churned out *Sacred Hoops*, the movement's most unapologetically Zen synthesis of sports, truth, and life. After leading the University of Kentucky to a national championship, Rick Pitino chipped in with *Success Is a Choice* (1997), whose title became one of Sportsthink's core maxims. Duke University's Mike Krzyzewski, known affectionately as "Coach K," contributed *Leading with the Heart* (2000), which brimmed with such memorable Lasordian insights as "a leader's ability to think on his feet . . . is of paramount importance."

Lasorda rode this first wave of Sportsthink, which was mostly about celebrity, charisma, cachet. It was a McLuhan-esque affair wherein the man was the message, even when the man *had* no message, or when the man's message was indecipherable. This is not said in jest. At one time the biggest draw, arguably, was none other than O. J. Simpson, who preached to standing-room-only crowds despite diction so poor that he could barely be understood. "It doesn't really matter what O.J. says," a booking agent told me with surprising candor. "It's just that he's here."

During the early 1990s, the evolving Sportsthink movement made cottage industries of O.J., Lasorda, Walsh, and just about everyone else who'd ever achieved anything on a gridiron, court, rink, track, or baseball diamond.

To be sure, demand for high-profile speakers remains strong. "Companies want to show employees how much they care about their success," Marc Reede of Nationwide Speakers Bureau told me. "The way to do that is to produce a top speaker." Reede's company delivers those speakers to clients including IBM, Coca-Cola, the Ford Motor Company, and Mutual of Omaha. Soccer sprite Mia Hamm has commanded Lasorda-like fees ever since her 1999 World Cup exploits; in return, she delivers such nostrums as "The person who says winning isn't everything never won anything" and "Many people say I'm the best women's soccer player in the world. I don't think so. And because of that, someday I just might be." Mike Eruzione, the affable captain of the gold medal–winning 1980 U.S. Olympic hockey team, has recently ridden the crest of a renewed patriotic fervor (not to mention a popular film chronicling his team's stunning victory). "Mike's the hottest sports speaker in the country," Reede told me in early 2004. "He had only seven or eight open days in February."

But in recent years, a funny thing happened on the way to the banquet hall: a gradual but inexorable shift from *event-based* to *culture-based* motivation, wherein Sportsthink became less about pep talks and more about daily business life. Corporate leadership now expected employees not merely to applaud the message but also to *live* it, dutifully importing as many aspects of sports as possible into the activities of the 9-to-5 workplace. Nowadays all this personal transformation takes place under the watchful eye of variously pedigreed noncelebrity consultants (like Karlene Sugarman, a consultant since grad school) who work on-site with corporate HR offices for weeks or months at a time, at $1,000 a day or more. Naturally, since the goals for today's Sportsthink are so much more ambitious, the program must be packaged differently; for starters, it must *be* a program, not just a book or a speech or a series of either. The key word, however, is *packaged*. Modern Sportsthink has been covered by a layer of intellectual, parascientific respectability—but when that layer is peeled back, one is still left with "ya gotta want it." As much as any manifestation of SHAM, Sportsthink forms an object lesson in how people desperate for easy answers (or wanting added consulting income) will impose order on chaos, filling in any inconvenient gaps, much as the human eye finds coherent images in a Rorschach inkblot.

Herewith, the overlapping precepts of what might be called the emperor's new attitude:

SUCCESS IS A CHOICE. Pitino said it explicitly, but many other Sportsthink gurus also preach that everything is within your grasp, that environmental obstacles can be overcome if you just follow Kirk Gibson's lead by calling on your psychic and emotional stockpiles. "Every moment of the day provides a new opportunity to take the fearful or fearless path," Jeff Greenwald, a former tennis pro and the founder of Mental Edge International, told me. "The sum of these choices will determine the quality of our performance with customers and coworkers and, ultimately, our results." This *attitude über alles* mantra grossly and unfairly oversimplifies the mechanisms of both winning and losing. According to Mark Fichman, PhD, an organizational consultant attached to Carnegie Mellon University, mental attitude is a "relatively small [factor in success] compared to your location in the social world to begin with." Archly, he adds, "It is easier to become president if your father was president." Fichman also underscores the logical flaw in selecting only successful figures, like Riley and Walsh, and asking them to reflect on the attitudes and behaviors that (supposedly) got them where they are. "When Bill Gates tells us he dropped out of school, that does not mean dropping out of school is a key to success," says Fichman. "Obviously if you looked at all the dropouts, you would not conclude it's a good thing to do."

THE INDIVIDUAL MUST NEVER WAVER IN THE FACE OF ADVERSITY. Like the palooka who gamely pulls himself up off the canvas after each knockdown, the dedicated employee is expected never to waver in his pursuit of the brass ring, no matter the battering he takes en route. This bespeaks heart, yes—but also a certain macho bluster. Because this bulletproof, bullheaded mind-set cannot always be shut off at will, it may bleed over into other areas of life, with untoward results. "People need to know that it's OK to falter sometimes," Benjamin Dattner, PhD, a principal in Dattner Consulting and a professor of organizational development at New York University, told me. "This approach of being constantly 'on' and never saying die is a key cause of burnout, if not potentially worse."

THE "GAME" COMES FIRST. Relationships, personal issues, extracurricular interests, even family—all take a backseat to the Almighty Job. This stricture has been especially hard on women, who already experience crushing pressure to choose between their domestic lives and careers. True winners aren't expected to avail themselves of such "easy outs" as the Family and Medical Leave Act, which allows employees to take time off from work to care for a newborn child or sick relatives.[1]

WINNING IS, INDEED, THE ONLY THING. Vince Lombardi's favorite declaration has taken on new meaning in corporate settings, where the lesson becomes "Nothing matters but the end result." Foreign to Sportsthink are such words and concepts as *compromise, conciliate*, and—perish the thought—*concede*. In the battle for market share, you don't create truces, you don't build bridges; you vanquish your enemy, period. This schema gives little credence to effort and does not take into account the fact that failure may occur for a variety of reasons. Critics link this axiom more than any other aspect of Sportsthink to the erosion of business ethics in recent decades. "Corrupt business practices have been with us since the dawn of business itself," John K. Mackenzie told me, "but the 'win at all costs' construct, imported from sports during the 1980s, greatly magnified the inclination to cheat." This was in fact the ethos captured with brutal clarity in such cinematic period pieces as Oliver Stone's *Wall Street*.

It may be useful to take a step back and ask whether Sportsthink even has true validity in sports itself. In fact, the emphasis on "mental attitude" in athletics is all-pervading, to the point that the tendency to reason backward from an observed outcome in order to find the psychic predisposition that caused it has gotten downright silly. When sprinter Michael Johnson won one of his gold medals in the 1996 Olympics, NBC's track announcers reeled off just about every SHAM-inspired cliché imaginable; the notion that Johnson was simply faster than his competitors seemed not to occur to anyone. After a seventeen-year-old Russian upset the heavily favored Serena Williams at the 2004 Wimbledon championship, NBC tennis commentator Ted Robinson gushed, "Maria Sharapova came out with a full-fledged belief that she was able to win a Wimbledon championship!" Again, it was Sharapova's *belief* that won Wimbledon, not her ability to return Williams's 120-mile-per-hour serves or to uncork laserlike forehands that ran poor Williams back and forth across the baseline all morning. Contests in all athletic realms are put before us as modern Homeric allegories—crucibles of wit, grit, and will. Today's victorious teams seldom credit talent or luck or even hard work, but rather the likes of "character" and "confidence" or, as Lasorda counsels us, "wanting it more than the other guy." Every key play of every game is explained in terms of the attitude—good or bad—that held the participants in its grasp at the moment the fateful play occurred. We hear of players who "refuse to lose"—basketball players who drive to the hoop with "fire in the belly," gridiron defenses who hold firm thanks to a "gut check," pitchers who get that final out "through sheer determination." On the other hand, a pitcher who gives up a decisive home run at an inopportune moment has "lost his concentration." Isn't it possible, just *possible*, that he merely lost his fastball, or threw a curve that failed to go where he'd aimed it?

Evidently not. This school of thought is seldom questioned in competitive athletics today. The players themselves parrot these arguments in interviews, crediting their success to everything but their physical skills. Notice that in the two different quotes about baseball superstar Barry Bonds at the top of this chapter, David Bell—relatively young and thus more likely a product of "ya gotta want it" brainwashing—talks about Barry Bonds's "confidence," which is what the *Morning Call* sportswriter focused on for much of the article. Only in the final paragraphs did the writer get around to quoting Hall of Famer Mike Schmidt. Coming as he does from a generation less steeped in the attitude-is-all blather of today, Schmidt quite sensibly notes that among Bonds's other miscellaneous attributes are extraordinary strength and hand-eye coordination. When you're trying to hit a baseball boring in at 96 miles per hour over a 20-foot-tall fence that's 350 feet away, those things can help.

Though one is tempted to play the topic for laughs, some observers feel that the possible long-term effects are no laughing matter, especially when this "killer mentality" is drilled into athletes as young as Little Leaguers—as it so often is by coaches who *think* they're doing the kids a favor.[2] Well-known sports psychologist Dr. Bob Rotella told me, "I worry about the guilt these spiels create in young men and women who may fail to perform for reasons that have nothing to do with 'dedication' or 'heart.' "

But you can't tell any of that to people raised on today's Sportsthink (or who make their living selling it). "Athlete is a *powerful* word," intones Dr. Patrick Cohn of Peak Performance Sports, who consults for IBM and other blue-chip companies. "Athletes walk with pride. Athletes aren't afraid of challenges. Athletes persist in the face of doubt and defeat." True enough. But left unsaid is: What does that have to do with you or me? The nonathlete reading such affirmations has no reason to look or feel confident. Athletes walk with pride or persist in the face of doubt because they have specific competencies in the realms in which they compete: the ability to run faster than most other humans, to reach more than ten feet into the air and jam a basketball into a hoop, to swivel on ice skates more deftly than most of us can maneuver on dry land. "That's where they get their confidence," observes Jim Bouton, a celebrated baseball iconoclast and the author of the legendary tell-all book *Ball Four*. In a line with clarion implications for anyone weighing the benefits of undertaking some hot new self-help regimen, Bouton told me, "They don't become confident simply by having some other athlete scream at them, 'Now go out there and be confident!' You can't just paste confidence onto yourself."

Jay Kurtz, the president of KappaWest, a leading tactics-based consulting firm, agrees. "We're coaxing people to buy into a conceit that's suspect to begin with, and even if they do buy in, there's almost no guidance on how to translate that conceit into useful practice," he told me. "It's all psychological gamesmanship." Kurtz argues that Sportsthink gurus "took a short, punchy, profitable metaphor and converted it into an extended, even more profitable metaphor. But it's still a metaphor." And like most metaphors, it breaks down under deeper scrutiny. Which may explain why leading Sportsthink aficionados fall back on the quasi-religious line that you "just have to trust it."

Whatever parallels exist between sports life and corporate life dissolve just beneath the surface anyway. For example, in the summer of 2004, as in every Olympic year, "Go for the gold!" became *the* dominant theme at major meetings and conventions, with company brass exhorting key personnel to emulate the qualities displayed by top Olympians. In fact, Olympic-level performances seldom result from camaraderie, consensus problem solving, and the other amiable behaviors HR departments assiduously tout. "Olympic medals," says Mackenzie, "often go to temperamental loners who shun teamwork and labor for years under conditions of obsessive personal sacrifice that few if any mainstream employees would tolerate." Adds Benjamin Dattner, "Tiger Woods makes his own bed when he stays at a hotel in a golf tournament, because he's such a perfectionist. But that same unity of focus that makes him a perfectionist might make it difficult for him to be a manager, or even to be very adaptable, in a corporate environment."

Kurtz, meanwhile, points out that Sportsthink miscasts the actual situation facing most companies that try to adapt it to their needs. "Sports like baseball and football are one team versus another. In business, you're hardly ever going up against just one team. So if you use the sports model, where you're engaging a single competitor at a time, you could outfox Competitor A but leave your flank open for Competitor B to kick your ass." Says Dattner, "In sports you may use different strategies, but everybody plays by the same basic rules. In the business world, this is not the case."

For such reasons, many observers believe that Sportsthink saps precious resources that could be put to better use elsewhere.

"Most of these regimens are a mile wide and an inch deep," says Kurtz. "Very few of them ever get down to the really gutsy things people have to do within a company to bring about meaningful change." Those "gutsy things," he says, include everything from workshops on defeating customers' specific objections to a top-to-bottom retooling of the corporate reporting structure to gutting a specific underperforming unit within that hierarchy. Kurtz particularly warns against instances in which Lasorda-like fervor is applied in the absence of skill: "The most dangerous people in the world are the highly enthusiastic incompetents: They're running faster in the wrong direction. If they don't know what they're doing, or have the wrong idea of what they *should* be doing, their 'will to win' could destroy them." Kurtz points to Apple Computer, which, twice in its history, came to the verge of extinction by using world-class exuberance to communicate a message that had little or nothing to do with the corporate world's then-current needs.

And yet . . . ah, the sheer power of that metaphor in a nation that simply *loves* (a) sports and (b) success. If (a) and (b) are combined, so much the better.

Consider Boise Cascade Office Products (BCOP), which forms a significant part of the Boise Cascade empire, a $7 billion business that ranked number 248 on the Fortune 500 list in 2004. BCOP once used a chart of a football field to depict its progress toward its annual quota (the "goal line") for sales to the rest of Fortune 500 America. The company mixed things up a bit by showing performance figures as "batting averages," a baseball stat.[3] But minor inconsistencies aside, the sports motif at BCOP extended beyond mere representations on a chart. The company taught new sales recruits to use sports imagery ("Think of yourself on the 20-yard line, about to kick the game-winning field goal!"). Specific sales plans drew from NFL playbooks, sometimes complete with Xs and Os. Members of a major-account team might be assigned the respective functions of quarterback, receiver, and offensive lineman, each function correlated to its closest customer-service analogue. (Administrative-support personnel are urged to view themselves as assistant coaches.)

The BCOP model is increasingly common nowadays, thanks in part to the growing roster of firms and lone gunslingers who aggressively sell the sports/business linkage. Peak Performance Sports targets the Fortune 500 with such "outpatient" programs as "Applying Sports Psychology to the Business Team" and "The Psychology of Performance: Lessons I've Learned Working with Great Athletes." Jeff Greenwald, formerly the world's number one–ranked tennis player over age thirty-five, takes his "fearless performance" aria to the sales teams of corporate America via one- to six-month coaching programs.

Greenwald, a clinical psychologist who also maintains a general practice, makes for an interesting case study. An irredeemably perky fellow who seems to preface every answer with "That's a great question!" he says he achieved his number one ranking by "getting my mind straight" and that he now hopes to help major sales organizations do likewise. Greenwald represents what might be termed a "more enlightened" wing of sports motivators who preach the importance of *de*-emphasizing outcome and concentrating instead on process. Top achievers, he insists, must learn to filter out extraneous concerns, the first of those being excessive concern about winning or losing per se. "Whether you call it intensity or mental focus or being in the zone," he says, "the bottom line is that you have to keep your mind on the specifics of what you need to be doing at that moment, and let the end result take care of itself."

Greenwald begins by interviewing key managers to diagnose the specific problem: a lack of teamwork, insufficient motivation among sales reps, or some other typical impediment to sales. He looks specifically at the nature of the coded messages being sent in communications between managers and reps. "Whether they realize it or not," he says, repeating a common SHAM incantation, "they're always communicating potent messages, to the staff and to themselves." He then segues to five core competencies that affect performance: confidence, "self-regulation" (the ability to control destructive thoughts and emotions), resiliency ("you have to be able to weather the ups and downs"), team chemistry, and the aforementioned ability to "focus." Greenwald teaches his pupils to "windshield-wipe away" negative self-talk. "People who exhibit poor performance tend to focus on the irrelevant at best, [the] counterproductive at worst," he says. "For example, they'll mind-read: Say they're giving a presentation and somebody in the audience looks like he's not interested. So they think, 'He's not paying attention to me. My speech is boring. *I'm* boring.' And suddenly they're out of their game. You need to windshield-wipe all that away."

Because this approach is doomed to fail without constant reinforcement from above, Greenwald encourages top-level managers to downplay results wherever possible. "I don't want managers focusing so much on whether the sale got closed. I want managers saying, 'Were you fearless today? Were you in the zone? What do you think you need to do next time?'"

Barry Epstein of Epstein Solutions, a satisfied Greenwald client and a former executive with Oracle, echoes the belief that "wanting it" alone is not the answer: "I think we've all had situations where we wanted something so badly, and that's exactly why we didn't get it." Yet mirroring the philosophical confusion in the realm (as in so many SHAM realms), Epstein also concedes, "If I'm a manager and my salesman comes to me and says he 'engaged' with the customer and 'felt fearless'—but he didn't sell anything—I'm going to say, 'That's very nice, but you're fired.'"

Which is essentially what Bethlehem Steel said to Steve Foucault, a onetime sales manager for the company, which undertook an ambitious sports-oriented training program in the late 1980s. "The awards ceremonies were the worst for me," Foucault told me. "They always gave the stuff to the people who 'went the extra mile,' as if to imply that the rest of us weren't trying hard enough. Well, I *went* the extra mile. I tried damn hard. I just wasn't as naturally gifted as some of the others. I always ended up feeling like a loser, and I wasn't the only one." Jim Bouton isn't surprised. "If everything is do-or-die, and you fail at whatever it is you're trying to do, you've delivered a potent message to yourself."

The biting irony is that the metamorphosis from pep rally to program has transformed Sportsthink from an innocuous placebo (or shot of adrenaline) to a much more aggressive form of "treatment" with potentially serious side effects. Sportsthink not only shares SHAM's propensity for building false and hurtful expectations, it also teaches people to look at their jobs, if not the world, through an overly simplistic, ultracompetitive lens. Life becomes a morality play in which winners win because of good character and losers lose because of a weakness of will or spirit.

It bears noting that no amount of can-do spirit was able to help Bethlehem Steel overcome global competition and the other external factors that made the company's prices uncompetitive. The steelmaker filed for bankruptcy in 2001 and faded into history two years later.

That Sportsthink has been oversold is incontrovertible. Most of its teachings, after all, are fairly generic insights about teamwork, cohesion, goal setting, positive thinking, and the like. Most leading sports speakers make free use of material that's only tangentially related to sports, or whose sports significance is obscure at best (thus lending further credence to the suspicion that the "sports" label is mostly an attention-getting device for delivering all-purpose SHAM pabulum). Sports psychologist Kevin Elko likes to give talks about "Finding Your 68," a reference to the uniform number worn by NHL star Jaromir Jagr. Born in the Czech Republic, Jagr favors the number because, says Elko, "it was in 1968 that the Russian occupation of Czechoslovakia occurred. So finding your 68 means finding the thing about you that makes you tick." And what then? "When you find what you want in life, you give it away, and even more will come back to you," says Elko.

Even when Sportsthink's affirmations make actual sense, says Mark Fichman of Carnegie Mellon, "I suspect you could reach similar conclusions if you looked at generalizing from any particular walk of life—say, the entertainment industry—to another." Clearly Greenwald's "windshield-wiper" technique could just as well be called *automotivethink*. Bouton, meanwhile, accuses his peers of "way too much sloganeering, hyping so-called methods that are hardly new or profound." Nor have they ever been tested in any meaningful way. Although there are plenty of anecdotal success stories, sports-related inspirational talks and business plans have never been empirically validated as a way of improving performance, capacity, innovation—anything. Benjamin Dattner finds this dearth of tracking intriguing, given the numbers mania of the sports world itself. "One of the great things about baseball and football, for example, is the volume of statistics available for benchmarking performance down to the most infinitesimal level. So if you want to emulate sports, then emulate sports: *Keep score!*" Fichman speculates that Sportsthink may be one of those things that nobody really *wants* to test. "We want it to work," he says. "We have too much invested in this, a lot of us, for it to be meaningless in the end." As a result, high on its intoxicating promise, "managers make assumptions, act on them, and never really verify if they are true," says Fichman.

The question arises: Why does Sportsthink have such boundless appeal, when its benefits are so sketchy and its risks so real? The answers say a lot about what America expects from SHAM generally, and why it buys in at such a high cost. Even Sportsthink's tireless advocates allow that many companies see it as a relatively painless alternative to more demanding types of consulting. "It brings people back to a simpler time in their life," says Mark Dixon, the director of sales and client services for Acosta Sales and Marketing, which for the past six years has booked sports speakers on behalf of the Southern California deli/bakery industry. "It reminds us of when we were younger, and more optimistic about life—a time when everything was still possible, and we were all going to play center field for the New York Yankees."

Sportsthink, then, plays to the Walter Mitty within people. The lure of the message is its hinted promise of transcendence—if Kirk Gibson could do it with his gimpy legs, sore back, and all, well, so can you. Maybe you can't hit that game-winning home run for the Dodgers. But if, as the movement's high priests claim, we all have within us an untapped reserve of mettle, then maybe you can learn to hit the winning home run for your company and, by extension, your career. Much as die-hard fans wear Allen Iverson's jersey or swing Alex Rodriguez's bat, we think we can absorb their success by embracing the cultural trappings that made them that way. Or so Sportsthink tells us.

After all, if success happens for magical reasons that have nothing to do with skill or wit or looks—if we can persuade ourselves that Gibson launched that homer because he flat-out willed it—then we too can rise above our limitations. As Tommy says, all ya gotta do is *want it.*

THE ENDURING METAPHOR

Sports-as-workable-microcosm-for-life has achieved something like ubiquity. As we'll see in the next chapter, many SHAM artists have begun calling themselves "executive coaches" and even the all-encompassing "life coaches." Politics, too, brims with sports references. President George W. Bush, when not spouting quaint Westernisms meant to remind America's enemies that thar's a new sheriff in town, likes to fall back on beefy allusions to the ballpark or the gridiron. Beltway wonks speak of *end runs* and *home runs* and *strikeouts* and *goal-line stands*, borrowing freely from the sporting lexicon in a manner that underscores its common meaning and impact.

This trend may have reached its zenith, or nadir, during Bill Maher's HBO show of February 20, 2004. The comedian and social satirist had as his guest Senator George Allen, Republican of Virginia. For a time the two men, both sports nuts, debated the financial underpinnings of the major spectator sports. Then Maher asked Allen a question about politics—specifically, why Allen had accused the Democrats of political obstructionism. Allen responded by arguing that Democrats in Congress had been guilty of delay of game as well as holding, that they were politically and ethically offside in their approach to governance, that they were preventing the president from throwing the ball down the field, that too many legislators had punted when they should have run with the ball. . . . It was a tour de force in extended metaphor made all the more impressive by the sense that Allen had delivered it off the cuff. When he was done, the audience hooted its appreciation, and even the famously unflappable Maher looked flapped. I could hardly help flashing back to my long-ago evening with Tommy Lasorda.

Lost in the adulation was the fact that Allen had grossly distorted reality, diminishing his subject by oversimplifying it. The process by which Congress makes law and sets policy is nothing like a football game, and we do injustice to that process by making it seem so. Sports-inspired oratory may produce wonderful sound bites and stump speeches, but it also encourages a win-at-all-costs outlook among politicians and their followers. As the two parties seek to vanquish each other, the best interests of constituents get lost.

Worse, America buys in. The simpleminded conceit becomes part of the national dialogue, defining how we feel about the subject, causing us to sort ourselves into teammates and opponents, winners and losers, white hats and black hats, red states and blue states. Despite all of Sportsthink's new precepts, inevitably followers receive the competitive message that overlays it all: *You're either on my team, or you're not.* Like the blurted, prejudicial courtroom remark that jurors remember long after the judge's admonition to "disregard it," Sportsthink's overarching ambition—to win the game—is what sticks, outweighing all that motivational pabulum or even those few potentially helpful aspects of process.

In the end, the great failing of Sportsthink, both within the corporate world and without, is one that plagues the self-help movement as a whole, and ultimately our society: the tendency to put forth one-dimensional answers to complex, heavily nuanced questions; the tendency to let our decisions be guided by empty prescriptives that are about as useful as that old Yogi Berra line: "Baseball is 90 percent mental—the other half is physical."

6

PUT ME IN, COACH, I'M READY TO PAY

> Soon a coach will be seen as someone you have as a matter of course to make your life run more efficiently, like an accountant.
>
> —Sunday Telegraph *(London), July 1999*

"You are the creator," says the Web site of Jane Ellen Sexton, "whether you like it or not. That responsibility is also your gift of empowerment. So how do you cooperate with you while honoring your own divinity?"

That last line does not contain a typo. "How do you cooperate with you" is the kind of question you'd expect from a self-described "intuitive life coach," especially one who also offers "channeling" for people whose self-help needs exceed garden-variety intuitive life coaching.

"Channeling," Sexton helpfully explains, "is the process where I connect with information that flows through me from dimensions outside of the earth plane for purposes of expanding reality. This information comes from a spiritual, non-intellectual level. The best way I would describe the process is that my ego and personality move aside, and I become the vessel for the information that is the most appropriate for you in the moment."

Though she may grope a bit in defining the process, Sexton has no trouble explaining that her services as an intuitive life coach cost $150 an hour—or $250 per ninety-minute session if you go the channeling route. But most clients should be able to get away with the basic life coaching, as it's the "experience" she has "most aligned with" since she became "certified to do spiritual work." Sexton also promises that "while I'm listening to you, I'm not focused on anything but you." At $2.50 a minute, that's comforting to know.

Marketdata Enterprises estimates that twenty-five thousand "life coaches" of various stripes are now active in the United States, about ten thousand of them working in corporate America alone. The International Coach Federation (ICF), founded in 1992 as the National Association of Professional Coaches, claimed seven thousand members worldwide by 2004; that's up nearly 200 percent in just four years. And ICF is just one of several fraternal bodies that (very) loosely oversee this new SHAM specialty. Technically, no life coach is answerable to ICF or any other regulatory body. Of course, civilian penalties may apply if coaches commit a provable fraud, but even that's unlikely to occur, since the nature of the promise is so intangible and, usually, nonspecific.

Life coaching is the Dodge City of SHAM.

"A HEAVY INDUSTRY"

As SHAM subcategories go, the coaching sensation—and it surely *is* that—remains in its infancy. In a major 2002 survey of coaching practices underwritten by the California School of Organizational Studies (CSOS), 42 percent of the respondents confessed to less than two years of experience. True, an elite corps of top managers has long sought counsel from an elite corps of personal consultants; for the right price, the right person could get Tony Robbins himself for an afternoon. But in recent years, coaching has gone mass-market with an astonishing trajectory: a growth rate the *Economist* in 2002 estimated at 40 percent per year. Dozens of Web sites lure browsers with names like coachville.com, mylifecoach.com, lifecoachtraining.com, and solveyourproblem.com. There is even inanimate coaching delivered straight to your desktop: A British product, LifeBuilder, claims to be "the only desktop Life-coaching and self-improvement programme available in the world and, at just £19.95 [about US$35] it's truly amazing. Whatever your goals, aims and dreams might be, take a look at LifeBuilder."

Like the regimens themselves, costs are all over the map. In business settings, coaches are so sought after that their hourly earnings often outpace those of counseling professionals with hard-won credentials. A top executive coach like Jeffrey Auerbach, who is also president of the College of Executive Coaching, may charge $400 or more per hour, easily exceeding the going rate for most established psychologists or psychiatrists. This is where the phrase "phone it in" takes on a whole new meaning. Despite the lofty hourly sums, coaches in many cases needn't show up on the premises. They'll typically make three or four thirty- to sixty-minute calls, and e-mail their invoices, flexing their coaching pursuits around their 9-to-5 jobs and other freelance activities. A case in point is Richard Brendan of Indianapolis. Aside from being a "Life Purpose" coach, Brendan produces and hosts the inspirational *Journeys-Fire* radio show (featuring "conversations on life and love with Activists of the Heart"), promotes himself as a speaker-for-hire, and serves as a director of the Indianapolis chapter of HealthNet, a major managed-care provider. He says he's also a lifetime member of the Dead Poets Society.

Though it's almost impossible to reckon a total dollar volume for all coaching activities, one can extrapolate from the CSOS survey. It arrived at a mean annual income of $37,500 for its 1,338 respondents, most of whom worked only part-time. (Those labeling themselves "executive coaches" reported an average income of $77,339.) If the $37,500 figure holds for Marketdata's estimated universe of twenty-five thousand coaches, the end result is just under $1 billion in coaching income.

"Coaching is becoming a heavy industry," Warren Bennis, a professor of business administration at the University of Southern California's business school and the author of the 1990 business classic *On Becoming a Leader*, told me in an interview. "It's an incredible story."

All the more so because many of today's life coaches were doing something else before the turn of the millennium; in a fair percentage of the cases that something had little to do with counseling, therapy, or training of any kind. "Whenever you get increased demand, and supply comes to meet it quickly, it doesn't necessarily have to be of the best quality," John Kotter, a professor of leadership at the Harvard Business School, told me. "If the demand is high enough, all kinds of muck will flow into the market."

That river of flowing muck has not prevented a steady complement of otherwise-savvy people (as well as some not-so-savvy ones, as we'll see) from putting their faith in coaching. Today, says Jim Naughton of *Psychotherapy Networker*, a magazine for professionals in counseling fields, life coaching is fast becoming "the equivalent of having a personal trainer." That's how mainstream the once-fringe concept has gone. *Fortune* magazine, in a long article on the subject, called executive coaching "the hottest thing in management."

The demand is such that companies sometimes will even try to make coaches out of people who didn't think of it on their own. For example, Linda Hill, a Harvard Business School professor, has reportedly been "inundated" with requests to coach.

Managers hire coaches to facilitate divisional change (and deflect the blame that often accompanies it). Midlevel staffers, no longer anticipating the continuity of employment or professional TLC that once was expected from the business world, have turned to coaches for guidance on how to improve their morale, get that last ounce out of professional productivity, and make better, more personally relevant decisions—both on the job and off. Personal coaches are "not just sticking to corporate matters," Bennis told me, "and that's really the whole point of it. They've widened the lens to encompass all areas of the person's performance. They'll ask questions like 'Does this job make you happy?' 'Should you even be in this line of work?' "

BIRTH OF A SENSATION

Coaching as we now know it debuted in the 1980s, probably with a Seattle financial planner, Thomas Leonard. Leonard realized that his successful young clients, though emotionally "whole" and hardly candidates for traditional psychiatry, nonetheless seemed to need more from him than just the usual tips on how to invest and shelter their formidable incomes. Years later, he would remember a moment of truth when he asked some of them if they wanted to talk more holistically about life. "They jumped at it," Leonard told *Fortune*. "They didn't need a therapist. They just wanted to brainstorm."

His career shifted from financial planning to full-time brainstorming, which at the time he called "life planning." He recalls that he "had an inkling there was something interesting and powerful about this idea." As mergers-and-acquisition mania took hold and widespread corporate downsizing destabilized the American job market, the hunger for Leonard's services grew. Some of his clients wanted to kick around alternative ways of making money, some wanted to learn how to de-stress, some wanted a pat on the back, some wanted a shoulder to cry on. Coincidentally, by this time the rise of managed care had left many mental-health professionals searching for other ways to earn a living, ways that were more recession-proof and less dependent on insurance reimbursement. They became ideal candidates for Leonard's more SHAM-like—and prepaid—training methods. Somewhere along the line, somebody used the word *coaching*, and within a few years Leonard was coaching other prospective coaches, who were often corporate burnouts or refugees from other areas of the conventional business world.

In 1992 Leonard kicked off a formal coach-training program he dubbed Coach University. At least in Leonard's mind, Coach U, as it came to be known, would professionalize and standardize the growing field. Leonard eventually sold Coach U to a protégé, Sandy Vilas. (Like many others, Vilas took an eclectic route to coaching: He had worked in the energy industry, in real estate, as a speaker, as a trainer, and as a stockbroker.) Under Vilas's leadership, Coach U became a life-coach incubator that today offers more than fifty "teleclasses"—that is, courses in coaching methodologies that are conducted via conference call.

What such instruction prepares coaches to teach today's America can be hard to say. Life coaching is such a slippery enterprise that even explanations of its appeal sound vaguely . . . well, slippery. Patrick Williams, the president and founder of the well-known Institute for Life Coach Training, has described his milieu as the process of "futuring" people. Harvard's John Kotter told *Fortune*, "As society moves from 30 miles an hour to 70 to 120 to 180 . . . as we go from driving straight down the road to making right turns and left turns to abandoning cars and getting on motorcycles . . . the whole game changes. A lot of people are trying to keep up, learn how, not fall off." (Reflecting on that quote, Kotter told me he was simply trying to describe the appeal of coaching from the perspective of an audience who may feel that their lives are spinning out of control in today's increasingly fast-paced world.)

Surely the life coach wears multiple hats. He or she is part consultant, part oracle, part cheerleader, part provider of tough love. (And as we'll see shortly, at least some of the male coaches might provide a less tough kind of love.) Not all of these hats always fit as well as they might, with the result that coaches, like most SHAMsters, sometimes get caught up in the logic of their own marketing efforts. On the Web site for the online coaching organization Paradigm Associates, life coach Mark Gibson begins, "Whether you believe you will succeed, or you believe you will fail, you are right." But Gibson makes a convenient U-turn: "Those who have a vague idea of what their full potential is, think that they can reach it alone. But let me ask you one question: Five years ago, when you imagined where you would be today, where did you see yourself? Are you there? Have you fulfilled your own expectations? . . . You can take charge of your life and how you want to live it right now, and the best person to help you plan the actions you need to take in order to get on the fast track to success is your coach." So while Gibson opens by arguing that *you can achieve whatever you think you can achieve*, just a few sentences later he's stating that even if you *believe* the sky's the limit, you probably can't reach the heavens without help—specifically, his.

Observers of the phenomenon say that these New Age therapists-sans-portfolio often function as full-service shrinks, though the coaches themselves vehemently deny any such thing, since those activities would constitute practicing psychiatry without a license. "I know the boundaries," one independent life coach told me. "I'm not here to put people in touch with their inner child. I'm here to help them as a tactician."

Still, the parallels between coaching and standard psychiatric practice are hard to ignore. Many life coaches begin with "diagnostics" intended to yield a reasonably valid personality profile of the customer. Typically coaches assign prep work that includes writing a journal of self-inventory; they may use formal tools like the Myers-Briggs Type Indicator. Having established a baseline profile of the client, a coach works with him or her on a "life blueprint" and eventually formulates a series of "action plans."

"To my ear," Bennis told me, "it sounds an awful lot like what psychiatrists and psychologists go to school for." But there's a critical difference, he adds: Calling the process *coaching* makes it especially attractive to men. "For men," Bennis remarks, "a lot of executive coaching is really an acceptable form of psychotherapy. Even nowadays, it's still tough to say, 'I'm going to see my therapist.' It's OK to say, 'I'm getting counseling from my coach.'" Martha Beck, a popular life coach and frequent talk-show guest, has echoed that argument, saying, "It's OK for a man to see a coach. In a lot of settings, it is not OK for a man to see a therapist." Like so many others in the world of SHAM, coaches achieve success by cannily packaging their supposedly easy solutions for their target market. In fact, many coaches who work with high-level male executives go out of their way to pump up the machismo factor. By some accounts they'll even act differently, putting on a swagger or affecting a more rough-hewn way of speaking. Perhaps it is not surprising, then, that according to Patrick Williams of the Institute for Life Coach Training, men make up a full 60 percent of the caseload for coaching while women represent 70 percent of the caseload in therapy.

While some of the coaches who appeal to male executives adopt a locker-room style, that doesn't mean life coaching is bereft of the usual SHAM jargon and catchphrases. The coach may "focus on helping our clients put vision into action, assisting individuals and organizations to be innovative in their thinking and actions, creating more challenging and cooperative work cultures, developing dynamic and useful programs that are effective in business and personal situations [through] state-of-the-art research [that brings] fresh, new approaches to our client systems. We offer these innovative approaches as catalysts for growth of both the individual and the organization." The preceding buzzword extravaganza comes to you courtesy of Elaina Zuker, founder of Elaina Zuker Associates, a coaching and organizational-development firm whose clients have included Avon, American Express, Bankers Trust, Chase Manhattan Bank, Citibank, IBM, MCI, and Sheraton Corporation. Such amorphous, jargon-laced patter is typical of corporate coaching, where one almost suspects that the point is *not* to communicate anything concrete.

Or sometimes it seems the idea is to communicate the obvious. Mary Bradford, a sales manager at Metropolitan Life, was introduced to life coaching by a friend. Bradford spoke every week with Talane Miedaner, an executive coach in New York City who had advised employees at corporations like Citicorp, Bear Stearns, Salomon Smith Barney, and Motorola.

Bradford had a habit of overpromising, a common foible among salespeople.

Miedaner told her to underpromise instead.

Those are the kinds of anecdotes that can cause teeth to gnash among people like Harvard's John Kotter, who have devoted lengthy careers to studying corporate mechanics in minute detail. "Yes, I resent it," Kotter told me. "When I see people throwing out junk, this river of mud, that is in *my* arena, and it piles on top of something I've done very thoughtfully and with a great deal of diligence and attention to detail over many years, well, you can't help but resent it."

Nonetheless, Bradford is not alone in swearing by the positive results of her coaching experience. In fact, feedback on life coaching is generally more positive than that for other SHAM products and purveyors, with companies often quoting measurable improvements in performance after coaches come in to dispense their wisdom. For example, a few years ago a regional manager for AT&T's aggressive Growth Markets division decided to bring in coach Cheryl Weir, who in her former professional life had spent thirteen years selling for IBM. Weir's coaching program cost $11,000 initially and about $2,000 in quarterly follow-up—but by the end of the year, revenue for the AT&T unit had grown 16 percent, double the previous year's growth rate. An AT&T executive later told *Fortune* she thought the company "earned back [Weir's fee] in a week." The ICF site prominently features one case study involving an unidentified Fortune 500 company where coaching produced a 529 percent return on investment (788 percent if you count the "financial benefits from employee retention"), according to Metrix-Global, a firm that specializes in quantifying corporate change.

Then again, reckoning a coach's provable bottom-line impact proves problematic, because companies often turn to coaches when they're undergoing other organizational changes. This makes it hard to separate out the results of the coaching from the results of the structural tweaking. But corporate managers who pay top dollar for a coach's services are inclined to view the process in the most favorable light; whether the payoff is quantifiable or not, there's a strong incentive to report success, because the price of reporting failure is simply too high. As Deborah Carr, a sociologist at Rutgers, puts it, "You have to remember that a manager who hires a coach is going to have to explain that line item to somebody higher up."

That focus on results now extends well beyond the corporate world. Just as people hire personal trainers when they're looking ahead to swimsuit season, they hire personal coaches when they're up against some fixed productivity deadline. And largely because of the broad social influences of Empowerment, whose most public face is Phil McGraw, increasing numbers of Americans are shouting, *I don't care what got me to where I am, just help me get to where I want to be.* Carr sees the pull-yourself-up-by-your-bootstraps message of today's coaches and allied advice givers as yet another form of rebellion against the Victimization theory that dominated public discourse beginning in the mid-1960s. Quoting a line that has become a catchphrase in the coaching movement, Carr told me, "Growth is hot, diagnosis is not. A lot of people today don't care whether Mommy spanked them once too often. They want to get beyond all that, and get on with it. And they want more personalized attention than they could get from Dr. Phil."

That same sense of forward motion makes the coaching craze perfect for a post-9/11 zeitgeist. In a sense, America as a whole finds itself thrust into a period of midlife reevaluation, suggests Carr. "Life coaching is solution-oriented and concentrates on the future," she told me. "It has an inherent sense of hopefulness, of moving past the darkness."

This may also explain why people who flock to coaches don't usually expect heavy doses of ethics—because ethical considerations have this annoying way of slowing things down. "Coaching is about teaching clients to do what works," says Carr. "It's like they're saying, 'I don't have time to be fixed, and I don't want to worry about how my actions might be judged by history. Just help me get from A to B.'"

And they're saying, *Get me there fast.* "Although people know instinctively that real change is difficult and long-term," says Benjamin Dattner, "Americans want to believe that a few sessions will fix everything."

But as one so often sees with the SHAM phenomenon, wanting to *believe* something will work—and having it *actually* work—are two different things.

THE REAL PROBLEMS

With more and more Americans turning to life coaches to solve their problems, it's important to ask, What qualifies someone as a life coach? A better question might be, What *dis*qualifies someone? "I do wonder about the vulgarization of coaching," says Bennis, who, make no mistake, regards *properly done* coaching as instrumental in molding the next generation of visionary business leaders. "I'm concerned about unlicensed, unqualified people doing this."

His concerns are not misplaced. Virtually anyone, whether he or she has attended Coach U or not, can anoint himself a life coach. "There are no bedrock qualifications, no unified approach to coaching, no clear and unimpeachable credentialing," Bennis points out. "Basically this is a business that flies under the radar screen of any sort of oversight."

The nonseriousness and laissez-faire nature of the enterprise is clear in the fact that even many of the top Web sites that offer life coaching also give the visitor the option of *becoming* a life coach. Indeed, the very first link on www.life-coaching-resource.com, even before the ones that click you through to the coaching help you presumably sought, reads, "Start your own coaching business." Imagine consulting a site for medical help and being greeted by the offer "Would you like to find a doctor . . . or become a doctor?"

Among the coaches *Fortune* interviewed for its story on the trend were a former certified public accountant, a low-level banking executive, and a marketing vice president for Bloomingdale's. Coach-training firms also have sprung up as independent entities, with their own respective standards and pseudoprofessional practices. ICF says that so far it has "made little headway" in its attempts to license coaching. What the organization *doesn't* say is that most of its own members aren't all that fond of such attempts; reputable though they may be, they regard standardization as the first step in regulation, and some surely fear that their individual methods might not pass muster. Plenty of coaches are doing just fine as it is, thank you. An unaffiliated corporate coach who asked to remain anonymous told me, "Their position basically is, if the federation is just a fraternal body where people get together to meet and swap stories over a beer, that's one thing. They're all for it. But when it shows signs of actually governing or licensing, that's where they draw the line."

The coaching boom of recent years even worries a lot of the more visible coaches, who make the familiar argument about the few bad apples and their effect on the bunch. Here too, however, one may intuit a more businesslike, unspoken motive: protecting market share against the encroachments of eager upstarts. Motives aside, there's no question that as the phenomenon spreads, attracting greater numbers of freelance coaches who are blessed with a pleasing persona and the gift of gab, hopeful clients risk being shortchanged.

Everywhere you look nowadays, you'll see an independent life coach hanging out a shingle, selling private-label motivation. For $3,000 an East Rochester, New York, couple, John and Seran Wilkie, will fix your life through the magic of—Seranism! That's their eponymous title for their thirty-hour course on how to put your priorities in order, live a happier life, work less, earn more, and (in today's iffy economy) save your struggling small business, should you happen to own one. Seran Wilkie, a religious junkie and former teacher of statistics and computer programming, has no formal training in psychology. Even so, she deems herself uniquely qualified to expound on the keys to happiness and help each person find his or her singular version of it. "Say you have a boss who's just stupid and he drives you crazy," she posits. "Ask yourself, 'If he's so stupid, how is he driving me crazy? He must be pushing some button on me, and where is that button?' And so forth. The program helps you see what really is." So far, the Wilkies say they have provided such enlightenment to about three hundred people.

The Sedona Method, named for the Arizona city where it originated, is a group-coaching technique pioneered during the 1970s by Lester Levenson and promoted most visibly these days by his avuncular pupil Hale Dwoskin. Dwoskin convenes a dozen or so individuals in a room and runs them through a wild inspirational potpourri that borrows freely and not always seamlessly from spiritualism, neurolinguistic programming, native American rituals, "trust exercises," and other activities, most of which have been discredited by the repentant magician and world-class debunker James Randi, among others. Dwoskin also coaches his participants to drop pens and throw chairs as "symbolic" ways of letting go of impediments to happiness and power. Though Dwoskin's book is titled *Happiness Is Free*, he nevertheless feels obliged to charge each Sedona participant $295. For what it's worth, Dwoskin is the author of what may be the single most vacuous quote ever to emerge from SHAM (and that's saying something): "Beingness is simply that state of 'I am' that is here before, during, and after every thought, feeling, and experience."

Even more troubling, evidence indicates that some male coaches prey on emotionally scattered women who have taken their lumps in life, are desperate for change, and don't mind spending a few bucks to sit down opposite some charming fellow with an easy smile who can help them figure it all out. By the end of a few such sessions, a transformation indeed may have taken place—the guy has gone from life coach to gigolo. "It's a great way to meet women," the anonymous independent coach told me. "In any case, whether you 'score' or not, they're paying you for your time." These coaches begin by publicizing relatively cozy seminars in smaller hotel meeting rooms, often on issues like "love enhancement" or "relationship readiness," topics apt to bring in women who've been stuck in a rut. Sometimes they start with hard-core financial advice, but execute a deft segue from money to happiness, happiness to love, love to sex (or "intimacy"). They smile and wink in all the right places; they encourage audience members to "get in touch via e-mail if you'd like to arrange for individualized coaching sessions." They meet any takers in coffee shops and restaurant bars, where they usually charge modest sums—$100 an hour or thereabouts—to "listen" and "suggest" on a "one-to-one basis." Where it goes after that depends on the signals they get from the client. A fiftyish Memphis woman we'll call Roxanne fell under the spell of just such a coach, and had "invested" a few thousand dollars before she realized that she was "really paying for his companionship," as she puts it. She blames herself for letting the situation get out of hand and still isn't quite sure the coach himself did anything wrong.

File this, then, under "a word to the wise": Women who seek honest advice, and nothing more than that, should beware of men who advertise themselves as "certified love coaches." They're probably certified con men, the whole thing is probably a scam, and it's probably the closest thing this society allows to legalized prostitution. This blatant line blurring is a particular sore spot with those who argue for regulation of the industry, for canons of ethics in almost all professional situations bar "real" therapists from becoming romantically involved with their patients.

Patrick Williams waves off the barbs tossed at his profession. He told *USA Today* that life coaching is an entirely valid approach to modern living, destined to "change the face of psychotherapy, helping people live a better life without the stigma of needing a diagnosis or a visit to a psychotherapist they don't want or need." But that brings us to what is arguably the most serious risk in the entire equation: Coaches who take all comers are almost sure to get a few with serious maladjustments that *require* intervention from skilled mental-health professionals. Experts worry that untrained or minimally trained coaches may fail to recognize when they're dealing with someone who is truly troubled—or, as *Psychotherapy Networker* editor Richard Simon writes, someone who needs more than "a good lesson plan and an enthusiastic cheerleader."

This is why it's critical for life coaches to make the distinction between coaching and actual psychotherapy—and to make that distinction *explicitly*. Alas, too many personal coaches depend on dwelling in that gray area between informal and formal help. "It's unrealistic," says Benjamin Dattner, "to expect a marginal life coach to bring up caveats that may cost him business, or may make a client think he needs several levels of help and helpers. The temptation is for the coach to want all that business for himself." In other words, not only do coaches shrink from making the distinction, but they actively imply just the opposite—that they're there to "fix what ails you," whatever that may be.

Even those at the top of the nascent industry show little enthusiasm for self-examination. If anything, they appear to revel in each new coaching inroad. ICF's own site features a link to a *Washington Post* article, "A Coach for Team You," about the large numbers of people who "are skipping the shrink and hiring a life coach instead," as the article's subtitle put its. If large numbers of Americans with serious psychological problems are consulting coaches instead of qualified therapists, clearly there's more to be concerned about than just what it wastes in dollars.

7

◇◇◇◇

KILLER PERFORMANCES: THE RISE OF THE *CON*TREPRENEUR

A failure is a man who has blundered, but is not able to cash in on the experience.

—*Elbert Hubbard*

Imagine, if you will, the sort of career one might fashion out of being stabbed, set ablaze, and shot no less than thirteen times. Drawing a blank? Meet Joseph Jennings. The former gangbanger and admitted drug dealer speaks to hundreds of schools each year as the founder and chief motivational theorist of Turning Point Inc. Jennings has traded being manhandled by cops for being backslapped by some of the nation's premier civic leaders—starting with George W. Bush, who in 2002 added Jennings to his Presidential Advisory Council on AIDS/HIV.

Jennings makes no effort to hide his unsavory past; in fact, it's very much his stock in trade. "A lot of times, the kids want proof. They'll say, let's see some bullet holes," the burly six-footer told me. "So I usually wear short-sleeve shirts. I carry the X-rays around, too." Jennings's tacky self-published autobiography, *Prisoner of the American Dream*, depicts him on its cover holding an assault rifle in each hand. The same basic image appears on Jennings's ultraslick Web site for Turning Point.

In a medium always looking for new wrinkles and methods of market differentiation, Jennings personifies one of the hottest and most controversial trends—what one might call *con*trepreneurship. The crimes differ, but what Jennings and his vocational think-alikes have in common is an instinct for profiting from the activities that once landed them in society's doghouse, if not its Big House. Caterpillars reborn as butterflies, these self-styled pitchmen (and a woman or two) inhabit a postmodern alternate universe in which battle scars and prison stretches merit prominent placement on a résumé and somehow render one uncommonly qualified to expound on fulfillment and success. The cast includes:

MICHAEL FRANZESE. If Jennings covers the gangbanger demographic, Franzese has carved out a comfortable niche as a Mob turncoat. As a bookmaking honcho in the Columbo crime family, back in 1986 he was ranked number eighteen on *Fortune*'s list of "The Fifty Biggest Mafia Bosses." But he ended up in prison, where he says he found God; *Vanity Fair* dubbed him the "born-again don." Since 1996 Franzese has been a fixture on the lecture circuit and at camps run by pro sports teams, who pay him to warn athletes about the dangers of gambling and other addictive, untoward behaviors. Franzese may be best-known for the 1997 pay-per-view special he produced, *Live from Alcatraz*, which featured top rappers and other celebrities in an effort to raise money for antidrug campaigns.

ANNE KELLY. Kelly is the founder and leading on-air personality of Recovery Radio. An erstwhile stand-up comedienne, Universal Studios tour guide, and singing-telegram performer, Kelly became a fixture on commercials and infomercials before she began taking more than a dozen Vicodin per day and "washing them down with 90 proof schnapps." Eventually she hit bottom. (Hitting bottom is a prerequisite for Recovery speakers; merely having your life go to pieces won't do.) Kelly, who likes to describe herself as a "homeless double felon," characterizes her seminars as "inspirational, motivational hours of pure hope." The keynote image on Kelly's Web site (perhaps inspired by Jennings?) is a small pile of Vicodin against the backdrop of a bottle of Jack Daniel's, and behind that, an ambulance.

TROY EVANS. Not every motivational speaker has an official bio that begins: "On November 12, 1992, Troy Evans was sentenced to 13 years in Federal Prison. He was convicted of five armed bank robberies, in three states, over a six-month crime spree, and was sent to the Federal Correctional Complex in Florence, Colorado. His neighbors included such notorious criminals as Timothy McVeigh and Terry Nichols." When Evans emerged from prison more than seven years later, he had two college degrees and, he says, a will to inspire. And so he developed a seminar presentation titled "From Desperation to Dedication: Lessons You Can Bank On." Among his more inspiring subtopics: "Playing on the Most Important Team" and "The Prison Inside You." His patter, like that of many felons-cum-philosophers, is suffused with a certain pragmatic amorality that emphasizes "getting on with it" above all else. "It's not important how we come to the events in our lives," he will say, dismissing those five armed robberies in one pat line, "but how we deal with them." Of his incarceration, Evans's materials observe that he was "plucked from the 'free world' to a world of steel and concrete," as if to imply that his loss of freedom had nothing to do with all that money he took.

STEVE ARRINGTON. Contrepreneurs tend to have colorful backgrounds, and Arrington's doesn't disappoint. He is a former navy frogman (specialty: bomb disposal) and chief diver for the Cousteau Society who once was honored by Ronald Reagan for saving the life of a drowning boy. He landed the job with Cousteau two years after his release from a California prison, where he'd been serving a five-year stretch for a drug arrest—but not just any drug arrest. Arrington had gotten himself mixed up in the infamous John DeLorean sting. In the backgrounder he has prepared for school principals, Arrington says simply that he speaks "from the perspective of someone who unfortunately made a marijuana mistake that directly led to my becoming a defendant in the John DeLorean drug trial." That statement leaves out a few steps (as well as any mention of the other drug that caused the whole DeLorean fuss). He made his "marijuana mistake" while still in the service, when he was caught selling a small amount of pot to another sailor; that ended his navy career and led him to an old millionaire friend, Morgan Hetrick, who hired him as a pilot and an aide-de-camp. Soon Arrington was piloting a small plane to a jungle hideout and picking up a quarter ton of cocaine from Hetrick's contacts in the Medellín drug cartel. Arrington then made a Florida-to-California drive for Hetrick in a car with more than sixty pounds of coke hidden under the backseat. The coke was meant for DeLorean. That's when he got busted. He says he was "relieved," as he had been looking for a way out "without ending up dead." In jail, he started to write a book that would warn young people away from drugs (the book would be published in 1996 as *Journey into Darkness*). He began making antidrug, personal-fulfillment speeches for churches, schools, and civic groups. In 1993 he left Cousteau to tour nationally and deliver multimedia presentations with such themes as "High on Adventure" and "Drugs Bite," incorporating snazzy clips of shark encounters and other high-seas derring-do. In his material he says, "My goal is to motivate youths to reach for their dreams and not make choices that can lead to nightmares." Today, he claims to have spoken in over fourteen hundred schools in forty-nine states. He also offers educational scuba-diving tours to Fiji.

RON COHEN. Cohen landed in prison on three separate occasions, for a total of eleven years, because of the Ponzi schemes through which he separated Dallas socialites from an estimated $80 million. Today, Cohen is a $150-per-hour consultant to a burgeoning roster of white-collar criminals, prepping them for how to cope with prison life. (Sample insights: "Leave the Rolex home" and "Don't start asking about a furlough or a conjugal visit the day you surrender yourself.") His Client Advisory Group operates out of a motel because, he says, "It's tough for an ex-con to get a rental." Cohen is credited with the neologism "Club Fed," which is used to describe U.S. prisons that boast such amenities as satellite TV, lavish buffet dinners, and workout facilities that few yuppie health clubs can match.

What the contrepreneurs get out of this is clear. Ron Cohen's $150-an-hour fee might not stack up well against the millions he used to embezzle, or even Tommy Lasorda's going rate, but it's a quantum improvement over the "Would you like fries with that?" wages for which so many repeat offenders must settle. Michael Franzese would rather talk to the Minnesota Vikings than a federal grand jury.

But why America buys in . . . now that's the question.

One possible answer is obvious enough. "It's sexy stuff," says Chuck Sennewald, a legendary figure in loss prevention who is not generally a fan of the movement but nevertheless perceives the appeal. "It's sexy, and it gets your blood going. People pay attention." Sennewald told me that he can see where a speaker's points, "if he has any," would resonate more when they're communicated "in a format like that, with bullets whizzing by and cop chases as a backdrop."

The rise of the lawbreaker/evangelist also bespeaks the American penchant for second chances. If these once-wayward souls have turned a glorious corner in their lives, it just naturally makes us feel better to help them celebrate it—to see them, hear them out, nod and smile at the uplifting things they say to us. Apart from anything useful that such people may contribute to the culture, the redemptive aspect alone has won the contrepreneur movement its share of kudos. Michael Ellis, a New Orleans defense attorney who has channeled his share of work to Ron Cohen, points out that on the whole society has become increasingly hard on the ex-con. "Post 9/11," Ellis told me, "you have the specter of background checks not only to get jobs and housing, but just to fly someplace." Amid that environment, Ellis asks, "How can you begrudge a person leaving jail for trying to make an *honest* living at what he knows best?"

Above all, perhaps, the career paths of Cohen, Jennings, and the rest illustrate the lengths to which society will go in its search for a fresh new spin, almost *any* spin, on overcoming life's daily challenges. Today, it's as if surviving an ordeal—even when it was self-induced—equips a person to teach the rest of us how to quit whining and make the most of life: *If so-and-so can cope with such-and-such, well then, my everyday struggles don't amount to much.* As with the traditional twelve-step Recovery movement, pain or dysfunction of almost any kind seemingly gives people a franchise to expound on the lessons of that pain.

"Not to be overly judgmental, but what it reminds me of is the old days, before there were Son of Sam laws" was an early take on the matter from Sam Knott, whom I interviewed several times on crime-related stories after the Christmas 1986 murder of his daughter, Cara, transformed him into a vocal advocate for victims' rights. "You'd have people who'd break the law, do horrific things, then they'd do books about it or sell the rights to their story and make a fortune. It was almost like doing the crime was a business strategy. Why do people like that deserve a platform ahead of people who always followed the straight and narrow?"

It's a good question, especially since the phenomenon isn't just confined to SHAM; contrepreneurship is visible throughout American society. IRS cheats reemerge as highly paid tax seminarists. Card sharks pitch themselves to Las Vegas as consultants. Shoplifters teach retailers how to enhance loss prevention and trim employee "shrinkage." Computer hackers draw six-figure consulting retainers from Fortune 500 companies that want to stop other hackers from crippling their systems.[1] The motivational-speaking circuit seems unusually eager to hear what the contrepreneurs have to say, and has provided a solid foundation from which they can build upward after their wrongdoing.

This, in turn, has caused some vexation among traditional consultants and other speakers who have managed to get through their entire careers without going to jail even once. "These guys are lifelong con artists, and this is just today's con," says Pat Murphy, a twenty-five-year veteran of the loss-prevention business and the CEO of the Web site LP Today. "My personal opinion is that they're still doing much the same thing they did before. It's their last laugh on the rest of us."

The director of the ethics program at the Wharton School of Business, Professor Alan Strudler adds, "It's hard to miss the irony. [When they speak in a corporate setting], these fellows get top dollar from many of the same companies who won't even hire for the most entry-level jobs without doing a background check."

UP CLOSE AND PERSONAL: JOSEPH JENNINGS

In a realm not lacking for characters, Joseph Jennings stands as a special case, and an instructive one for understanding how these SHAM artists gain traction.

For two decades beginning in adolescence, Jennings enjoyed a heady if nerve-racking lifestyle financed by drugs and gangbanging. He portrays himself as the product of a tough childhood orchestrated by a domineering father who taught him, above all, "how to survive." Jennings steadily ascended his neighborhood's thuggish pecking order, in part through sheer brazenness. Not content with the normal risks of drug dealing, he began hijacking shipments bound for competitors. By his early twenties, his drug business had furnished him with a large home and swimming pool, fancy clothes, gold jewelry, a Rolls-Royce—"anything I desired," he told me, not without some pride. Eventually he moved to Southern California, where he rubbed elbows with Hollywood and music-industry types (whom he now declines to identify because, he says, he was their supply chain to mind-altering substances and other illicit items).

Jennings's personal epiphany took place while he plotted a murder, and a flamboyant one at that: He intended to use a .45-caliber submachine gun to kill a social worker who'd had the audacity to question his fitness as a parent. But the night before he was supposed to do the deed, his pregnant wife began to hemorrhage. On the way home from the emergency trip to the hospital, Jennings found God. God told him it was time to go straight. (For the record, baby and mother were both fine.)

Jennings's speaking career "started off like any other adventure," he recalls. "You knock on doors." He landed some local gigs, and before long the doors on which he was knocking belonged to school-district superintendents. Today he estimates that he speaks to about four hundred thousand kids a year, in as many as ten schools per week. "Things have come along," Jennings admits, when asked how he's doing financially. "In the beginning I drove everywhere. Now I fly." He charges $950 per assembly. Patron organizations like the Detroit Lions bring him in to speak to multiple area schools, where he spreads his tough-love gospel of responsibility and personal choice.

"In every assembly," he says, "there are kids who've thought about committing suicide in the last thirty days. Probably half the audience doesn't have a biological father at home. You've got girls who've been raped ten years ago; their self-esteem is so low. A lot of young blacks are still operating under a slave mentality. They don't want to read;

they think manhood is about having babies. You have to attack that mind-set."

Does he think he can achieve that in one talk? Jennings replies somewhat obliquely, by criticizing society's other quick fixes, like those urban recreational leagues now in vogue: "You take a twelve-year-old killer and you give him a basketball, you know what you have? A twelve-year-old killer with a basketball. As soon as he's tired of playing basketball, he's gonna kill. You have to change his heart." And does Jennings really believe he's the right man for the job? "Look, brother," he says, "what we do is a start, at least. Nobody else is doin' it."

Asked whether he ever senses any skepticism about his fitness to be speaking in schools, Jennings says yes, but only in the so-called good schools—and not for the reasons you'd expect. He says the resistance he encounters there is less about any skeletons in his closet than about the skeletons in theirs. "You have to realize, I would say probably 60 percent of the schools I go to are all white," he says. "The problem in the white community is, they prefer not to talk about it. It's about denial." He recalls one particular school where "all hell broke out after I spoke. Turns out 65 percent of the girls started talking about how they'd been molested. People got upset. Why? Because I brought it up! Not because fathers and grandfathers were raping their daughters!"

Some incidents have been more inspiring, Jennings says. He tells the story of the time he was speaking in Florida and a white football player rushed up to him after his performance. The boy was in tears. "He told me, 'You saved me, you saved me.' It was almost frightening. And he said, 'Saturday we have a prom, and in my drawer I have a .38, and after the prom I was going to blow my brains out.' And he said, 'I heard you say it's OK, you can change your mind about things.' And he did."

For all his preachments about possibility, Jennings's track record with his own children—there are more of them than gunshot wounds, fourteen in all—has, he admits, been spotty. One son is now in jail for murder. "He was out in Napa, and this guy, a priest, picked him up and tried to molest him. And my son killed him," Jennings says simply and without much evident emotion. But that sad experience has only sweetened his feelings about the success enjoyed by his other kids. "The most awesome thing was taking another son to college," he says, describing it as the most rewarding moment in his life to date. "Because on one hand I raised a child and taught him everything I'd learned, and it wasn't enough. But when we drove up and got my other son enrolled and went to his dorm room . . . I mean, he's eighteen, he's captain of the rugby team. He's doing great for himself. See, he broke the cycle. The kids who come out of hell, they have to break the cycle. They have to break the curse."

JUST ANOTHER CON?

It's not easy to know how to think about a Joseph Jennings. He raises interesting, provocative questions. But such questions are seldom addressed with intellectual rigor, because—as is so often true of "inspirational" messages—no attempt is made to gauge the long-term effects of his programs. People unthinkingly endorse Jennings and his stated agenda without examining in any meaningful, empirical sense whether he stands to do any good—or harm. It's just assumed that because Jennings *seems* like a good guy and is *striving* to do good, good is what will come of it.

But as with Sportsthink, it's worthwhile to ask about the takeaway. What's the message that sticks here? Is it really about redemption and honor at long last? Or, from the kids' perspective, is it more along the lines of *how fucking cool* it must have been to live the underground lifestyle Jennings describes? For every football player who backs away from suicide, how many other kids get off on the idea of the pricey cars and prominent scars and just the sheer machismo of it all?

Which is why parents might have some questions about a school's choice of motivators. School districts often plan these events without specifically informing parents of the nature of the presentation; they simply send home a note stating that they're having a guest motivational speaker, and they may or may not ask parents to sign off on the child's attendance. Would parents really choose a guy like Jennings to deliver inspiration to their kids? If a school can afford just one or two speakers a year, why pick Jennings? Why not opt instead for an unblemished role model who can offer the life lessons and the positive message without the dope and the body count? Even someone like Tommy Lasorda (or perhaps someone younger whom kids wouldn't instantly dismiss as a fossil) might be more to a parent's liking.

And what of the speakers themselves—are they really sincere? A few years ago, Terry Lanni, the MGM Grand chairman and then–Nevada gaming commissioner, was asked for his take on felon-turned-seminar-speaker Bill Jahoda. Like Michael Franzese, Jahoda had run a large mob gambling operation, but now he was crisscrossing the nation preaching the evils of gambling. Lanni didn't mince words. "I don't find much credibility in a person who operated as he has indicated he operated in an illegal fashion preying on people," he told the *Las Vegas Sun*. "Now he's suddenly determined that he's found religion, and as a result of that, he's a more accepted human being. I find that to be reasonably despicable."

I've interviewed a number of the key players in the contrepreneur movement, and it's true that in unguarded moments they'll say things that hint at the very inner stirrings they take such pains to deny when onstage. Listen closely and you might hear a wistful longing for the bad old days—maybe in a felicitously timed sigh, or the quick note of unalloyed glee that creeps into an account of some memorable caper. They may ride with the hounds now, but you wonder if their hearts are with the foxes after all.

When I asked Jennings if he ever daydreams about his long-ago rogue lifestyle, he was forthright. "Well sure, brother!" he said, laughing in such a boisterous way that even over the phone, I could almost see his eyes flash. "I ain't smoked weed in eighteen years, but you can't tell me I didn't have fun doin' it!"

It's there, too, in Kevin Mitnick, a former hacker who has gone from being the world's most infamous computer criminal to a high-paid corporate consultant; he calls his venture Defensive Thinking (and he suffered the ignominy of being hacked several times in his first few months of operation). When I interviewed Mitnick, he offered preening remarks about the advantages he offers corporate America over "the people who came up through the system and studied [computer] penetration through labs and textbooks, instead of out in the real world." That one swipe left no doubt that Mitnick still prides himself on what he was able to accomplish before he traded his black hat for a white one. This same sentiment was on display at a recent Def Con, the hacker convention that is held each year in Las Vegas. The whole tenor of the event has changed through the years. Once an underworld-chic gathering whose highly caffeinated attendees met in smallish groups to share their latest antiestablishment exploits, Def Con has evolved substantially into a mainstream forum on network security—if not an actual job fair for Fortune 500 companies. In one recent year, some members of the community showed up wearing T-shirts that bore the simple, heartfelt lament "I miss crime."

In fairness to the felons, most do accept responsibility for their former lives. Ron Cohen told me, "I've never shirked the fact that I've made some very, very bad mistakes, and that yes, I'm guilty. But what do they want me to do about it now?" Joseph Jennings points out that he's a living, breathing example of the fact that healing is possible. "When the lecture comes from somebody who's always been in a position of authority, often it falls on deaf ears," he says. "I'm not proud of what I did, but it gives me a credibility with the kids who most need to hear my message. I was where they are now."

Fairness also compels us to mention the one very specialized market segment whose need for help is most acute and whom ex-cons may be uniquely qualified to serve: America's sizable population of other ex-cons, now estimated at thirty million and growing by six hundred thousand each year.[2] This is where Ned Rollo comes in. Rollo, now in his early sixties, pleaded guilty at age twenty-three to manslaughter and was sentenced to seven years' hard labor at Louisiana's infamous Angola State Prison. Upon his release he was shocked at the degree to which society shunned him and appalled at the paucity of options available to people who had done time. He began working as an advocate for ex-cons, at first slowly and locally, on a shoestring. There were setbacks: People and institutions fought him, and he struggled with his own demons. Eventually, however, he founded OPEN (Offender Preparation and Employment Network). Through OPEN, Rollo seeks to show other former felons that the glass really is half full; he is, as the *Dallas Observer* put it, "a kind of Tony Robbins for the penitentiary set." Toward that end, he wrote *99 Days and a Get Up: A Pre- and Post-Release Survival Manual for Inmates and Their Loved Ones* (rereleased in 2002 with an amended subtitle: *A Guide to Success Following Release for Inmates and Their Loved Ones*), which is fast becoming required reading at federal lockups across America. The Texas prison system alone ordered forty thousand copies. He has also appeared on *Good Morning America, Donahue*, and—need I say it?—*The Oprah Winfrey Show*. Today, Ned Rollo is recognized as one of the nation's top authorities on reintegrating convicts into society, even by those with formal credentials in penology.

So take heart, Martha Stewart. There *is* life after house arrest.

PART TWO

◇◇◇◇

THE CONSEQUENCES

8

YOU ARE ALL DISEASED

Sometimes we feel guilty because we *are* guilty.

—*Promotional line for* Late-Night Catechism, *the "one-nun" comedy show*

To many people, SHAM gurus like Phil McGraw, Tony Robbins, and John Gray have become the face of the self-help movement (in part because they like to plaster their faces on books, videos, and in some cases coffee mugs and nutrition bars). But another segment of the movement has earned many millions of loyal followers even though it lacks celebrity leaders and endorsers. It, too, has a face: the face of anguish, ineptitude, and self-pity.

As we have seen, the Recovery movement experienced its own boom along with the SHAM explosion of the late 1960s. It was a period during which the so-called disease model took hold and reigned supreme. The 1935 debut and subsequent success (at least in its membership rolls) of Alcoholics Anonymous led in 1953 to Narcotics Anonymous, in 1965 to Overeaters Anonymous, in 1970 to Gamblers Anonymous, and in 1979 to Cocaine Anonymous. (Some say the last group was spun off from Narcotics Anonymous so that chic Hollywood types wouldn't have to rub elbows with gritty mainliners in the Nelson Algren tradition.) Today the menu includes Adult Children of Alcoholics, Artists Recovering Through the Twelve Steps Anonymous, Codependents of Sex Addicts Anonymous, Debtors Anonymous, Emotional Health Anonymous, Nicotine Anonymous, Pills Anonymous, Prostitutes Anonymous, Sexaholics Anonymous, Survivors of Incest Anonymous, and Workaholics

Anonymous. By no means is that a comprehensive listing. There are even programs for "cleanaholics," who are too often lumped with genuine sufferers of obsessive-compulsive disorder, a very real and troubling psychiatric disorder that afflicts an estimated four to six million people.

In fact, despite the ardent rebuttals from the likes of Dr. Phil and Dr. Laura, Recovery has earned perhaps the most mainstream respect of any segment of SHAM. Judges routinely sentence offenders in a variety of cases to programs inspired by AA's original twelve steps. People naturally conceive their underperforming relatives, friends, and coworkers as unfortunate slaves to miscellaneous dysfunctions. Moreover, those glum views are codified in many personnel-policy manuals, which put companies in the bizarre position of making special allowances for their least productive workers.

But for all its acceptance in so many settings, the Recovery movement suffers from the same problems that plague the rest of SHAM: It hasn't been shown to provide much help to those whose needs it supposedly addresses. And it could actually be doing them—and society as a whole—real harm.

One of the most damaging aspects of the Recovery movement is its insistence that most if not all of us are "diseased," which brings us to the title of this chapter. Since Recovery is so much about confessions, I'll offer one of my own: I stole the title from comedian and social satirist George Carlin, who used it for a scathingly irreverent HBO special. Carlin himself might have stolen it from the lexicon of Victimization, which, if it's about anything at all, is about being wounded, psychically *damaged* in such a profound, personality-shaping way that only through years of grueling therapy can you learn to cope (but never *overcome*, since in the land of Recovery, addictions and dysfunctions, like diamonds, are forever). You'd think a plague so horrid and haunting would befall just a small number of us, but such is not the case, we are told. With so many different programs for so many different dysfunctions, Recovery casts such a wide net that almost no one fails to get caught in it.

Ergo: You are all diseased.

But there is a larger point here: If you are *all* diseased, it really means that *we* are all diseased—that society itself is diseased. Far from backpedaling in the face of such ludicrous inferences, many gurus have made that very point explicitly. Anne Wilson Schaef put it this way in *Co-Dependence: Misunderstood—Mistreated*: "When we talk about the addictive process, we are talking about civilization as we know it." For anyone who still didn't get it, Schaef later titled a book *When Society Becomes an Addict*. A key chapter of Robert Burney's book *Codependence: The Dance of Wounded Souls* bears the title "Normal Families Are Codependent." He's not being ironic. In *Recovery: A Guide for Adult Children of Alcoholics*, Herbert Gravitz and Julie Bowden described the addiction phenomenon as the "visible tip of a much larger social iceberg" that, the authors speculated, afflicts "as much as 96 percent of the population."

If true, this would mean that in a nation of some 295 million people, a mere 11.8 million of us (or roughly the population of Pennsylvania) are emotionally whole.

Does it sound cynical to note that the more classes of people one can paint as dysfunctional, the broader the market for the antidysfunction product or "belief system" one is selling?

Schaef, Burney, et al. may be right about our dysfunctional society—but one can plausibly argue that they've got the cause and effect backward. Given Recovery's viselike grip on the self-help community for much of the past forty years, no one should be surprised that we have a society that thinks of itself as diseased, a society that suffers from maladies that did not exist in any measurable sense before SHAM itself got involved.

RECOVERY'S LONG SHADOW

Though in recent years the rise of SHAM's Empowerment wing has dulled some of Recovery's luster, the movement's effects continue to be strongly felt. We see its shadow most prominently in the culture of blame that has been sold to an audience eager to excuse its own failings;

the legacy of that philosophical bottom-feeding surely will be with us for decades to come. We see it in the justice system, in educational policy, in child-rearing protocols, in marriage counseling—in too many meaningful areas of modern life to cover in just one book. It turns up in the melancholic language of political demagoguery, and even in mainstream campaign rhetoric. The most compelling political slogans of recent vintage—"Are you better off today than you were four years ago?"—would not have flown as well in the 1950s, when Americans had not yet been trained to consider their own plight in terms of federal beneficence. "Once upon a time, if you weren't 'better off,' you wouldn't have looked to Washington for an answer," the late historian Stephen Ambrose told me when I was publisher of the *American Legion* magazine and he was one of our marquee writers. "It wouldn't have occurred to you to think of your station in life in the context of government policy. For better or worse, it was your life, and you owned it."

Times change. Many of us now renounce ownership of our lives. And so if we've had trouble getting married or staying married, or getting along with people, or staying employed; if we smoke or drink or shoot up; if we beat our kids or wives or girlfriends, or have both a wife and a girlfriend; if we drive too fast, shop too much, defer too often to those around us; if, despite all that fast driving, we can't get to work or other appointments on time, then—we've been conditioned to think—it's because we have something inside of us over which we have no control, or because someone else did something to us from which we and our inner children never quite recovered. Our neighbors have been encouraged to accept us in our state of weakness or dissolution, just as we have been encouraged to accept them.

You say you don't remember anything terrible being done to you as a child? You're in denial. You're *repressing*, which is framed as a dysfunction in its own right, so you're damned if you do, damned if you don't. The late 1980s and 1990s witnessed the astonishing rise of "repressed memory syndrome," wherein great hordes of reasonably well-functioning adults who had never before recalled a single moment of childhood trauma suddenly began recalling, en masse and in great detail, lengthy patterns of childhood abuse. Dozens of women and some men prosecuted or sued their aging fathers, uncles, brothers, babysitters, teachers, or other authority figures from their pasts. In some cases the targets of this retroactive scrutiny admitted a degree of guilt. In other cases, however, the memory itself proved spurious—either implanted or otherwise induced in the course of therapy, or "autosuggested" by intense media coverage of the trend.[1] Even when such allegations prove false, lives can be ruined. For example, in the mid-1980s, shocking accusations of sexual abuse at the McMartin Preschool in Manhattan Beach, California, became front-page news, creating paranoia among parents and spawning other sex-abuse investigations. Four years of investigation, followed by two trials spanning three more years, failed to produce a guilty verdict against a single defendant.

The McMartin ripple effect was all too real. Americans began seeing the phantoms of child abuse behind every curtain. By the mid-1990s, Boy Scout leaders, youth-sports coaches, and high-school band teachers were being accused in such numbers that in 1997 the prominent Canadian newsweekly *MacLean's* ran a cover story with the subhead "Youth leaders warn that an atmosphere of suspicion makes it difficult for them to function." People were turning in their neighbors. Doctors were turning in their patients. Even film developers were turning in their best customers: In 1989, David Urban snapped candid photos of his wife and fifteen-month-old grandson as she gave him a bath. The photo lab at Kmart reported him, and a Missouri court later convicted him of child pornography, though the case was overturned on appeal. Similar ordeals befell Cynthia Stewart of Ohio, who, like Urban, took bathtime photos of her eight-year-old daughter, and William Kelly of Maryland, who dropped off film including nude photos that his daughter and her playmates took of one another. Elements of several of these stories were weaved into the plot of the 2001 TV movie *Snap Decision*.

It's easy to scream abuse when the term is defined so vaguely and generically as to include just about anything. It's easier still when the culture tells you that you would have turned out just fine had your parents not destroyed your "essential self" by trying to mold you into a tractable, well-mannered citizen. Here, as in so many areas of SHAM, we encounter a fragile pyramid consisting of a baseless supposition posited as fact, then used as the foundation for further suppositions: the seductive folklore of the "pure-hearted child" that permeates so much of Victimization's jargon. Judith Martin—best known as "Miss Manners," but also a former *Washington Post* correspondent, a novelist, and a social critic—may have put it best in a speech at Harvard University in 1984: "The belief that natural behavior is beautiful and that civilization and its manners spoil the essential goodness inherent in all us noble savages is, of course, the Jean-Jacques Rousseau school of etiquette. . . . [It] survives in the pop-psychology and 'human potential' movements of today, and in the child-rearing philosophy that has given us so many little—savages. . . . The idea that people can behave 'naturally,' without resorting to an artificial code tacitly agreed upon by their own society, is as silly as the idea that they can communicate by a spoken language without commonly accepted semantic and grammatical principles."

My intent is not to trivialize or explain away the genuinely awful things that do happen to innocent people. Rather, my purpose is to establish that in the normal course of American life, truly awful things happen to comparatively few of us. That is by definition. If it were not the case, "we probably wouldn't consider such things 'awful' in the first place," says psychiatrist Sally Satel. We would not react to stories of horrific abuse with as much shock and outrage because, for better or worse, we would view such events as "business as usual." When the aberrational becomes commonplace, it is no longer aberrational. It is simply life. In reality, many of the episodes and practices Victimization taught us to regard with loathing—maybe your father spanked you a bit, or your mother took a drink or two—really are, or were, just part of growing up.

You'd never know that from the titles of the movement's signature works: *Toxic Parents: Overcoming Their Hurtful Legacy and Reclaiming Your Life, The Doormat Syndrome*, and *Raising Children in a Socially Toxic Environment*. If you're in decent shape yourself, there's always the problem of interacting with the dysfunctionals around you: *Toxic Coworkers: How to*

Deal with Dysfunctional People on the Job; Coping with Toxic Managers, Subordinates, and Other Difficult People; and *I Thought I Was the Crazy One: 201 Ways to Identify and Deal with Toxic People.*

As you can see, they're big on toxicity in Recovery circles. And they're *huge* on shame; thousands of self-help books have focused directly on the concept. Notable among them: *Soul without Shame: A Guide to Liberating Yourself from the Judge Within; Shame and Grace: Healing the Shame We Don't Deserve; Letting Go of Shame; Shame: The Power of Caring; Shame and Guilt: Masters of Disguise; Facing Shame: Families in Recovery; Released from Shame: Moving Beyond the Pain of the Past; Women and Shame: Reaching Out, Speaking Truths, and Building Connections; Fear and Other Uninvited Guests: Tackling the Anxiety, Fear, and Shame That Keep Us from Optimal Living and Loving*; and—in the category of "all-time longest and most unwieldy title built around a single concept"—*I Can't Believe I Just Did That: How Seemingly Small Moments of Shame and Embarrassment Can Wreak Havoc in Your Life—and What You Can Do to Put a Stop to Them.*

Plenty of other books have been devoted to *codependency*, a concept that is widely misunderstood, perhaps because the explanations advanced for it defy understanding. In the bible of the movement, *Codependent No More* (1987), Melody Beattie defined the codependent as "one who has let another person's behavior affect him or her"—which doesn't exclude too many of us—"and who is obsessed with controlling that person's behavior" (which probably describes all of us at some time in life). The trouble is, anyone who does not spend his or her life in a cave is bound to care for, or depend on, other human beings, at least to some degree, and the ensuing emotional bond will not always produce happy results. Beattie's definition, moreover, hinges on a precise and delicate common understanding of the words *obsessed* and *controlling*. No such consensus exists, "or likely is attainable," writes John Rosemond, a psychologist and syndicated columnist.[2]

Despite such ambiguities, *Codependent No More* at one point spent a hundred consecutive weeks on the *New York Times* best-seller list, selling some two million copies. Anne Wilson Schaef's *Meditations for Women Who Do Too Much* (1991), which offered its own slant on codependency, sold more than four hundred thousand copies. My personal favorite in this crowded field is *Codependency Sucks*, by Linda Meyerholz, MS, which shows a feral, manic-looking man who appears on the verge of throttling a very pained-looking woman. The book is published by Love 'n' Support Publishing.

Nor was this necessarily a girlie thing. John Bradshaw's *Bradshaw On: Healing the Shame That Binds You* sold some eight hundred thousand copies, persuading a generation of men that they, too, were entitled to feel crappy about themselves and their upbringing. It was Bradshaw who popularized the notion of the inner child and who gave American culture the downbeat neologisms *rage-aholic* and *toxic shame* (the latter, perhaps, under the theory that if the two words resonated so well individually, why not seek a synergistic effect?). And there was Robert Bly, National Book Award–winning poet (in 1968) and self-proclaimed "father of the expressivist men's movement," who in 1990 penned *Iron John: A Book about Men*. The book is a quasi-allegorical folk tale in which the title character leads readers, presumably men, on a journey of gender- and self-discovery. What male readers mostly seemed to discover was that they were sick of being nagged by women and stereotyped by feminists. *Iron John* became a touchstone for disaffected men, almost surely making them far more resentful of women and feminism than they ever needed to be. It also made Bly a top draw in the workshop movement (though Bly himself, it should be noted, disavowed the book's more misogynistic interpretations).[3]

For many Americans, books and informal workshops haven't been enough. *American Demographics* reported in March 1992, at Recovery's peak, that twelve million Americans were attending meetings of at least one of the nation's half-million support-group chapters. Still today, more than a decade after the publication of Marianne Williamson's *A Return to Love: Reflections on the Principles of A Course in Miracles*, seminars by the high priestess of New Age fulfillment sell out almost as quickly as Clay Aiken concerts, as do the $150 workshops run by John Bradshaw. As Archie Brodsky, a senior research associate in the Program in Psychiatry and the Law at Harvard Medical School, told me, "For certain individuals, this whole self-help and Recovery phenomenon is more potent and addicting than any narcotic. People's appetite for this stuff is unquenchable." Hence Recoveries Anonymous, which describes itself as a "Twelve Step program . . . especially for those who, despite their best efforts, have yet to find the recoveries that they are looking for." In other words, if you're not quite sure there's anything wrong with you, don't despair—we'll *find something*.

In sum, Victimization and Recovery have relentlessly encouraged ordinary people with ordinary lives to conceive of themselves as victims of some lifelong ailment that, even during the best of times, lurks just beneath the surface, waiting to undo them.

Needless to say (though almost nothing commonsensical is "needless to say" in the context of SHAM's teachings), it is not automatically dysfunctional to face life with assorted traumas and trepidations our parents imbued in us as children. On the contrary, it is entirely functional to fear certain things, for such fears help safeguard us from pain, humiliation, and even death. In any case, as Sally Satel and other vocal critics of Recovery will tell you, we're not children anymore. Today as never before, perhaps—given the genuinely apocalyptic threats unfolding around us—Americans have an obligation to themselves, their families, and society to quit whining, stop comparing notes on who is more diseased, addicted, or dysfunctional, and just tend to business.

Recovery exhorts Americans and America to do just the opposite, creating whole new categories of addictions and diseases for which there is often little, if any, foundation. "Psychology continues to support disease models of addiction despite an inadequate research base," Franklin Truan, a clinical psychologist, observed in the *Journal of Psychology*. Speaking of alcoholism specifically, Michael Hurd told me, "At best, the 'disease' concept is a loose metaphor."

What's more, the Recovery ethic strongly implies that a genetic predisposition exists for whatever ails us. In the case of the physical dependencies—alcohol, drugs, eating, smoking—this genetic component frequently is stated outright. A much-quoted study of overeating, for example, refers to a person's physical size as his or her "biological destiny." In making these declarations, Recovery leaders seem undeterred by the fact that "the scientific foundation for these sweeping assertions is flimsy at best," Satel told me.

No matter how flimsy the evidence, by dint of sheer repetition the message spun by Recovery's champions has won over the American public: A 1997 Gallup poll showed that almost 90 percent of respondents regarded alcoholism as "a disease." Interestingly enough, another 1997 poll, this one among physicians who actually *treat* alcoholics, showed that 80 percent of the doctors thought alcoholism was plain old bad behavior.[4] But amid the ongoing national mood of empathy, understanding, and political correctness, that is not the kind of poll that gets headlines.

MUCH ADO ABOUT . . . WHAT, EXACTLY?

Perhaps the most striking feature of SHAM's Recovery wing is the mainstream credibility it enjoys despite the dearth of evidence supporting it. The questions start with the progenitor of all Recovery, Alcoholics Anonymous, with its 2.2 million members worldwide.

If we are to believe AA itself, then yes, its program would seem to offer some benefit. The organization quotes a success rate of about 40 percent, which traditionally has been considered admirable, given the thorniness of the problem. But there is no shortage of observers, among them former AA members, who allege in opinion pieces and widely read Web logs (blogs) that AA plays fast and loose with its numbers. (Try, for example, www.orange-papers.org or www.brothersjudd.com/blog/archives/009208.html.) Even government agencies, including the National Institute on Alcohol Abuse and Alcoholism (NIAAA), have had a hard time puncturing AA's wall of secrecy and anonymity.

"It's been a very difficult group to study," Ann Bradley, a former alcoholic and now NIAAA's resident authority on relevant analyses, told me. "It's really something we still don't know a great deal about." Bradley says she does see signs that AA is "becoming somewhat more cooperative in working with outsiders."

In its official posture on AA, NIAAA treads lightly. Its overview of the program says, "Although AA is generally recognized as an effective mutual help program for recovering alcoholics, not everyone responds to AA's style or message, and other recovery approaches are available." The agency also concedes that AA's "efficacy has rarely been assessed in randomized clinical trials."

Others have been more forthright in challenging AA's effectiveness. In October 1995 the *Harvard Mental Health Letter*, a publication of the esteemed Harvard Medical School, pegged the *spontaneous* cure rate among alcoholics—the percentage who shake the addiction on their own—at between 43 and 82 percent, depending on the study criteria. As many as one-third of those, Harvard reported, were able to give up booze cold turkey. In short, Harvard's research indicated that alcoholics who *don't* try AA have a better chance of kicking the habit than alcoholics who *do*.

If Harvard's ranges seem a bit wide and the numbers a bit imprecise, consider what NIAAA's Bradley told me: "In 1994 we reviewed all of the research to that point—125 different studies!—and it was like apples, oranges, grapefruits, and bananas. People had used so many different measures of the disease, and what constitutes addiction, and what constitutes dependency, and what constitutes being cured." Bradley describes sorting through the morass of discordant data as "the most awful experience of my life."

Still, there is further evidence for the notion that recovery-minded individuals might be better off skipping AA or derivative programs. The ambitious work of the behaviorist Stanley Schacter suggests that individuals who try to lose weight or stop smoking on their own are more successful than those who try formal twelve-step programs. Indeed, in study after study, decade after decade, the demonstrable results of Recovery regimens—90 percent of which are based on AA's storied twelve steps, according to the American Psychological Association—have been inconclusive at best. In his exhaustive 1983 work *The Natural History of Alcoholism*, Dartmouth psychiatrist George E. Vaillant looked at four decades' worth of clinical trials and added an eight-year study of his own. He concluded that no evidence indicated that treatment of alcoholism in any form yielded better results than an individual could achieve just by letting the addiction run its course. Vaillant's conclusions drew angry denunciations in Recovery quarters, but they have never been scientifically refuted. Discussing the voguish treatments for various physical addictions, Franklin Truan observed, "None of the models presented is more effective than others or more effective than no treatment."

It's also hard to ignore an analysis first published in the *American Journal of Psychiatry* in August 1967. Researchers followed 301 people who had been arrested for "public drunkenness" in San Diego and were randomly assigned to three groups based on the nature of the court-ordered follow-up: no treatment, referral to professional counseling, or Alcoholics Anonymous. Finishing dead last—with almost 50 percent rearrested during the following year—were the eighty-six individuals sentenced to AA. Second best was the group receiving the counseling. And most successful at staying out of jail? Those receiving no treatment at all. Now that's self-help.

Whatever the initial cure rates may be, eventual relapse after treatment is shockingly high—between 50 and 90 percent, depending on the addiction and the study. For starters, we know that a fair number of people—possibly more than half—listed among Bill W.'s "First 100," that inaugural class of AA members, fell off the wagon and/or died within a short time after being "cured." Other accounts put the "First 100" itself at fewer than forty core individuals.[5]

Such evidence lends credence to allegations that by characterizing addictions as "lifelong diseases," AA-based platforms actually lay the groundwork for their own failure. If Alcoholics Anonymous has been adept at persuading society of any one thing, it's that even after an alcohol abuser stops drinking, he or she remains a "recovering alcoholic" or "dry alcoholic." One of the most eloquent critics of the twelve steps, Michael J. Lemanski, writes in the *Humanist* that such programs "offer what is, in reality, the antithesis of therapy. There is no cure." In any case, research through the years has cast doubt on the cardinal AA belief "once an alcoholic, always an alcoholic." Studies by the

RAND Corporation and by separate Scottish and Swedish teams, among others, have uncovered a sizable percentage of former alcoholics who reverted to social drinking without also reverting to lives of chaos and heartbreak.

The knowledge base on addiction and recovery surely would be far deeper had not AA, throughout its history, vigorously opposed independent research that sought to test its premises. For their aggressiveness in stamping out critical thinking even among members, AA and its sister organizations have invited comparisons to cults.[6] Lemanski has described AA's materials as follows: "The reader is told that, within meetings, only Al-Anon 'conference approved' literature can be read and discussed; sources of information from outside the program are not to be used because they 'dilute' the spiritual nature of the meetings. . . . Therapy, therapists, and professional terminology are also taboo," a position that frustrates group members who desire to supplement their twelve-step efforts with input from medical or mental-health professionals. Many addicts find such outside reinforcement essential. The scientific journal *Alcoholic Research and Health* conceded in 2000 that "AA affiliation without professional treatment has not routinely resulted in improvement." On its Web site, the National Institutes of Health notes that "even people who are helped by AA usually find that AA works best in combination with other forms of treatment, including counseling and medical care."

That observation is not surprising amid mounting evidence that alcoholism is seldom a problem unto itself but rather may have a root in depression or anxiety. In 2004 NIAAA released the results of what it describes as the "largest ever" study of the "co-concurrence of psychiatric disorders among U.S. adults." The study revealed a significant overlap between people suffering from alcoholism and people suffering from mood or anxiety disorders. Extrapolating from its representative sample of 43,000 Americans over age eighteen, NIAAA estimated that many of the 19.4 million Americans who meet the diagnostic criteria for substance-abuse disorders (alcohol, drugs, or both) are also among the 19.2 million Americans who meet the criteria for such mood disorders as clinical depression and manic disorders and/or the 23 million who suffer from such anxiety disorders as panic attacks, phobias, and generalized anxieties.[7] For the many people in those overlapping groups, it is doubtful that AA alone would work.

Even so, when AA fails to bring about the desired results, the organization projects blame back on the sufferer—a common ruse in the world of self-help. "If an individual in AA, for one reason or another, doesn't make adequate progress, the typical view is that he or she isn't adequately 'working the program,'" writes Lemanski. "The usual prescription, then, is to attend more meetings. The program can never be the problem." (Another way of looking at it is that while Victimization doctrine holds that your problem is not your fault, if you can't overcome that problem using the sanctioned twelve steps, well . . . it's your fault.)

AA's defensiveness and inflexibility has created ample room for other groups to enter the Recovery market. Women for Sobriety (WFS) presents a typical case history. Now a 150-chapter organization based in sleepy Quakertown, Pennsylvania, WFS was formed in 1975 by Jean Kirkpatrick, a heavy drinker who had drifted in and out of AA for decades (not to be confused with the former ambassador to the United Nations). Kirkpatrick, who died in 2000, was unhappy not only with AA's decidedly male tenor but also with some of the core aspects of the organization's philosophy. "In AA meetings, they rehash their drinking stories over and over," WFS administrator Becky Fenner told me. "I think that kept bringing up so much guilt in Jean that it actually made her feel worse. She wanted to get beyond the horror stories and the guilt." Further, says Fenner, "At Women for Sobriety, we don't have a higher-power concept. We encourage our women to take full responsibility for their own actions, instead of turning it over to something in religious or spiritual terms. We want them to work on their own self-worth."

Moreover, applying the AA model can be problematic when the malady doesn't lend itself to the dogmatism of the twelve steps. To use the most obvious example, the abstinence-only approach that sounds reasonable enough when the demon is alcohol becomes a tougher sell in a group like Sex and Love Addicts Anonymous (SLAA), where one is dealing with a pastime that you can't reasonably expect people to foreswear now and forever.[8] The result, in SLAA's case, is a middle-of-the-road stance that incorporates most of the AA liturgy but also acknowledges that "there are no absolutes for sobriety in SLAA." By its own admission, the organization hopes to promote a "healthy attitude" about sex at the same time that it decries promiscuity as a ruinous evil and refuses to specify just how much sex constitutes promiscuity. Members are even told to be wary of "sexual anorexia," an unhealthy avoidance of sex that may result from an overreaction to the program.

Some find these behavioral gray areas difficult to negotiate. Parallels have been drawn to the old Catholic-school enigma, wherein young girls learned that sex is both a "grievous sin that will destroy your life and send you to burn eternally in hell" and a "great blessing and a joy that you should one day bestow upon your husband lovingly and without hesitation."

Such problems highlight the complications that result when twelve-step programs are adapted to a vast array of problem behaviors or "dysfunctions." If twelve-steps programs can't be depended on to solve the tangible problems for which they were created, can they be counted on to help people cope with airy psychological constructs like "codependency" that can't even be defined, let alone quantified.

DYSFUNCTION BOULEVARD

No matter how confusing its methods or its metaphors, and no matter how questionable its success rate, Recovery is here to stay. Based on nothing concrete, people who should know better will continue to call everything an addiction or dysfunction or disease so that they may then employ tactics that have never been shown to work. In part, says Franklin Truan, this has to do with a natural human need for mastery of one's environment. "Having an answer to a problem, whether or not it is valid, gives the individual a sense of control over something that previously may have seemed uncontrollable," he wrote in the *Journal of*

Psychology. Money further complicates matters: "The perception of addiction as an incurable disease," Truan continued, "provides the professional and lay community with the opportunity for unlimited and never-ending treatment, which has become a lucrative business."

For such reasons, we're well served by taking a brief tour down Dysfunction Boulevard. Consider these five overlapping messages of the twelve steps and the Recovery movement.

1. YOU'RE DAMAGED GOODS

"Once, people used to shrug off a bad day as a bad day," says David Blankenhorn, the founder and president of the Institute for American Values and the author of 1995's controversial social critique *Fatherless America*. "No matter how bad things were on Monday, there was always Tuesday." That uplifting sense of renewal is the very source of strength the twelve-step programs undermine, he told me: "Instead of just looking at ourselves as being in a rut, [the Recovery movement] teaches us to see ourselves as having a permanent condition of some sort. The condition becomes how we define ourselves."

There may be a way of rising above it, if you confess your weakness (steps 1 and 2 in the twelve-step paradigm) and entrust yourself to The Program and/or The Guru (steps 3, 6, and 7). But whatever is wrong with you will always be there, much like herpes, waiting to flare up again.

As with any incurable disease, there are bound to be complications and side effects, some of which, we're told, are every bit as bad as the principal malady. The litany of these secondary afflictions is lengthy and sobering: post-traumatic stress disorder, obsessive-compulsive disorder, other "opportunistic" addictions, to name just a few. It is often said that people raised in dysfunctional environments become prime candidates for substance abuse, spousal abuse (either as abuser or victim), overeating ("food addiction"), and so forth. The literature of Recovery tells us that abused children are far more likely to become sexually disordered adults, the specific manifestation depending on the parent who did the abusing and the nature of the abuse.

Harvard's Archie Brodsky says the movement's self-fulfilling fatalism is clear in the lexicon: "People are always 'in recovery.' They're never 'recovered.'" This can lead to what some have called a "cop-out syndrome," wherein people not only explain past failings in terms of their malady but also lay the groundwork for future failings: I'm an adult child of an alcoholic, so therefore what can you expect of me? What can I expect of myself?

In support of such philosophical criticism, Brodsky cites a RAND study of adolescents attending Alateen meetings. Although the majority of the kids did show short-term improvements in schoolwork and overall "adjustment," most settled back to their old ways within a year—and 36 percent actually did *worse*. "The seminars gave them psychological 'permission' to see themselves as failures," Brodsky told me. "Before the seminars they were discouraged. After the seminars, they felt *flawed*."

2. GOOD IS BAD

Despite the ferocious optimism embodied in the twelve written steps, the programs do not, in practice, accentuate the positive. A nihilistic view of life and living is stitched into the very fabric of Recovery. Convincing people who are "in denial" of the gravity of their condition and its dominion over their daily lives often requires a harrowing psychological battering from the group. Akin to what you sometimes see in "interventions" taken against substance abusers, this battering may entail constant retelling of their most regrettable moments (the sort of tedious immersion in self-loathing that led Jean Kirkpatrick to splinter off from AA) and/or coercive introspection in which members learn to see the hidden pathology beneath their unremarkable memories of childhood. "In the world of codependency," Wendy Kaminer wrote in *I'm Dysfunctional, You're Dysfunctional*, "families are incubators of disease: They manufacture 'toxic' shame, 'toxic' anger, 'toxic' self-doubts, and any number of 'toxic' dependencies. Codependency books lead you back through childhood to discover the many ways in which you've been abused and the 'negative messages' you've internalized. . . . Readers are encouraged to reconstruct their own pasts by drawing family trees ('genograms') charting their legacies of abuse."

Says Brodsky, "It's hard to overstate just how traumatic and psychologically destructive that single 'revelation' can be. You grow up loving and trusting your family, your parents. Now you're told they were the source of the unhappiness or any lack of achievement in your life." How, he asks, could that not play havoc with a person's ability to trust other aspects of life that "seem good on the surface"?

Their faith in even the most sacred of life's institutions rudely shattered, many people emerge from Recovery skeptical and suspicious. As Kaminer has suggested, those raised on Recovery regimens often believe nothing, and believe *in* nothing. Recovery's emphasis on discerning the covert patterns in behavior teaches twelve-steppers to catalog the bad things that happen to them under preconceived notions of Victimization and a supposedly hostile universe.

To understand how Recovery theory can stand a good thing on its head, consider the spate of programs designed to combat "love addiction." One popular program, Irresistible Chains, drives its followers, primarily young women, to a Web site that includes a subsection called "The Addiction Hits Campus." Love is described as a "social dependency constellation," a symptom of which is "the need to cling to one human object for love and support." The site recounts the tragic saga of Jody Agler, an Indiana University student whose travails began when she met fellow student Jeremy Lantz and "had feelings for him immediately." Eventually, through much counseling and soul searching, Agler learned to distrust the euphoric connection she felt with Lantz; she also learned that such connections may be counterproductive for her in general. The site goes on to quote Stanton Peele, a psychologist and addiction therapist who points out that some folks "devote their whole lives to one person, closing off all shutters and doors." In fairness to Peele, he is not a fan of twelve-step theory. Still, he states here that love bears "a striking resemblance to drug use," a theme the site reinforces again and again. Anne Wilson Schaef picks up the same disillusioning theme in such best sellers as *Escape from Intimacy* and *Meditations for Women Who Do Too Much*.

3. IT'S ALL ABOUT *YOU*

It has been observed that people in codependency workshops are not the nicest folks to be around. That's because anticodependency therapy comes across as an endorsement of selfishness.

"To the extent that it works at all, it has to be criticized for causing an overreaction away from caring about other people," Steven Wolin, a professor of psychiatry at George Washington University, told me. "The 'recovering codependent' tends to keep people at arm's length. It's a classic pattern. They go from one extreme to the other, and if you confront them on it, they'll tell you, 'Well, I'm better off looking out for myself.'" Wolin says he isn't always so sure.

The so-called Me Generation of the 1980s already had worked up a head of steam by the time Melody Beattie's *Codependent No More* burst on the scene. "Many factors played into the deteriorating marriage climate in the 1970s and 1980s, of which the Recovery movement was just one," says the social scientist James Q. Wilson, whose classic work of social commentary, *The Moral Sense*, deals in large part with the breakdown of American institutions over the past half century. But there's no question that Beattie's 1987 book was a perfect fit with the zeitgeist or that some people embraced its arguments who shouldn't have. At the height of self-determination fever, some women, filled with a sudden need to escape the drudgery of day-to-day life, began walking out on their "unsatisfying" marriages (and sometimes their blameless, wide-eyed children). The 1980s featured the highest average divorce rate of any decade in American history, never dipping below 4.7 percent per 1,000 population. That's about double what it was in 1955. (In the next chapter we'll see in more detail how SHAM has adversely affected marriage and relationships.)

4. ALL SUFFERING IS CREATED EQUAL

When an influential voice like John Bradshaw draws outrageous analogies between children of alcoholics and Holocaust survivors, he encourages a loss of perspective that isn't helpful in a society struggling to fine-tune its moral bearings and rank its collective imperatives. Reacting to the Bradshaw argument, David Blankenhorn says, "Having annoying or even emotionally dysfunctional parents is not the same as physical abuse. An occasional episode of spanking cannot be compared to living through the Holocaust."

It can be argued that pain is pain—that when you're hurting, it matters little whether others consider your pain trivial in the grand scheme of things. This argument, in fact, underlies so much of Recovery. As noted in point 3, *it's all about* you. You're allowed to think of your own needs, to *put yourself first*. On the other hand, it does matter to society that so many of its supposed citizens have devolved into whiny, Seinfeldian solipsists who rank their fondness for "emotionally unavailable" lovers on a par with world hunger. "The process of coming to adulthood is about learning to make value judgments and assign priorities," James Q. Wilson told me. "It's about seeing yourself in the context of something *larger* than yourself and your own selfish needs."

One would think a key ingredient of personal growth and emotional health is the ability to understand gradations of suffering, to develop a certain resiliency in dealing with disappointment, to discern the all-important distinction between needs and mere wants.

Yet to hear the folks in Recovery tell it, an individual's quest to have his private pain validated is the single most deserving enterprise on the planet. "It's beyond navel contemplation," says one psychiatrist who asked not to be quoted in this connection. "It's asking other people to feel sorry about the lint you find there, and then to help you remove it."

The ironic (and often, for the Recovery groups themselves, self-defeating) result of this psychosociological free-for-all is a kind of desensitization. After listening to the complaints from drunk people, fat people, sad people, oversexed people, incest survivors, divorce survivors, people who can't get a date, people who wish they could stop dating partners who hurt them, and on and on, we become jaded. Sick of trying to sort through the mess, we begin to assess the various (self-)interest groups without meaningful regard to the merit of their claims; we simply assign the greatest value to the squeakiest wheel.

5. IT'S NOT YOUR FAULT

Some years ago I began surveying my college classes on their feelings about the Clinton presidency. Did Bill Clinton's romantic indiscretions—and his subsequent lies about them—in any way reflect on his fitness to govern? Resoundingly, semester after semester, my students said no. It is true that college students, on average, take a more bohemian approach to life than most people and thus are more inclined to shrug off promiscuity. But their reasoning intrigued me. I recall one young woman who casually explained, "Women were his weakness, that's just how it was. I don't think he could control it." And the lying? "Well, what do you expect the guy to do? Admit it in front of his wife and the nation?"

A male student chimed in: "People always try to cover up for the bad things they do, don't they?"

My unscientific classroom polls hinted at the outlook with which those students grew up, and which is now rampant in society: Each of us has some weakness, something inside us we *can't control*—and *that's how it is*. What's more, since nobody wants to admit a weakness, well, *what else are you gonna do but lie*? Why, it's just plain common sense!

If that sounds plausible, ask yourself how far you're willing to take that logic. What about Ted Bundy's "weakness"? The boys at Enron? Were Uday and Qusay Hussein suffering from "damaged inner-child syndrome"? (I've purposely taken the argument to extremes, because Victimization theories have been employed as murder defenses in this country.) Once you start making allowances based on people's weaknesses, where do you draw the line? And who gets to draw it? If a person has no power over his or her weakness, how does society credibly decide whose weakness is tolerable and whose isn't? Having gone that far, how does society justify blaming people, much less punishing them, for acts that are beyond their control?

A popular answer: *We draw the line where society gets hurt.*

But we do *not* draw the line where society gets hurt. Not consistently, and not neatly, either. Often we draw that line based on how well blocs of people with a shared "weakness" have sold their message of Victimization and self-disciplinary impotence. Let's return once more to that original class of victims. Though America finally shows signs of reaching the limit of its patience with drunk drivers, it was not always thus. In 1967 the American Medical Association (AMA) burst forth with its revisionist conception of alcoholism as a disease. This did not happen out of the blue. Alcoholics Anonymous and leading psychiatric organizations, as well as factions of the legal community, had long been pressuring the medical community to give alcoholism a biological underpinning.[9]

For the first half of the twentieth century, alcoholics were handled more under the criminal model than the patient model; they were thrown into drunk tanks rather than tucked into beds in emergency rooms. If and when they did land in hospitals, they were commonly treated as "charity cases," with the cost of their care often coming directly out of a hospital's bottom line. There was no formal mechanism for obtaining insurance reimbursement of any sums hospitals spent on the care of alcoholic-related disorders. More important, society's unsympathetic view of the affliction left doctors with little basis for urging health insurers to set up or subsidize rehabilitation plans. The AMA's revised stance, in essence, took substance-abuse therapy out of the exclusive province of private groups like AA and made it mainstream. It also allowed psychiatrists and psychologists to submit for reimbursement for whatever counseling and therapy they provided to addicted patients. While many of those in the vanguard of this movement meant well, one cannot overlook the more venal motives on the part of at least some of those among the AMA establishment who represented the hospital interests and certain medical specialties. Put bluntly, they saw the unrealized profit potential in alcoholism.

Today, on any given day, seven hundred thousand Americans receive treatment related to alcohol abuse or dependency. As a rule, this care is either fully reimbursed by individuals' insurance or underwritten by blanket policies carried by employers. In addition, a major 1998 survey pegged the direct cost of alcohol's medical consequences at $18.9 billion, much of which, again, is now covered under health insurance. The AMA policy also opened the door to pharmacological approaches to treating alcoholism, as well as still more insurance reimbursement of sums spent on drugs such as disulfiram and naltrexone.

In sum, an entire new industry-within-an-industry has sprung up—all based on little or no hard evidence, especially none that existed in 1967.

"It is astonishing how far some of my colleagues have gone in stretching the limits of what we really knew about the mechanism of substance abuse, which isn't much," Sally Satel told me. She is especially critical of those doctors and medical researchers who were the earliest voices in positing an "alcoholism gene." "There is no peer-reviewed evidence for any such conclusion," she says. "Reputable medical institutions that in any other setting would never dream of committing themselves to a position without hard science nonetheless leaped on the bandwagon when it came to this one subject."

Given this mainstream stamp of approval, twelve-step catchphrases soon began showing up in courtrooms. When Salt Lake City's *Deseret News* ran a five-part series on drunk driving, the paper revealed that even some defense lawyers complain about the judicial system's lax handling of DUI lawbreakers. Noting that her clientele consisted of "a constant stream of repeat offenders," an unidentified attorney pointed out, "The first thing they say to a judge is that they're in counseling. They say they have jobs and families to take care of. To have defendants dictate their work schedules for the judges to work around, it's ridiculous." According to a lawyer I spoke with, a motorist facing sentencing in Nevada told the judge, "Your Honor, I am appalled by what I did out on that highway"—note the due observance of step 5 in the twelve-step sequence—"but I ask the court not to forget that *I am a victim, too. I'm a victim of the genetic disease of alcoholism* [italics added]."

Courts have accepted such arguments despite the fact that society most certainly gets hurt because of drunk driving. According to an ambitious study prepared in May 2002 for the American Automobile Association Foundation for Traffic Safety, 40 percent of all highway fatalities in 2000—that's 16,653 deaths in a single year—"involved at least one drinking driver, bicyclist, or pedestrian." That's a fair amount of "hurt."

Interestingly, if the drunkenness-as-disease paradigm doesn't mitigate the treatment of impaired drivers as well as it once did, that is largely because another group of victims rose up in an aggrieved chorus: Mothers Against Drunk Driving (MADD). Members of MADD could describe losses that were rather more tangible than those cited by the Recovery side. For example, Susan Bragg, a MADD victim advocate in Texas—which led the nation with 1,745 alcohol-related deaths in 2002—has argued, "Victims must deal with so much throughout the process. Worse yet, during plea agreements, victims are made to feel guilty if they don't support a plea agreement or an early release from prison. Victims say, rightfully so, 'We didn't put ourselves in this situation. Why are we made to feel otherwise?' "

MADD advocates and other critics of judicial leniency also point out that society isn't likely to solve this problem by coddling the drunk driver, at least not if the statistics can be believed. According to the study prepared for the AAA Foundation for Traffic Safety, in 2001 American drivers took an estimated 80 million trips in which their blood-alcohol level exceeded the legal limit. Since only 1.55 million drunk-driving arrests occurred that year, the study calculated the odds of being arrested during any one such trip at more than fifty to one. The report concluded that authorities could "convince more drunk drivers to change their behavior"—note: *behavior*, not *dysfunction*—pointing out that states that have taken such aggressive steps as zero-tolerance prosecution and lower blood-alcohol limits have substantially reduced the problem. Evidently drunk driving is a disease one can be cured of by watching other sufferers go to jail.

Which brings us back to Bill Clinton's adulteries and society's blurry lines. I often suggested to my classes that Clinton's "weakness" was not as innocuous as is typically believed, or at least as is typically portrayed in the media. Leaving aside his treatment of the assorted women in his life (including his wife), Clinton caused significant damage to a great American institution—the presidency. His behavior undercut the leverage chiefs of state are supposed to enjoy with other branches of government. Certainly his nonstop legal entanglements and eventual impeachment distracted him from concentrating fully on governance. What presidential business went untended while Clinton focused on defending his personal behavior from constant attack? We may never know how many ill effects the nation suffered as a result.

My classroom arguments fell on deaf ears. Sometimes students would actually groan. "I hear people say those kinds of things and I want to scream, *Oh, grow up, America!*" one young woman said. She opined that the problem during the Clinton years was not the man himself, but America's prissiness, combined with its lack of sympathy for Clinton's "being human." This was the same student who, earlier that semester, had chastised critics of actor Robert Downey Jr. for their failure to grasp "the tragedy of his addiction." She wasn't alone. Much of Hollywood and not a few editorialists rallied to Downey's defense after one of his many tumbles off the wagon, condemning his detractors as "judgmental" or "mean-spirited."

We have the Recovery movement to thank for the fact that nowadays the people who criticize wrongdoers are the sinners, while the wrongdoers themselves are simply "being human."

As all of this implies, viewing dysfunctions as diseases has profound social consequences. If the alcoholic's want of drink (or Bill Clinton's want of women, or Winona Ryder's want of that extra handbag) is as much an ineluctable symptom of some hardwired biological imperative as the leukemia victim's proliferation of white blood cells, then questions of right and wrong become moot. If we do what we do because we must, then what difference does it make whether we should or shouldn't have done it?

Recovery's bedrock assumption—that you're not evil or venal, you're simply exhibiting symptoms—lays the groundwork for an amoral view of life. It explains why today's society goes to extraordinary semantic lengths to separate the criminal from the crime. A person who makes his living robbing liquor stores isn't necessarily a common thief anymore; he's a person "involved in an ongoing criminal enterprise." We shouldn't really impugn *him*, as a person, because he may have *no control over what he's doing*. I could cite innumerable cases of this mentality in action, but a particularly telling example was the defense mounted on behalf of Rosemary Heinen. The former Starbucks corporate manager embezzled $3.7 million from her employer, then splurged on diamonds, Rolexes, grand pianos, hundreds of Barbie dolls, and nearly three dozen new cars. Yet according to her lawyer, Heinen wasn't greedy, unethical, or corrupt. No. She was a tragic example of "impulse control disorder."

Melody Beattie was right when she asserted in *Codependent No More* that "guilt makes everything harder." But . . . isn't it supposed to? Sally Satel, like many rational observers, is perplexed by the suggestion that we should refrain from calling a spade a spade. During an interview with John Stossel for his ABC News special *Help Me, I Can't Help Myself*, Satel was asked how she felt about the psychiatric industry's admonition to use the word *alcoholic* sparingly so as not to "stigmatize" people. Satel refused to flinch. "Why would you want to take the stigma away?" she replied. "I can't think of anything more worthwhile to stigmatize."

"There are things that shouldn't be that easy for people to do," says David Blankenhorn, pointing out what should be self-evident but has become less so amid the moral relativism of the past quarter century. "Guilt originates in conscience. To deny guilt is to marginalize the conscience."

A NATION OF HUMPTY DUMPTIES?

It's the oldest dictum in sales and marketing: "Find a need and fill it." Clearly unhappiness represents a more solid base on which to build a Recovery movement than contentment. Happy people aren't trying to recover from anything; nor do they go looking for massive amounts of help. That's why the impresarios and self-styled healers of the twelve-step world went one better than finding a need: They *created* a need by devising a twisted metaphysic wherein caring about people equals codependency, self-sacrifice equals masochism, raising obedient children equals child abuse. If there is a particular genius to Recovery, it's as a marketing tool, not a personal-salvation program.

For the individual consumer, Recovery may be worse than merely wasteful. "The problem with a lot of it," says James Q. Wilson, "is the unfortunate and diabolical human tendency to reject the good news while embracing the bad."

Think about that in the context of the harrowing and relentless psychic pounding visited upon people during the early stages of Recovery. Though a (sincere) Recovery workshop tries to impart a dual message—this is why you're broken; this is how you can be fixed—the part about being broken is what sticks. Therein lies the supreme and fatal paradox of Recovery, and of so much of self help in general: It is easily capable of persuading followers that they're gravely flawed. But getting people to the next step—that they can change—is a major stretch. Many in this created class of victims never attain "wellness."

As Harvard's Brodsky puts it, "In too many cases, the 'I'm a loser' part stays with you long after you've given up on the remedy."

The result is what some label the Humpty Dumpty Syndrome—wherein you're taken apart, but your pieces can't be put back together again. "It's like the guy who's got a little something wrong with his car, some relatively minor thing, so he figures it's not worth going to the mechanic," one psychologist told me. "He buys the shop manual, puts the car on blocks, gets the thing taken apart just fine. Then he finds out he can't get it back together right. And now it won't start at all. He's much worse off than he was before."

In societal terms, it's bad enough when misguided but sincere people reach out to others they perceive to be damaged. It's far worse when the charlatans get into the act, knowing as they do that they can sell their books, fill the seats at their seminars, or boost the ratings of their TV specials only by persuading large numbers of us that we're less happy than we thought, or we're afflicted with some dreaded dysfunction we didn't know we had.

Is that really what we want? A nation of diffident Humpties, teetering on the edge of that wall, above a boulevard of uncertainty and regret? A society beset by a curious, paralyzing combination of self-doubt and self-interest: a country made up of 295 million Individuals-with-a-capital-*I* who are endlessly second-guessing not just the choices they make in their private lives but also the most critical issues of social policy? In hyping the hope of "Recovery," SHAM has left us more troubled than ever.

9

LOOKING FOR LOVE . . . ON ALL THE WRONG BASES?

We live in a society that's very selfish.

—Raoul Felder, divorce attorney to the stars, answering a Fox News anchor's question about why the divorce rate is so high, July 2004

If there's an overriding message to this book, it is this: Even if you've never turned a single page of a self-help tome or heard the first word of wisdom depart the lips of some newly ordained self-improvement deacon, the way you live your life has been affected, if not transformed, by SHAM and its canons. There is simply too much of it in the environment: on TV, in magazines, embedded between lines of dialogue in the latest Bridget Jones movie or some other Hollywood blockbuster. You may hear it in the patter of friends who have been reborn as part of Dr. Phil's flock, or read it in the codes of behavior spelled out in your company's personnel-policy manual. Over time—as is true of anything that enjoys near-constant repetition—SHAM's program for better living has a way of sounding plausible, inevitable, "normal." The most incorrigible skeptics fall prey to passive reinforcement.

Nowhere is this truer than in that bedrock area of human interaction where self-help's efforts have been most concentrated through the years: love and relationships. And once again, it becomes clear that the "payoff" has not been as advertised.

In the course of my decadelong tenure as a Little League coach, I watched gloomily as divorce touched more than half the families whose kids played on my teams. Over that same period, among the several dozen employees who came and went at the bank where my wife worked, most of the marriages also came and went. During the final year of her employment, her crop of eight coworkers boasted just one intact union other than our own. More recently I taught at a large Midwestern university, and while I never formally surveyed my students, classroom discussion made clear that many of them reported their grades to (and solicited money from) more than a single set of parents.

The pace at which couples uncouple has shown a modest decline in recent years. Even so, the current rate—four divorces for every one thousand members of the population—remains about double what it was in 1960. Generally speaking, the younger you are nowadays, the worse are your odds for fulfillment everlasting. An extremely complex demographic analysis by the Census Bureau, "Number, Timing and Duration of Marriages and Divorces: 1996," showed that a twenty-five-year-old man has a 53 percent likelihood of being divorced at least once in his lifetime; a woman of the same age does just slightly better, at 52 percent. As troubling as how many of us get divorced is how *fast* we do it: A third of divorces occur before couples reach the unremarkable five-year plateau. Should the trend continue, we may need to rethink our traditional notions of marital longevity and the commensurate awards for same. Diamonds suddenly seem a fitting tribute for any couple who makes it to the ten-year benchmark.

The ramifications of this trend are dire. Census Bureau figures reveal that the nuclear home is about to sink into minority status among today's infinite array of family-living arrangements. Just 50.8 percent of American households consist of a married mother and father and children whose conception awaited the conception of the marriage itself; that figure was 67 percent in 1970. A quarter of the nation's children now live in broken homes—or, to use the current euphemism, "alternative families." Despite such euphemisms, however, Americans are coming to realize that this rampant dismantling of households cannot be good for the children left behind: Statistics on crime, drug abuse, and teen pregnancy leave scant room for dissent. "There comes a point," David Blankenhorn told me, "where the ugly numbers drown out the politicized debate. We've reached that point." And one might argue that many of the parted adults themselves suffer because of divorce.

To be sure, SHAM alone cannot be held responsible for these dismal trends. Other reasons for the rise of the divorce rate have been amply chronicled. Working wives are less dependent on men for financial sustenance and thus no longer have to suffer marital problems in silence. Concrete notions of morality rooted in Judeo-Christian ideals have given way to freedom of choice and situational ethics; as one comic gibes, we're wont to act these days as if Moses had handed down the "Ten Suggestions." The past quarter century has witnessed the destigmatization of most of the taboos—single parenthood, abortion, adultery, and divorce itself—that once militated for the traditional family unit. Then again, the evidence indicates that SHAM has contributed to this destigmatizing and to the blurring of right and wrong.

Even more important, of all the factors affecting the grim numbers on divorce, the most virulent—and paradoxical—may be the very self-help outreach that was supposed to make everyone happy. The various twelve-step programs and their myriad less-structured imitators emphasized breaking the cycle of victimhood by not being so solicitous of others, in the process also teaching followers to worry less about any collateral damage inflicted in the course of pursuing their own needs. Like a social Ebola, the cry of "codependent no more!" has broken out of that small core group of perpetual victims for whom such admonitions might be necessary; it now infects the mainstream with the supposedly empowering message that the best way to foreclose being a loser at love is to never put your feelings fully at risk in the first place.

Empowerment and Victimization have inflicted a curious double whammy on relationship-minded Americans. SHAM tells people to expect the moon (after all, "you deserve it") while browbeating them for letting themselves become victims in the past and reminding them that anyone with even a shred of dignity would *never* let that happen again. It's not hard to see how this fulminating obsession with emotional self-preservation would spell death for true love. Like doctors in a cancer ward who avoid becoming too involved with dying patients, many Americans today approach their wedding day with a reserve that can't help but handicap the marriage.

For example, they draft prenuptial agreements and refuse to commingle assets. Though in its September 2002 items on prenuptial agreements *American Demographics* could report no "concrete numbers" on their latter-day rate of incidence, the magazine noted that "anecdotal evidence" strongly suggests a trend toward prenups, "especially as more people are giving matrimony a second, third or fourth try." In the American Bar Association publication *Attacking and Defending Marital Agreements*, Laura Morgan and Brett Turner report that about 20 percent of couples embarking on second marriages obtain a prenup, compared with just 5 percent of couples who are having their first go-around.

Moreover, couples postpone having children, in part for financial reasons, but also because they "want to make sure the marriage works first." The Centers for Disease Control and Prevention reported in 2003 that the average age at which American women have their first child had reached an all-time high of 25.1, compared to 21.4 in 1970. Today, as David Frum of the American Enterprise Institute observed in a 2003 column for the *Wall Street Journal*, "marriage is a continuum, a series of gradations between true singlehood and formal matrimony."

Another sign of the distance kept in more and more marriages: Couples take separate vacations and glory in the notion that each partner "needs his/her space" to "grow as a person"; a contingent of young marrieds, probably small but still significant, create customized arrangements between the parties that slice large loopholes in traditional marital dogma to accommodate greater sexual freedom.

Does that sound like a recipe for marital bliss?

Now SHAM wants to help dig America out from under the relational rubble its philosophies have helped create. It's not unlike a doctor injecting you with some frightful disease, then telling you that for a small extra charge, he'd be more than happy to show you his home remedy for it. And SHAM's cure is as bad as the disease.

In a sense, SHAM has been "about relationships" since the 1960s, when Thomas A. Harris and his mentor, Eric Berne, began selling theories of "transactional analysis" as a better way of learning to engage with those around us. Today, though, SHAM targets the relationships sector with an unprecedented vigor. Once lightheartedly described as "advice to the lovelorn," SHAM's concerted efforts in the area of nurturing, fixing, and/or ending romantic relationships is what year after year attracts the greatest influx of new authors and other self-appointed experts. Each "expert" has his or her own special spiel or spin. Each hawks a steady stream of products and services to an audience of people desperately trying to work out the kinks in their love lives. In most cases the SHAM artists are targeting the *same* desperate audience, according to Jennifer Ortiz, publisher–relations manager for Marketdata Enterprises, which tracks the business side of the self-help industry. "'Relationships' is where you probably see the largest contingent of repeat customers," Ortiz told me. "They're always thinking the next book or seminar is going to make the difference."

Needless to say, that desperation mind-set is not lost on the gurus.

THE TROUBLE WITH MARS AND VENUS

SHAM's most prominent relationships guru might well be John "Mars and Venus" Gray. It's hard to imagine that during the ultra–politically correct 1990s someone could have built an uncontested SHAM franchise by reaffirming almost every stereotype about gender-identified emotions and behaviors. But that's what John Gray did. While Gray-as-political-dissident is a bit of a stretch, David Blankenhorn remarks, "At a time when the women's movement had been pressuring America to regard men and women as identical beneath the skin, he came right out and said it—men are from Mars, women are from Venus. What more is there to say?" Gray's legions of fans, especially women in relationships, saw him as speaking to an elemental truth that sensible people knew in their hearts, even if they weren't allowed to utter it publicly.

The trouble with Gray, as with most SHAM gurus, is that he goes too far. On the basis of little or no science—at least that he shows his readers—he presumes to know everything about what makes men and women, respectively, tick. And he does so in purple prose that would mortify Jacqueline Susann herself. He speaks of a woman's "hunger for love within her soul" as she "surrenders once again to the deepest longing within her feminine being." Lying nearby, meanwhile, is a man who yearns for his woman's "warm and wet responsiveness."[1]

Even once you get past the language, Gray's specificity in describing the sexual differences between the genders is striking. Gray states that a woman engages in sex to experience a heightened form of love. A man has sex to be released "from all his frustrations." Great sex "is soothing" to a woman. Great sex "strengthens" a man, who regards his woman's fulfillment as his "ultimate quest and victory."

But Gray's most eyebrow-raising contention may be this: "The difference between a man and a woman is that she doesn't feel her strong desire for sex unless her need for love is first satisfied."

Is that so.

In a 2003 study appearing in the *Journal of Sex Research*, Terri Fisher, PhD, a psychology professor at Ohio State University, sifted through questionnaires completed by 201 unmarried, heterosexual college students, 96 men and 105 women. The students were separated into three groups. All were instructed to complete a questionnaire about their sexual attitudes, experience, and behavior, and the age at which they first had sexual intercourse. Members of group 1 filled out the questionnaires while hooked up to a polygraph machine that, they were told, would reveal any attempts at dishonesty. (The machine was a ruse: It didn't actually work, but the students didn't know this.) Members of group 2 filled out their surveys alone in a room and were told their answers would be anonymous. Members of group 3 completed their surveys alone in a room, but with the researcher sitting right outside, with the door open. They were told the researcher might see their responses.

When the answers were tabulated, it was clear that social influences had played a large role in shaping the responses. Women who thought others might see their answers reported an average of 2.6 sex partners; women who had privacy but were not subject to impeachment by the "lie detector" reported an average of 3.4 partners; and the women hooked up to the polygraph machine reported an average of 4.4 partners. Interestingly, the men's answers didn't vary very much regardless of the test conditions; average responses fell in a narrow range between 3.7 and 4 partners for all three groups. While the difference is small, it bears noting that, in this survey at least, the most sexually active women were *more* sexually active than the most sexually active men—4.4 partners for the women versus 4 partners for the men. And among the groups that were presumably most "honest"—those hooked up to the polygraphs—the sexual tendencies and attitudes expressed were roughly the same for men and women alike.

"Women appear to feel pressure to adhere to sex-role expectations, which is to say, to be more relationship-oriented and less promiscuous," Fisher told me. But she underscores that if her survey can be believed, only women's *attitudes* differ from men's—not their actual appetites or behaviors. To the extent women "differ" from men in their sex drive and proclivity for libertine behavior, Fisher concludes that it's because of social expectations, not genetic code. She is now skeptical of most historical assumptions about women's sexual attitudes. Other studies, as well as a number of telling public-opinion polls, are on Fisher's side, not Gray's.[7] Perhaps both men and women are actually from Saturn.

THE PROMISES OF DR. PHIL

Phil McGraw first asserted a serious claim to the lonely-hearts territory in 2000, when he published *Relationship Rescue*. One of SHAM's cleverest cross-promoters, McGraw that fall released his *Relationship Rescue Workbook*, in which he wrote, "The two books are designed to be companions." Translation: "If you haven't yet bought *Relationship Rescue*, get with the program." Though the workbook was well received by Phil fanatics, some grumbled about the amount of material the two books share—a somewhat surprising development, since SHAM buyers have a history of uncomplainingly purchasing the same books from their favorite gurus over and over again.

McGraw gives relationship-minded readers and viewers regular doses of SHAM's usual black-or-white affirmations. For example, *Relationship Rescue* is a tour de force in the overly optimistic view of personal omnipotence that typifies, and derails, so much of Empowerment.

"Your relationship is in trouble," McGraw argues, "because *you* set it up that way. . . . You set it up that way by actively, consistently, and efficiently designing, programming, and choreographing your entire lifestyle to generate and then support a bad relationship. You have chosen to live in a way in which no other result could occur."

To make such sweeping remarks in the absence of context not only is philosophically flawed but may be psychologically irresponsible, according to Judith Wallerstein, PhD, a psychologist, researcher, and leading relationship expert. "There are people we meet, and sometimes marry, who turn out to be very different from what we thought they were," Wallerstein told me. "Sometimes *we* turn out to be different from what *they* thought we were, or what *we* thought we were." Indeed, there is such a thing as bad luck or being in the wrong place at the wrong time with the wrong partner. There is such a thing as being duped or making an honest mistake. While preachers of Victimization eradicate notions of personal responsibility and therefore can offer easy ways out of difficult relationships, McGraw and others go so far in the opposite direction that they can leave individuals no choice but to consider themselves failures if they cannot make their relationships work. That is to say, McGraw's Empowerment patter may ultimately lead to a sense of Victimization.

Though McGraw's simplistic advice does not serve individuals well, in the end he possesses that special talent, present in all great SHAM impresarios, to inspire blind faith in his followers. Regardless of what McGraw says, what fans hear is "Deliver yourself unto me, body and soul, and I will lead ye to the promised land."

THE RULES

It's been a decade since a pair of then-married New Yorkers, Ellen Fein and Sherrie Schneider, ignited a cultural firestorm and gave currency to a set of long-whispered dating maxims with their *New York Times* number one best seller *The Rules: Time-Tested Secrets for Capturing the Heart of Mr. Right. Salon* writer Mark McClusky lampooned the book as a "bizarre combination of Pavlovian psychology and Danielle Steel romance," but Fein and Schneider have undeniably had a major impact on relationships in this country, and as a result on the relationships sector of SHAM.

Fein and Schneider's original man-hunting manifesto bespoke an abiding cynicism about men (and perhaps women and relationships as well) in codifying its thirty-five-point romantic formula, which the authors said had been handed down from mother to daughter since first being posited by a friend's grandmother at the turn of the century. *The Rules'* directive to women was simple: Play hard to get and you dramatically improve your odds of being, well, gotten. The authors admitted in one TV interview that this wasn't exactly rocket science, that their book consisted of "stuff that every woman sort of knows instinctually." For example, "Don't accept a Saturday night date after Wednesday" is a code by which single women have lived for generations. But, said the authors, no one had formulated that mentality into a complete "dating system" and put it all down in black and white.

That could be because *The Rules* sets forth one of the most diabolical stratagems for finding "true love" ever published. To begin with, some of Fein and Schneider's rules seem awfully arbitrary: "End phone calls after 10 minutes." And many seem awfully manipulative: "Don't call him, and rarely return his calls." Most rules are both arbitrary *and* manipulative: "If you are in a long-distance relationship, he must visit you at least three times before you visit him." Others smack of something one might expect from Donald Trump: "Close the deal—Rules women do not date men for more than two years." The authors also encouraged a Barbie doll approach to life that sounds patronizing (to women) and anachronistic and rankled not a few female reviewers. To wit: "Never leave the house without wearing makeup. Put lipstick on even if you go jogging!"

Nonetheless, the book sold more than a half-million hardcover copies and begat the predictable series of follow-ups: *The Rules II: More Rules to Live and Love By, The Rules for Marriage: Time-Tested Secrets for Making Your Marriage Work* (released as Fein was filing for divorce from her husband of sixteen years), and most recently *The Rules for Online Dating: Capturing the Heart of Mr. Right in Cyberspace.* The sequels continue the authors' tradition of arbitrariness and manipulation, while incorporating additional off-the-cuff canons that hardly could apply with every type of man (or woman) in every situation. From their book on marriage: "Give [your husband] 15 minutes alone when he comes home" because "you don't want him to feel smothered." And, they lectured wives, "Whether you like it or not, your husband determines your sex life. Whether your husband wants it all the time or is not that interested in sex, you will be happiest if you adjust yourself accordingly." Some feminists accused Fein and Schneider of setting back women's quest for sexual equality by several eons. Other critics deemed the "Rules" amoral. But the authors refused to apologize for their books. "It's not about fairness," Fein said in an interview. "It's about what works."

Certainly it worked for the authors, spawning a cultlike generation of so-called Rules Girls who remained faithful to Fein and Schneider as they transformed themselves into The Rules Consultation Corp. (TRCC). Nowadays Fein and Schneider have a particularly strong online presence. An e-mail consultation with TRCC normally costs $150, paid in advance, but distressed daters can ask a "quick question" for $50. Phone consultations are available for $175 for forty-five minutes, after an initial fee of $200. Bargain-minded Rules Girls may be interested in Fein and Schneider's package of six forty-five-minute phone consultations for $900 or eight consultations for $1,000. A woman who thinks she's already got it together may even wish to get in on the action: She can become a Rules facilitator for $1,000, organizing her own workshops and support groups.

A decade after Rules-mania hit, critics continue to wonder how anyone can expect to build a committed, trusting relationship on a foundation of gamesmanship and manipulation, if not outright deceit. "I understand the emphasis on creating that aura of mystery, and maybe there's some validity to it," Judith Wallerstein told me. "But when you make rules like 'don't tell him too much about yourself too soon,' well, is he really getting to know the person he's falling in love with?"

In time, the book provoked an impassioned albeit underwhelming rebuttal from Barbara De Angelis, *The Real Rules: How to Find the Right Man for the Real You*. De Angelis's advice? To meet a man who values you for who you are, be who you are.

THE HIGH CONCEPT

Even before *The Rules* and *Men Are from Mars, Women Are from Venus* emerged on the national scene, erstwhile marriage counselor Robin Norwood authored the successful book *Women Who Love Too Much* (1985) and the usual spate of follow-ups. Norwood came out of SHAM's Recovery/Victimization sector, and her chapter titles show it: "If I Suffer for You, Will You Love Me?" "Loving the Man Who Doesn't Love You Back," "Beauty and the Beast," "Dying for Love," and "When One Addiction Feeds Another" (which seems an appropriate title for the self-help movement itself). Most of the ills that plague women in relationships can be blamed on the family, according to Norwood. "We cannot cover in this one book the myriad ways families can be unhealthy," she writes. "That would require several volumes of a different nature." Like so many others preaching the gospel of Victimization, Norwood turns everything topsy-turvy, almost making it sound as if you'd be better off with leukemia than with the ability to love deeply.

Even if Norwood's perspective seems excessively dour, her success has inspired a plethora of imitators. Both Robin Norwood and John Gray reveal a key trait of some of the most successful SHAM gurus: the ability to find a punchy, "high-concept" approach to familiar territory. The importance of high concept is clear in Gray's career: He outlined most of what would become his best-selling ideology in a prior work titled, prosaically enough, *Men, Women, and Relationships*. But it took the high-concept Mars/Venus label to put Gray on the map. Notable among today's high-concept hopefuls is Susan Nolen-Hoeksema, author of *Women Who Think Too Much*. Upon first hearing the title, I thought her book would be a zesty send-up of Norwood's book, but it turned out to be a serious, unabashedly derivative attempt to play off Norwood's success.

Here, in her own words, is Nolen-Hoeksema's three-point program for helping women conquer the problem she references: "The first step to freedom is to break the grip of your thoughts so that they don't continue to pull you down further, and eventually smother you. The second step is to climb out of the muck onto higher ground where you can see things more clearly and make good choices about what directions you should go in the future. The third step is to avoid falling into the trap of overthinking again."

Clearly, Nolen-Hoeksema doesn't really mean that women "think" too much, in the sense of rational deliberation. Rather, she refers to some women's excessive consciousness of their feelings and obsessive need to take the pulse of all relationships. A better title for her book would have been *Women Who Love Too Much*. But that was already taken.

Other recent contenders underscore the importance of the high concept in a crowded self-help market. Gary D. Chapman produced *The Five Love Languages* (and, needless to say, a raft of spin-offs); the reader might wonder what those five languages are, but the answer turns out to be nothing the average SHAM reader hasn't heard many times before. Mira Kirshenbaum came forward with *Our Love Is Too Good to Feel So Bad*, a title that, aside from being catchy, appeals to the common tendency to question a relationship; by the end of the book, however, one realizes that Kirshenbaum has essentially rewritten her previous best seller, *Too Good to Leave, Too Bad to Stay*. Sherry Argov has written *Why Men Love Bitches: From Doormat to Dreamgirl—a Woman's Guide to Holding Her Own in a Relationship*; the plucky title might indicate a direct approach, but in fact the author constantly waffles and qualifies her statements in a way that undercuts the book's meaning and practical application (for example, Argov exhorts readers to be "kind yet strong").

THE SINGULAR WORLD OF WOMEN'S MAGAZINES

While stacks and stacks of books dispense relationship advice, the influence of women's magazines cannot be overlooked. To no small degree these magazines devote themselves to preparing their readers to find men, please men, and keep men. Today's trendiest and most popular women's magazines also rely heavily on their Web sites and frequently drive readers there for amplification (sometimes including interactive features) on relationship-oriented themes. We'll leave to others the larger political and social implications of a publishing movement that purported to empower women as a gender, then ended up teaching them largely how to paint themselves, primp themselves, and acquire enough sexual know-how to keep a man satisfied and at home. Instead we'll focus on the content itself and its direct impact on those who consume it.

The industry has come a long way since insiders referred to the keynote women's publications as the "seven sisters," and a feature in one of those "sisters," "Can This Marriage Be Saved?" in *Ladies' Home Journal*, represented the gold standard of relationship advice.[3] Today's front-runner in providing SHAM content would have to be *Cosmopolitan*, which in recent years has become notorious for its racy cover lines ("He Wants to Put His *What* Where?") and frank reader-diagnostics ("Do You Turn Guys On? Take Our Simple Test"). Since its inception under Helen Gurley Brown, and especially later under Bonnie Fuller, *Cosmo* claimed the lucrative middle ground between the politically charged feminism of *Ms.* and the girlie, socially uninvolved narcissism of, say, *Glamour* or *Mademoiselle*. Over the years, *Cosmo*'s formula for success (especially at locking up the coveted eighteen-to-thirty-four advertising demographic) has nudged even its most conservative competitors toward the more licentious end of the scale, such that today, cover lines on once-staid *Redbook* feature promises of "The Best Sex Ever!" juxtaposed against the usual pie recipes and diet plans.

Here again, however, are signs that the *intended* effect—equipping women with every trick of the romantic/sexual trade—may not be the *actual* effect. "For the average woman, measuring up to the exalted sexual standards set in *Cosmo* is nigh impossible," the independent-minded feminist Camille Paglia has written. Surveys on the relatively low level of sexual satisfaction among single females would appear to confirm this. For example, a 1994 study by sociologists Linda Waite and Kara Joyner, "Emotional and Physical Satisfaction with Sex in Married, Cohabiting, and Dating Sexual Unions: Do Men and Women Differ?"

showed that married women are markedly happier with their sex lives than the *Sex and the City* types to whom *Cosmo* appeals. Similarly, in a small but intriguing 2003 research project by Eric S. Blumberg, PhD, "The Lives and Voices of Highly Sexual Women," only fifteen of the forty-four women who admitted to the title characterization reported "relative satisfaction" in their current sexual relationships.

Further, one has to question the wisdom of telling readers only half the story—equipping them in a technical sense without putting that technique in any ethical context—thus yielding the impression that sexual virtuosity alone will guarantee a woman lasting contentment. In *Spin Sisters* Myrna Blyth accuses *Cosmo* and *Glamour* of indoctrinating women in the notion that "narcissism is an advanced evolutionary stage of female liberation," and that a "predatory" approach to dating and sexual relationships is "the most important step in [a woman's] personal liberation." Such an approach has to cause feelings of confusion and self-doubt when women learn that sexual intimacy in the real world is not quite as antiseptic, painless, and consequence free as it seems to be in the pages of *Cosmo*.

The final insult is that the self-help matter offered by women's magazines sometimes isn't even responsive to real-world problems, or, at least, the problems of real-world readers. A few years ago I asked a young editor I knew, who'd recently taken her third job in that segment of the industry, how her latest magazine managed to tease such great letters out of its readership month after month.

"We make 'em up," she said with a coy shrug. "We decide what kind of mix we need for the issue, or if there's some really provocative theme we want to cover. Then we write a letter to fit."

ADVICE IN NINETY SECONDS

People who seek feedback on relationship issues, and who don't want to wait for Phil McGraw's next book or John Gray's next seminar, have two other major places to turn: the telephone and the Internet. Both deserve some analysis.

Laura Schlessinger is not America's only radio shrink, and at least in matters of dating and relationship building, she may not even be its premier one. Dr. Joy Browne has positioned herself as talk radio's foremost expert on practical advice for finding a good relationship. Her books covering various aspects of the subject include *Dating for Dummies, The Nine Fantasies That Will Ruin Your Life, Getting Unstuck*, and *It's a Jungle out There, Jane*. Unlike so many others in SHAM who call themselves doctors, Browne actually is entitled to use the descriptor. She holds an MA and a PhD from Northeastern University and did postdoctoral work at Tufts Medical School. Later she spent time as a therapist in private practice and then as the director of social services for the Boston Redevelopment Authority. Browne even has won kudos from the American Psychological Association, and from *Talkers* magazine, which voted her Best Female Talk Show Host two years running.

Another in the growing list of *The Oprah Winfrey Show* alumni, Browne emphasizes that her advice is "compassionate" and "practical," which most interpret as a none-too-subtle swipe at Schlessinger's moralistic shrillness. Everyone in SHAM has a pet phrase, and Browne's is "What's your question?" (a softer version of Dr. Laura's snappish "So what's your question for me?" usually said to a caller who has gotten herself in a pickle that Schlessinger finds despicable). Though Browne has never quite hit Schlessinger's heights, she has a loyal following among the lovelorn and has never inspired the rage and contempt that seems to build so naturally in so many of her rival's listeners.

Where Browne goes astray is that she buys into the conceit that confidence comes before success or other "factual" attributes. Early in her book *Dating for Dummies*, she outlines her theory that success in dating—like success in just about everything—flows from self-confidence. "So let's talk about this confidence thing," says Browne in her chatty style. "Are some people—the gorgeous, smooth, successful among us—born with it? Nope! These people got to be successful and smooth by *appearing* to be confident." It's the type of omnibus statement SHAM thrives on.

The evidence, alas, does not support Browne's optimistic statement that attitude is all that matters. Daniel Hamermesh and Jeff Biddle, researchers at the University of Texas, have devoted considerable attention to the specific impact of looks on success. Their work appears to show that the job market clearly and substantially rewards beauty—something people are born with. People judged "strikingly attractive" by the survey's information gatherers earned, on average, up to 10 percent more in salary than less-attractive peers, even after adjusting for education and other factors. No matter which profession Hamermesh and Biddle looked at, they found the same phenomenon. In the legal profession, better-looking lawyers of both genders earn more money by their fifth year of private practice than less-attractive lawyers, and the skew widens further with time. Good-looking male attorneys, the researchers found, also have a much higher probability of ascending to partner than their more ordinary-looking colleagues. Hamermesh found the same thing when he looked at the University of Texas itself. Faculty members whom students considered "good-looking" got higher ratings as teachers. (The bad news for the good-looking is that in some studies physical attraction has been *negatively* correlated with honesty and overall concern for others.)

What's more, if you're ugly, don't commit a crime, at least in Texas. A 1991 study of fifteen hundred defendants by sociology researchers Chris Downs and Phillip Lyons showed that Texas judges impose meaningfully sterner sentences on the unattractive felons who come before them. Even doctors aren't above considering beauty. Studies show that doctors spend more time with attractive patients and have a better, ahem, bedside manner with them. Other studies suggest that good-looking people generally date other good-looking people. This is especially true of good-looking men. The message would appear to be that despite Joy Browne's simplistic statements about the power of "confidence," an ugly duckling can summon up enormous confidence and still not land that date with Halle Berry or Brad Pitt.

SHAM partisans might argue that physically attractive people possess more self-confidence, and they'd surely have a point. Looking in the mirror and seeing Brad Pitt or Halle Berry staring back at you no doubt does wonders for your mood. But the correlation with success that researchers consistently find is with the *beauty* part, not the *confidence* part. If Joy Browne and others were correct—if confidence were the marker for success, not beauty—then the statistical correlation between beauty and success would not be as clear as it is. And you can't will yourself to be beautiful.

You can't will yourself to be omniscient, either, but that doesn't seem to stop Laura Schlessinger. Her much-maligned fondness for jumping the diagnostic gun—even in the course of a ninety-second phone call—compounds the problem for those seeking romantic help via the telephone. During an August 2004 radio show, Schlessinger spent the first half of a call chiding a young caller, "Marilyn," for expecting men to be more like women. Marilyn had begun the call by voicing the fear that her boyfriend of seven months was "unable to attach," possibly because of his "abusive" upbringing; she said she'd like him to "open up" more to her. Cutting the young woman off in the midst of several fumbling attempts at greater specificity, Schlessinger launched into one of her favorite tirades, on how today's society has conditioned women to expect wimpy men.[4] Schlessinger strongly implied that Marilyn should count herself lucky to have a more traditional, masculine man.

I asked Dr. Michael Hurd how he would have handled Marilyn's situation. "I'd want to know more about this guy," Hurd told me, "especially when I hear the caller hinting at an 'abusive childhood.' I definitely would've explored that angle, when you're talking about a guy who presents as cold and emotionally withdrawn." Depending on the nature of the abuse, says Hurd, "what that girl could have on her hands is not so much a traditionally masculine man, but a time bomb. A good therapist might recommend that he needs some counseling himself."

The old Laura Schlessinger, having rendered her verdict, might have voiced some perfunctory expression of goodwill to Marilyn ("Got it? Good luck now") and moved on. But Schlessinger more recently has been attempting greater empathy, giving callers more time and latitude; she'll allow them to hang on through a break (an extraordinarily rare occurrence earlier in her radio career), and she instructs not a few of them to "be sure and call me back and let me know how it all worked out now, OK?" This kinder, gentler Dr. Laura could have to do with some personal epiphany in the wake of her own travails, or it could have to do with her keen awareness of the attrition in her ratings as well as in the number of stations carrying her show. Regardless, Schlessinger did not immediately dispose of Marilyn this day. And when the frazzled young woman finally managed to get a word in edgewise, she gave Schlessinger a concrete example of the behavior that distressed her. She explained how, that very morning, when she'd tried to pin down concrete plans for that evening, her boyfriend had put her off by saying, in essence, "I'll see how I feel when I get off work and if I feel like it, I'll call you."

Clearly taken aback, as well as offended on Marilyn's behalf—one could almost feel the little hairs on the back of Schlessinger's neck perking to attention—the talk-therapist at this point reversed her field. The boyfriend was no longer a "traditionally masculine man," but a self-centered brute who "didn't care about Marilyn." Suddenly the biggest question in Schlessinger's mind was why Marilyn had wasted seven months on this bum.

It's almost impossible to overstate the significance of what happened during that phone call. A young woman came to Dr. Laura with a problem. Dr. Laura leaped to a conclusion about the nature of the problem and chided the caller, in essence, for being silly. Had the call ended there, as Hurd tells us, a fair amount of damage could have been done to Marilyn. But we can't be overly happy about what finally *did* happened, either, says Hurd. "Anybody can have a bad day. And in spite of what I said before about any red flags in this guy's background, I hate to see people giving relationship-ending advice based on a phone call. In any one phone call, you're seldom getting a good feel for the nature of the problem." In the end, he says, it's further evidence that when life-changing issues like relationships are at stake, "you shouldn't be turning to pop psychology for answers."

THE ANSWER IS JUST A CLICK AWAY

You may recall Wendy Kaminer's snarky observation that what mostly distinguishes self-help gurus from laypeople is the former group's ability to "write well enough to get a book deal." The Internet eliminates even that "credential," modest as it is, thus further lowering the bar. It allows people who *couldn't* get a book deal to direct-market their self-published (or, increasingly, e-published) wares and become viable niche players in the burgeoning relationships market. The Internet, after all, is where busy and bar-averse singles of all ages increasingly run to find their actual partners, so it stands to reason that they'd go there for advice on partnership as well. The rise of the Internet opened up SHAM's relationship wing to anyone with a modem and a Web-design tool.

We're less interested here in actual dating sites like eHarmony.com and Match.com than in the cornucopia of other sites proffering all that essential wisdom on the mental game of romance.[5] There are thousands upon thousands of such sites (a Google search under "relationship advice" yielded 197,000 hits), each offering "indispensable" advice for hopeless romantics, for people about to embark on relationships, for people who regret having embarked on the relationships they're in—in short, for every possible permutation of relationship state-of-being. While many of these sites purport to offer free services, the truth is that nothing online is free. Eventually you receive a pitch for something that isn't free. A Web page run by self-described "relationship coaches" Susie and Otto Collins, cheerily headlined "For Anyone Considering Leaving a Relationship or Getting a Divorce," is typical of the group.

"Dear Internet Friend," they begin warmly. "If we guess correctly you're in either one of two situations. One—you're unhappy in your current relationship and are trying to decide whether to stay or go. Or two—you've already made the decision to leave and you want to make sure you're making the right decision." Leaving aside the issue of whether the two questions are basically the same question asked two different ways, the Collinses continue, "You're about to discover some of the most important questions you need to ask yourself in order to make the clearest, most empowered"—there's that word again—"decision possible about whether to Stay or Go. By reading the information on this web page you'll also discover a powerful new resource that will give you fresh new insights into your current relationship." After a few more paragraphs of that, and some confessions about how their own relationship weathered a period of turmoil that taught them profound lessons, and then a series of lines exhorting you to take a "true, honest and truthful" look at your own relationship, the Collinses finally get around to that "powerful new resource"—their own book, *Should You Stay or Should You Go?* The Collinses swear that *Should You Stay or Should You Go?* is the book they wish *they* had had when they were going through their own tough times. They finish up with a list of things their book will do for you, number one of which, startlingly enough, is "help you know whether you really want to stay in this relationship or move on." They also emphasize that "although we do give our opinion and insights about some of the issues, these decisions are yours and yours alone," lest you feel like calling them at home, after you've read the book, to ask, "Well, Susie and Otto, should I stay or should I go?"

Order *Should You Stay or Should You Go?* and you will receive, absolutely free, no less than *seven* bonus products. That includes two additional books by the Collinses, *Creating Relationship Magic* and *Love Lessons*, and such "special reports" as "6 Keys to Healing After Leaving a Painful Relationship." The "regular price" for all this wisdom is $59, but, of course, if you "order now"—the words form a clickable blue link—you get it all for just $34.95. And if you can't wait another minute before deciding whether to stay or go, a downloadable version of the book is available to you as soon as the bank approves your credit card.

Notice how Susie and Otto Collins have niched their approach to the marketplace—the whole Stay or Go conceit. The Collinses have learned and applied the cardinal rule of online marketing in a world in which each of us has been taught to see ourselves as a special-interest group. If you have a relationship or are desirous of having a relationship, any kind of relationship, with any kind of partner, there is a site that purports to address your special needs, even though, in most cases, the "special needs" part is just a smoke screen, a way of packaging generic insights that could apply to any relationship under almost any circumstances. Deciding whether to "stay or go" is not that different from deciding whether your relationship "works," which is not that different from "fixing your relationship" (or "rescuing your relationship," as Dr. Phil might put it), which is not that different from understanding "what you really want in a relationship," which is not that different from evaluating your "relationship fitness." And yet, by coming at the topic from so many different angles, online purveyors of SHAM succeed in segmenting and subsegmenting the marketplace, thereby cleverly reselling the same advice with myriad different labels, just as Hollywood keeps making the same slasher movies with different titles (or sometimes the same title, with a II or a III or a IV after it, if they've got a bankable commodity like Freddy Krueger to work with).

ROMEO IS HEMORRHAGING

So where has all this SHAM-administered advice brought us?

An editor I know at the *Washington Post* took his wife to a cozy Georgetown restaurant for their tenth wedding anniversary. Amid the mood lighting and champagne, they were nonetheless subjected to the conversation of a young couple in an adjacent booth who spent all of dinner swapping bond-fund appraisals, high-tech esoterica—everything but sweet nothings. Before long the editor's wife leaned over to him and whispered, "I feel like I'm back at the office." In my own travels, I've come upon similar scenes many times. I once wrote about a particularly striking experience in a trendy café in Manhattan, where I spent two hours surrounded by way-cool twenty- and thirtysomethings. I saw exactly one couple that night who displayed *any* outward signs of affection toward each other. They cooed and occasionally kissed, and, for those unforgivable sins, were greeted with smirks and muttered putdowns by others in attendance.

These are anecdotal cases, but I don't think anyone would dispute that by and large, romance—the true, swooning, Cary Grant/Grace Kelly kind—is dying, or at least on life support. Young men and women are "hipper" today. They laugh at chivalry and frown upon public displays of affection. Though many social influences come into play here, the combined forces of SHAM indisputably contribute to the mix, taking the spontaneity and magic out of love.[6] SHAM kills romance by making courtship (another word that seems like a vestige of a bygone era) programmatic and premeditated, something to be regarded with cynicism. Romance is the abandonment of self-discipline; romance is reckless, and SHAM preaches, above all, self-control, the conscious triumph of will over impulse. This is why SHAM's cure for the demonstrated romantic malaise of the past quarter century is as bad as the disease itself—if not worse.

The process begins with books like *The Rules*, which rigidly define "acceptable" mating rituals and promote empty, unfelt gestures—often at the expense of the felt ones—and moves on through the various support groups and Web sites that emphasize emotional reserve while reminding men and women of the gulf in understanding and mutual respect that eternally separates them. How could generic rules that supposedly apply to everyone *not* take much of the mystery and mystique out of dating? Today, it's as if the seeker of love is seeking not a person but rather a representative of a certain gender. People learn to look for the stereotype, not the individual, and they relate to one another and respond to one another on that misguided, impersonal basis. Here, more than anywhere else, is where George Carlin's sly line about the folly of "self-help" acquired from outside the self stands in bold (and comic) relief. Can a person really look outside himself for "rules" on love that are *personally, individually* relevant and resonant? This shop-manual approach to dating precludes that glorious alchemy between one singular man and one singular woman that produces an enduring, highly individualized coupleness.

And as SHAM edges away from romance, it edges toward pragmatism. Many young women (including many of the female students I met in my seven years of teaching college) seem to have forsaken any timeless romantic idylls in favor of a much more utilitarian take on the mating dance. Check the tenor of personal ads run by the fairer sex. Increasingly they spend less time effusing amorous whimsy—"Wanted: soul mate for long moonlit strolls"—than laying out specific criteria men must meet in order to establish their fitness for a relationship. *Professional* and *financially secure* are terms one sees a lot in such ads. Not that long ago I saw an ad from a woman who lusted for a suitor with "a clean credit report." This is not to imply that women should seek out unstable bankrupts. But clean credit?

The simple truth is that no one can orchestrate real love or even honest chemistry. No one can explain why people feel love for those they feel it for. The only certainty is that men and women are going to be drawn to the people they're drawn to. In SHAM's defense, some people do make poor choices in affairs of the heart, and many seem to be attracted to exactly the wrong people. (Consider that while in prison, serial killers like David "Son of Sam" Berkowitz, Richard "Night Stalker" Ramirez, Ted Bundy, and even the openly gay Jeffrey Dahmer received cards, smoldering letters, panties, and earnest marriage proposals from adoring women.) SHAM's relationship gurus try to warn their followers away from making bad decisions in love. It's an admirable endeavor . . . but does it work? *Can* it work? By inducing people to embark on relationships that go against their basic wiring, does SHAM not set them up for failure? Will they be happy? If everything in a woman's system is telling her to find a biker instead of a banker, is her marriage to the banker going to succeed? And can SHAM ever really cure her of her lust for the biker? Is there any reputable evidence of SHAM's ability to do that?

Moreover, what are the costs of *trying* to do that? Of making both genders so overly, obsessively concerned with the *process* of love?

"This may sound a bit odd," one writer who has worked in the Relationships field told me, "but since we're talking about love and marriage, I'd make the comparison to an orgasm. Especially for a woman, the more you obsess over having one, plan for it, and expect it, the less likely it is to happen. So I suppose you could argue that the very act of planning for love in a mechanical kind of way is what prevents it from happening." Pausing for a moment, the writer adds, "Come to think of it, it's the same thing with a man and an erection. You can't usually *will* one." No. And you can't will falling in love.

But you *can* make people cynical and hard-bitten. You can remind them so often of the dangers of finding Mr. Wrong that they second-guess every romantic spark that ignites within them. You can lecture them ad nauseam about the eternal battle of the sexes or the inherent difficulties in cross-gender communication. You can remind a woman nonstop that men really just want to get laid, while reminding a man that women just want to go shopping on his dime. By doing so, you contribute to a climate wherein both genders believe in nothing, trust in nothing. This speaks to the less-than-optimal investment that too many young people have in the relationships on which they embark, even when that relationship is a marriage. Loath to play the fool, they hold back something of themselves in anticipation of a better alternative.

Today's young marrieds are infinitely better equipped for life, in the practical sense, than my generation ever was. Ask them about their financial plans for ten or twenty years down the road, and they'll have a ready answer. Many of them are already laying the proper groundwork for prosperity, or at least a reasonable measure of security. But ask them to picture what their marriages will look like ten or twenty years from now, and you may well get a blank look. Not a few of them will blurt something like "I'm not thinking that far ahead right now. I'm taking things a day at a time." Some of the people who give that answer will leave a relationship the minute it "stops working" for them. Yet they know enough to hold a tech stock through the market's cyclic gyrations.

Susan Allan is the founder and director of the Divorce Forum, a Santa Barbara–based counseling agency and a popular Web site on matters matrimonial. When I asked Allan why we have so much divorce today, she gave a simple answer: "We have more divorce because marriage isn't based on unconditional love."

Nothing ventured, nothing lost. Or so we tell ourselves.

10

I'M OK, YOU'RE . . . HOW DO YOU SPELL *OK* AGAIN?

> You can see the glass as half full or half empty. But either way, it's still half empty.
>
> —*Anonymous*

In contrast to SHAM's characteristic way of doing things, let's start with a few objectively measurable facts. Herewith, a sampling of the cheery news from the American educational system:

National Scholastic Aptitude Test (SAT) averages were first made available in 1952. Between 1952 and 1963, America's national SAT score held fairly constant at 478 out of a possible 800 in verbal aptitude, 502 out of 800 in math. This, despite a 400 percent surge in the pool of high-school students taking the SAT. (In the earliest years of the test, only the most motivated students signed up for it. Gradually the SAT became a rite of passage for college-bound students.) In 1963 there commenced an *eighteen-year decline* in test scores, which, by 1981, had bottomed out at 424 for verbal, 466 for math. In 1982, scores rose for the first time in two decades—by two points in verbal, one point in math. The low test scores have produced a serious kill-the-messenger response, wherein critics blame the test itself.

In 1998 the Amsterdam-based International Association for the Evaluation of Educational Achievement released the results of its Third International Mathematics and Science Study (TIMSS), involving twelfth graders from twenty-three nations. In combined math and scientific literacy, the United States placed fourth from the bottom, ahead of only Lithuania, Cyprus, and South Africa, those historic hotbeds of scientific innovation. In advanced math, the United States outpaced only Austria. In physics, American kids finished dead last.

Inclined to discount any one study? Here's another: The Programme for International Student Assessment (PISA) ranked students in thirty-two developed countries. Thirteen countries had better results than the United States in science, fourteen tested higher in reading, and seventeen bested us in mathematics.

As worrisome as the TIMSS and PISA results themselves were the apologias mounted by defenders of the U.S. system. Dudley Herschbach, a Harvard chemistry professor and Nobel laureate, told the *New York Times* that maybe we do "let kids wander all over hell in high school, but that preserves some energy for later when it is better spent." Gerald Bracey, an author and education consultant who has long been an unflinching defender of the beleaguered system in which he works, said the low scores probably showed nothing more than that other cultures are good at teaching their students how to take tests; U.S. schools, on the other hand, "are nurturing more creativity" in our kids.

And the rationalizations go on and on. North Carolina's annual test scores in fourth- and seventh-grade writing competency were so low in 2002 that district officials did what any of today's self-respecting education administrators would do: They threw out the scores. "We don't have any confidence in the results," explained Phil Kirk, the chairman of the state board of education. Note that Kirk blamed the *results*, not the schools or the curriculum. In any case, more than half the state's fourth-graders failed the writing test. Districts in Texas and Florida, equally embarrassed by their children's scores, ditched the results as well.

In fairness to Kirk, Bracey, et al., one could proffer several explanations for why test scores have fallen, particularly when it comes to declines in verbal fluency. As a people, we don't speak as formally as we once did. We've gotten lax, careless. We have presidents who, in delivering major policy speeches, say "ain't" and "nu-cu-lar," and we have had vice presidents who spell *potato* with an *e* at the end. We've also incorporated into mainstream expression increasing amounts of street dialect (think *Ebonics*) and other linguistic corruptions. Hollywood has further reshaped the culture. Can America really expect kids growing up with *Goodfellas* and *8 Mile* to diagram sentences written in the queen's English? Moreover, American schools contain an ever-larger population of immigrant children whose parents are disinclined to give up their native tongues.

Fine. Forget about the verbal. How about math?

What sinister social influences are causing kids in droves to multiply 5 by 7 and get 43? In what culture or country does 19 minus 14 equal 8? Granted, verbal skills play a role in every aspect of education, so language barriers (be they cultural or semantic) will affect the quality of learning. But we see the same problems, the same dour long-term trends, in relatively homogenous school districts, where everybody, including the teacher, speaks pretty much the same brand of English—or Spanish or Tagalog. And then you have the nettlesome fact that some of the highest achievers (including, year after year, finalists in the National Spelling Bee) are the children of recent immigrants. If language is such a barrier to education, how do we explain *that?*

Or could it be that such immigrant kids come from homes where the emphasis is "You'd better learn your ABCs" instead of "Now how do you *feel* about yourself today?"

The reference to children's feelings is not made in jest. In fact, no discussion of the problems that plague our education system can ignore the self-esteem movement, which gained respectability nearly four decades ago and has become a guiding force in America's schools. It's doubtful that any major cultural movement has been bureaucratically endorsed based on flimsier evidence—or been responsible for more disastrous results—than the attempt to imbue American schoolchildren with self-esteem.

"So many of the ills associated with the current malaise in public education can be associated, to a greater or lesser degree, with the emphasis on students' egos and feelings over their academic progress," Roy Baumeister, a professor of psychology at Case Western Reserve University and a leading critic of America's overselling of self-esteem, told me.

"Overwhelmed by pressure to be nurturing, to feed the students' emotional selves, educators are forgetting their basic mission. And we'll be paying the price for that for decades to come."

As we'll see, the self-esteem movement in schools was yet another outgrowth of SHAM. As the modern self-help movement exploded in the late 1960s, more and more Americans began focusing on their own feelings, taking the cue from author/psychiatrist/SHAM guru Thomas A. Harris and asking themselves, "Am I OK?" Given Harris's premise that many people are "not OK" precisely because they were somehow damaged in childhood, it was only natural that some "experts" would turn their attention to how to prevent such damage in America's children.

The result of that campaign—the rethinking of America's grade-school system in a way that undercut its commitment to quality education—offers one of the clearest and most instructive lessons in how SHAM's failings can hurt us all.

FORGET PERFORMANCE—FOCUS ON *FEELINGS*

It's been observed that there are two ways to guarantee high scholastic performance. The first is to expect a great deal from students and implement systems that force them to live up to those expectations. The problem here is that some kids won't make the cut. They're going to feel left out; indeed, they may be left *back*. That will hurt their feelings, take a toll on their social lives, and, we're led to believe, haunt them forevermore.

That brings us to the second way of guaranteeing performance: Simply set expectations so low that no one fails. And tell kids to be happy with the results.

Silly as that sounds, in recent years the latter "method" has become a popular strategy (if not the operative strategy) in American schools. Instead of encouraging excellence, educators have decided to banish failure by defining it out of existence—while at the same time persuading America's schoolchildren that they are automatically *special, wonderful, brilliant*.

Thanks to the emphasis on self-esteem, our schools now give ungraded tests (that is, when tests aren't forgone entirely); are plagued by the outer-limits degree of grade inflation known as "grade creep"; ban most competitive games during gym class or even recess periods; and, above all, replace hard-core, carefully planned, historically documented curricula in math, English, and the sciences with touchy-feely, free-form, ad hoc exercises and "play activities" meant to teach students how to "make nice." If they teach anything at all.

Gone, for the most part, is the open posting of grades, which would humiliate those who failed tests or even those who didn't do as well as some peers. In jeopardy of a similar fate, at least in some educational precincts, are verbal classroom exercises, which of course can highlight the student who is unprepared or less skilled in a given subject. Educators who openly display any behaviors or attitudes that compare students unfavorably to their classmates can expect a talking-to from on high. This is not to say that teachers should be permitted to force students to sit in the back of the room wearing dunce caps. We've come a long way since such draconian measures. But how does a teacher motivate higher performance without first calling attention to a student's substandard performance? And, of course, the teacher who gives his dressing-downs in private leaves himself open to charges of harassment from resentful students.

Even *favorable* comparisons hold hidden danger. Hailing some students as examples of excellence in open class can make other students feel inferior.

It's not hard to see how this leads to less quality work. The superior student is denied the opportunity of having his or her work praised, with all the positive feedback such praise provides; the rest of the class is deprived of peer role models. Policies at many "enlightened" schools go so far as to discourage educators from tolerating "teacher's pets," thus putting teachers in the unwelcome position of having to blunt the natural enthusiasm of their most motivated, upbeat pupils. (Apparently we don't care all that much about the *good students'* self-esteem.) If the choice is between (a) having a small group of students stand out in a way that makes the rest of the class feel bad or (b) having the entire class perform in a uniformly mediocre but collegial way, many schools would opt for (b).

In all this, the focus—as in most areas where self-help has done its dirty work—is on *feelings* over thoughts, *intent* over outcome, *contentment* over productivity. School districts have methodically disconnected pride from performance. As John K. Rosemond, a developmental psychologist and a syndicated columnist, has observed, in an Alabama elementary school where reading scores are abysmal, students walking through the front door each morning see their reflections in a mirror overhung by a banner telling them: "YOU ARE NOW LOOKING AT ONE OF THE MOST SPECIAL PEOPLE IN THE WHOLE WIDE WORLD!"

It doesn't end there. Consider a typical lesson plan in self-esteem building, culled from an idea-swapping Web site that helps teachers "more meaningfully connect" with their classes. The theme of the lesson, posted by Bonnie Custer of St. Agatha School in Portland, Oregon, is "feeling flashbacks." Custer employs a "cooperative learning structure" called "Mill and Mingle" to enable students to share feelings and build a sense of community. After reminding prospective users that her lesson should not be used until "these feelings have been discussed and modeled," Custer lists the requisite materials for this lesson: ". . . cards with Feelings (for visual learners), tape recorder or record player, music appropriate for grade level, space to move around freely." Thus prepared, students segue into the Mill and Mingle activity itself, which goes like so: "While music plays students circulate through classroom. When the teacher stops the music, they form pairs by turning to the person closest to them. The teacher calls out a feeling (use cards, also, as cue for visual learners) and the pair shares with each other a time when they have felt that way." Custer suggests as some possible feelings "happy, angry, embarrassed, lazy, scared, frustrated, shocked, loved, proud, important, curious, pleased, bored, disappointed, upset, joyful, sad, surprised, terrific, alienated, ashamed, worried." She also recommends that teachers have students identify similarities and differences in feelings shared and then "write about this experience of shared feelings in their journal." The process, Custer says, should be "repeated several times."

One might ask, is this really what kids go to school for? Shouldn't teachers spend more time actually *teaching*? According to some experts, no. "Healthy kids can teach themselves what they need to know," writes Grace Llewellyn in *The Teenage Liberation Handbook*. Such attitudes once motivated Supreme Court Justice Hugo Black to observe, "Children need to learn, not teach."

In some schools, standards have fallen so low that simply showing up is treated as a real achievement. In one Long Island, New York, school district, a program rewarding "perfect attendance" was bastardized to the point where a student could qualify by showing up in class for any given period of three consecutive weeks. A student who achieved that modest benchmark got not just a commemorative award—but free pizza, too!

Another teacher told me about his middle school's "Happy Board," where students advertise milestones of significance to them: "Some of the stuff that gets posted is surreal. 'I'm a woman now. I got my period.' 'You should see my dad's new SUV!' That kind of thing.What does that have to do with the school? Or even true self-esteem, for that matter?" The teacher's school also features occasional assemblies during which the student body gets to stand up, en masse, and applaud itself.

If the goal of such activities is to promote self-esteem, how do educators imagine the students will fare once they enter less coddling environments? After all, when they eventually enter the workforce, the Long Island students won't be feted with pizza parties or earn raises for managing to show up at work for three straight weeks. And the children who are taught to stand up and cheer for themselves "just because" might one day encounter situations their egos have not been conditioned to handle, or where the criteria are fixed and inflexible. Not too many med-school registrars' offices worry about hurting candidates' feelings.

It's as if school administrators and teachers believe that merely by having life happen to them all students earn the right to feel self-esteem. That diminishes the worth of the genuine self-respect that comes from having applied one's self to a true challenge. "The mechanism of self-esteem," John K. Rosemond told me, "is that you faced up to a task that, at least to you, was of uncertain outcome. You don't feel real self-esteem unless you've tackled something you didn't necessarily know you'd be able to master when you first undertook it." Getting your period or just observing your father's new SUV in the driveway hardly qualifies.

What's odd here is why so many educators would assume that high expectations automatically destroy children's self-worth. Thanks to the film *Stand and Deliver*, featuring a sterling performance by Edward James Olmos, many Americans are familiar with the work of Jaime Escalante, a teacher who pushed his class of inner-city academic discards to remarkable performances—in calculus, no less. But there's another story that, though less well known to the public, has become legendary in education circles (indeed, several people I interviewed for this book mentioned it without prompting). It's the story of a Chicago public-school teacher named Mary Daugherty.

One year, the story goes, Mrs. Daugherty found herself confronted by a class full of sixth-graders who were so clueless and intractable that she suspected many of them had learning disabilities. So one day, while the principal was off the premises, she broke a hard-and-fast rule: She looked in the file where student IQ scores and other relevant data were kept. Daugherty was amazed by what she found: Most of her students had IQs in the high 120s and 130s—near-genius level. One of the worst offenders had an IQ of 145.

Mrs. Daugherty did a great deal of soul-searching that night. She concluded that the blame for their conduct and lackluster performance was hers and hers alone; she had lost this class of brilliant minds by boring them with low-level work. So she began bringing in difficult assignments. She upped the amount of homework and inflicted stern punishments for misbehavior. By the end of that semester, Mary Daugherty had engineered a 180-degree turnaround: Her class was one of the best behaved and most accomplished in the entire sixth grade.

Impressed—and, frankly, stunned—the principal asked Mrs. Daugherty how she had managed such a dramatic turnabout. Haltingly she confessed her secret raid on the IQ files and how it had changed her approach to teaching the class. The principal pursed his lips, smiled, and told her not to worry about it. All's well that ends well, he told her.

"Oh, by the way," he whispered as she turned to retreat to her classroom, "I think you should know: those numbers next to the kids' names? It's not their IQ scores. It's their locker numbers."

One reason Jaime Escalante and Mary Daugherty remain exceptions is that social pressure makes it difficult to hold kids accountable for actual learning. New York City's mayor, Michael Bloomberg, learned this firsthand in January 2004 when he announced his plan to hold back third-graders who scored in the lowest of four levels on citywide math or English tests. The plan would end the common practice of "social promotion," which essentially passes children along to the next grade regardless of whether they've mastered the competencies taught in the previous grade. Critics railed against Bloomberg, many of them viewing social promotion as an important means of ensuring self-esteem, since it prevents kids from feeling like losers as they watch their friends ascend to the next grade. Iowa state senator Maggie Tinsman was similarly attacked in 2003 when she spearheaded legislation to halt the social promotion of Des Moines grade-schoolers in order to stress to schools the importance of reading. "If we are 'the education state,'" argued Tinsman, using a tagline popular among Iowa's boosters, "we must very strongly say, 'yes, we want every child to learn to read.'" Tinsman's critics denounced her remarks as "harsh" and even "racist."

Some states have proposed "conditional grades," a sort of between-grade limbo, where underperforming children go until they can join their peers at the next level up. Descriptions of such programs typically include counseling support and other expensive incidentals. The budgetary impact of these plans is significant: $30 million a year for Des Moines, as much as $1 *billion* for New York City, by some estimates. Such are the lengths to which we'll go to avoid bruising the feelings of kids who can't—or won't—do their work.

"The term 'self-esteem' has an almost incantatory power these days," writes Mike Schmoker, an elementary-school teacher, in *Education Week*. "Every discussion in education takes a bow in its direction." To educators, says Schmoker, self-esteem is "less a quality to be slowly earned than one quickly and easily given."

For more than seven years I have taught college, mostly to upperclassmen, and I can testify to the prevalence of the same easy, lowest-common-denominator thinking, even among students competing for a place in today's Darwinist job market. Students who've been awarded a B-minus—for work that merited less—will come to your office in tears. They are products of an educational system (and, indeed, a society) that has conditioned them to think they're entitled to be shielded from the ignominy of being "second-rate." And if they somehow get less than that, it's somebody else's fault: the teacher's, the system's, the school's. Not theirs.

Of course, before someone can get a really good job, it helps to get into a really good college, which is why grade inflation has reached down to high school as well. Figures from the College Board, which oversees the SAT, document this decay. In 1972, when data first began to be collected, 28 percent of college-bound seniors reported having an A or a B high-school average. By 1993, *83 percent* had an A or a B average. During this same period, the average SAT score fell by thirty-five points. Again: lower achievement, better grades.

This may also create a fractious climate at home by driving a wedge between students who are essentially majoring in self-esteem and parents whose notions of a quality education are not quite so laissez-faire. At school, little Samantha is told she's unique, special, wonderful. At home, Mom and Dad don't understand what Samantha has done that's so special or wonderful, especially when she just came home with a math test on which half the answers were wrong or an essay full of terrible grammar and misspellings.

"Why can't you be nice to me like Mrs. Rosenberg!" yells Samantha, on the verge of tears. "I'm never good enough for you!"

To which the hapless parent replies, "But honey, three times five isn't nine."

"*So?* The teacher said it was a good effort! Why can't you ever be happy with anything I do? Why can't you be happy with the fact that I'm *trying*?"

Faced with these situations, California, Michigan, and other states have allocated funding for programs designed to teach the *parents* how to better relate to their underperforming offspring and thus not dissipate all that heady smoke being blown at school.

The nonstop emphasis on safeguarding the student's self-esteem is such that teachers—already an underpaid, embattled group that we should be trying to support and ennoble—feel even less positive about their jobs, finding themselves at the mercy of arbitrary rules and ambiguous policies that may end their careers, or worse. In school districts nationwide, teachers can be fired for offenses against their students' self-esteem—and then, on that basis, sued by the parents of the sulking child. One San Diego school district maintains a code of ethical conduct for teachers that bizarrely prohibits them from "actions and/or activities that in any way might cause a student to feel bad about himself or herself respective to their [*sic*] peers." A new hire might reasonably ask, And exactly what does that exclude? If anything?

"The standards are so broad that they could be read to prohibit just about anything and everything," a twenty-year New York City teacher told me. "It's an eye-of-the-beholder thing. If the student ends up feeling bad, you did something wrong." Rightly, he asks, "I don't mean to whine, but I'm a credentialed professional who's been doing this for two decades. I care about my students, and I take pride in my job. Where is the concern for my self-esteem?"

HOW DID WE COME TO THIS?

It's safe to say that the impetus for the academic self-esteem movement came straight from Napoleon Hill and the other SHAM impresarios who preached, *Believe it, achieve it.* But many influences coalesced into what we see in today's schools. The leaders of the self-esteem movement borrowed freely from the available rhetoric. They created a garish patchwork of unproven theories and inconclusive data, using whatever small shreds of material helped their cause while discarding the large bolts of tightly rolled fabric that didn't fit their free-form patterns.

Amid the counterculture fervor of the 1960s, radical-chic behavioral theorists began fretting about how America was forcing orthodoxy down its students' throats, worrying too much about their math skills and not enough about their souls. But these theorists also argued that if we showed students we cared about them more as people, they would begin to add and multiply like little Einsteins.

Through self-esteem, in other words, we could have it all!

Pressed on the subject, many of the early gurus invoked turn-of-the-century education pioneer Maria Montessori. Montessori's clinical analysis of children's learning habits led her to endorse a form of passive education wherein children taught themselves about life by interacting with their environment. After becoming Italy's first female physician in 1894, Montessori returned to college to study psychology and philosophy. She became a professor of anthropology in Rome, then abruptly gave up both her university chair and her medical practice to work in close quarters with a group of sixty children. In 1907 she founded her famed Casa dei Bambini, or Children's House, incubator of the so-called Montessori method of education. She first visited the United States in 1913 and won quick support from such American notables as Alexander Graham Bell, Thomas Edison, and Helen Keller. By the 1960s Montessori-style education had caught on with progressive, high-minded suburban types—the "station-wagon Socrates set," as an editor friend of mine called them. At around this same time, of course, the nascent self-help movement was exhorting each of us to search for a "personal truth" (supposedly) free of orthodoxy-enforcing strictures.

A watershed event occurred in 1970. Theodore Sizer, then dean of the Harvard Graduate School of Education, together with his wife, Nancy, edited an enormously influential critique of current educational methods titled *Moral Education*. The Sizers condemned just about everything identified with the cultural values communicated via the American educational system: from the frontier ethic to the *McGuffey Readers* to the hierarchal classroom to any "performance metrics" (grades, to you and me) that sparked "terror" in the hearts of young students. The Sizers propounded a "new morality" that prized, above all, students' rights and inherent beliefs. In this brave new world of ethical relativism and the democratized classroom, "teacher and children can learn about morality from each other," the Sizers explained.

Moral Education made discussions of self-esteem and student empowerment de rigueur in teachers' lounges and especially at major educational confabs. Soon self-esteem became a sufficiently weighty topic to justify its own conferences: A February 1986 gathering in San Jose, California, begat the National Association for Self-Esteem (NASE). (Among the key players at the landmark California Self-Esteem Conference was Jack Canfield, who went on to write and edit the homespun, best-selling *Chicken Soup for the Soul* series.) Five years later the NASE board got around to defining the subject of its existence: "Healthy self-esteem" was "the experience of being capable of meeting life's challenges and being worthy of happiness." Today the organization promotes such books as *The Feelings Storybook*, described on the NASE Web site as "a sensitive and heartfelt book for children of all ages, including the child within each of us. . . . *The Feelings Storybook* provides an expansive vocabulary for the developing reader and acts as an excellent assessment tool for emotional growth."

The explicitly bracketed "self-esteem movement" dovetailed nicely with a second phenomenon, "affective education," which emphasized subjective psychological growth ("Who am I?" "What do *I* really want in life?") over cognitive learning ("Never mind who I am or what I want; can I do simple arithmetic?"). Since its formal 1975 debut with a personal-growth program called Quest, affective education has flourished wildly, with about three hundred such programs now being marketed to U.S. school districts. Some popular ones include Pumsy (Pumsy being the program's green dragon mascot), DUSO (Developing Understanding of Self and Others), and Free the Horses. In general these programs are not actually part of the curriculum; instead, trained facilitators work with groups of children in an assembly-hall setting or even off campus. Corporate sponsors or civic groups such as Kiwanis or the Lions Club often pick up the tab.

Affective-education proponents were near-manic about avoiding the preachiness that tends to characterize attempts to sell a values-based curriculum. Thus, by its very nature, and to some extent by design, affective education undercuts the participant's belief in moral absolutes.

Hoping to empower children and solidify their notions of self, most such programs teach them to make decisions based solely on personal criteria: "Would this make me happy?"

Here, for example, is how an affective-education facilitator might frame a discussion of armed robbery (and this is not an exaggeration):

> If you rob a bank, yes, you may come away with a sizable sum of money.
> But there's a high probability you'll get caught and go to prison for a spell.
> And you may have to hurt some folks in the bargain.
> Hurting other people may make you feel bad.
> Plus, prison is not an especially nice place to be.
> So you'll want to carefully weigh your feelings on robbing that bank.

The question of whether it's simply *wrong* to rob a bank—and/or hurt people—does not figure in the equation. In fact, affective-education trainers are specifically warned against introducing their own "value judgments" into the class discussion.

It's not hard to see how affective education's moral neutrality would irk parents whose ethical goals for their kids are somewhat loftier. (That is, if parents even know the specific content of these programs. After all, who is going to object when little Johnny comes home with a circular announcing a "program to boost your child's confidence and self-esteem"?) Even some of the early advocates of affective education have recanted. One of its founders, W. R. Coulson, PhD, has admitted that he might have made a costly mistake in pushing affective education. "Youthful experimentation with sex, alcohol, marijuana, and a variety of other drugs has been shown to follow value-free education quite predictably," he lamented.

Coulson is right. For example, when researchers at the University of Southern California compared students placed in affect-oriented drug-education programs with students receiving no such education, they found that those enrolled in the "preventive" program increased their use of tobacco by 86.4 percent, alcohol by 42.4 percent, and marijuana by 74.2 percent.

BUT AT LEAST THEY'LL FEEL GOOD ABOUT THEMSELVES—WON'T THEY?

Self-esteem is one of those things we make reflex assumptions about—that is to say, we assume it's a good thing. But scant evidence exists to show that self-esteem really *is* good for children. It may even be bad for them.

To begin with, young children probably do not understand the emotions that all this feel-good blather is supposed to foster within them. A well-meaning newspaper reporter visited a New Mexico school whose self-esteem program had children begin the day by chanting:

I feel good about me
I feel good about me
Me is something
It is very good to be

When the reporter asked one child, "How does it make you feel when you say that?" the boy first crinkled up his face as if not understanding the question. Then, under prodding, he replied with visible agitation, "I don't know. It's just something they make us say. Like the pledge of allegiance."

This should surprise no one, because researchers themselves don't even seem to know what self-esteem is or precisely how it figures in human development. The NASE, remember, took five years to produce a definition of self-esteem that in essence reduces to the tautology "self-esteem means feeling good about yourself." The broader field of psychology continues to debate the concept and its real-world implications.

"There is simply no consensus on what self-esteem even *is*," Paul Vitz, a professor of psychology at New York University and the author of *Psychology as Religion: The Cult of Self-Worship*, told me. "There have been thousands of psychological studies on self-esteem. Often the term *self-esteem* is muddled. It becomes whatever the person doing the study wants it to be . . . a label for such various aspects as self-image, self-acceptance, self-worth, self-love, self-trust, et cetera. The bottom line is that no agreed-upon definition or measure for self-esteem exists."

In scholastic settings, even the most basic correlations you'd expect—between being good at something and feeling good about something—may not exist. A 1989 study of mathematical skills compared students in eight different countries. American students ranked lowest in mathematical competence. Korean students ranked highest. But the researchers took an added step: They asked the students to rate how good they *thought* they were at math. The same American students who fared so poorly on the objective portion of the test had the highest overall opinion of their math skills. The Koreans, who aced the test, were their own harshest critics. "The best way to develop *real* self-esteem in children," Michael Hurd told me forthrightly, "is to teach them how to think."

OK, but if self-esteem isn't helping kids become students, at least it should help them become better, happier citizens. Right?

Not necessarily. Albert Bandura, a psychology professor at Stanford, concluded on the basis of an extensive multiyear study that self-esteem has little or no effect on either personal goals or skill-based performance. Pointing to his colleague's study, Vitz says, "There is no evidence that high self-esteem reliably causes or prevents anything, good or bad. A lot of people with high self-esteem have caused quite a lot of trouble for society."

Roy Baumeister, of Case Western Reserve, goes further than Vitz, actually positing a causal relationship between high self-esteem and *destructive* behavior: "It turns out that many hit men, genocidal maniacs, gang leaders, and violent kids have high self-esteem, *not* low self-esteem, which is the typical association some people have automatically tended to make."

As Martin Seligman asked in "The American Way of Blame," an essay for the *APA Monitor*, "In the last year there has been a cascade of multiple murders in school by American boys. In the 1950s there were none. What changed?" Certainly society itself changed in myriad ways, but Seligman argued that the "inner world" of these children has changed as well. As he put it, "They're taught mantras like, 'I am special,' and some of them come to believe it. A surefire recipe for violence is a mean streak combined with an unwarranted sense of self-worth."

John Rosemond agrees that teachers and parents who embraced the "liberate the children" view may have badly underestimated the potential barbarism of children who are not given a directed moral education. Left untouched by civilizing forces, the "self" for which this new view of education wants you to feel "esteem" may not be worthy of it. "To be honest," he told me, "I don't think there's been any profession that has wreaked more damage on the culture than psychology."

Even psychiatrists who pooh-pooh the notion that America may be raising a generation of homicidal maniacs have their own concerns about self-esteem as it's presently taught in schools and embraced by too many doting parents.

"One of my pet peeves is to hear parents praising kids' accomplishments as if they're professionals," Ralph López, a Manhattan pediatrician, told me, describing a phenomenon he calls "overindulged child syndrome." "A child who draws very well is a 'wonderful artist,' a child who dances well is a 'great dancer.' Praise the *event*, certainly—what the child did—but don't label the child himself or herself. All you do is fill them with unrealistic expectations." López says that "kids who have had too much positive reinforcement don't do as well in the workplace. They're overdue for a crash landing."

If you want to see this phenomenon at its outer limits, check out each season's early episodes of *American Idol*, when Simon, Randy, and Paula gleefully separate the wheat from the chaff. Note the way rejected contestants further humiliate themselves by expressing outrage after rendering a performance that failed in every way. It speaks to a culture in which all of us, steeped as we are in *I'm OK—You're OK*, behave as if we think *everything* we do is OK. Says Vitz, "People brought up on that mentality have come to believe that society's standards and criteria are not nearly as important as the way we see ourselves."

Is this really what we want? Is this the kind of blind, mindless sense of self that America hopes to stoke in its young?

THE BIGGEST LITTLE VICTIMS

If self-esteem-based education has been a dismal disappointment overall, it has been an unqualified disaster for one group of students: boys. Far from nurturing confidence, the currently entrenched pedagogy has taught America's boys and young men to question their own worth. It does this by rewarding qualities boys typically lack—docility, emotionalism, sensitivity—and punishing qualities they're more likely to possess: competitiveness, outspokenness, stoicism. Ironically, despite its determination to downplay winning and losing, the self-esteem movement, by privileging introspection and sentiment over action and intellect, naturally sorts the genders into winners (girls) and losers (boys).

Martin Seligman has written powerfully of the self-esteem movement's "frightening" impact on America's young men, and he's not alone. In a May 2003 *Business Week* cover story titled "The New Gender Gap," Michelle Conlin wrote of a "stunning gender reversal in American education. From kindergarten to graduate school, boys are fast becoming the second sex." Nor do boys have any real choice in the matter; the only alternatives are dropping out or being banished. As Leon Podles, author of *The Church Impotent: The Feminization of Christianity*, lamented to Karl Zinsmeister, editor of *American Enterprise* magazine, the educational system countenances boys only "if they will agree to behave like girls."

Significant numbers of them say "no thanks"—particularly those from the lower-income families for whom education offers the best prospects of breaking the cycle. "Among kids in families earning $80,000 to $100,000 per year, girls are 8 percent likelier to be on a college track than their brothers," says Podles. "At family incomes of $10,000 to $20,000, the skew swells to 56 percent." Using U.S. Department of Education numbers, *Business Week*'s Conlin points out that by 2010 there will be 142 women receiving bachelor's degrees for every

100 men; by 2020 that ratio could be 156 women to every 100 men. Conlin runs through some other startling statistics: "Once a boy makes it to freshman year of high school, he's at greater risk of falling even further behind in grades, extracurricular activities, and advanced placement"; boys are 30 percent more likely than girls to drop out of school; and more than 70 percent of special-education students are boys.

Three decades ago, just as self-esteem-based education was gaining favor, educators rightly recognized that girls weren't learning as well as they could be and sought to close the gender gap. Conlin, referring to the "Girl Project" that resulted, writes, "The movement's noble objective was to help girls wipe out their weaknesses in math and science, build self-esteem, and give them the undisputed message: The opportunities are yours; take them. Schools focused on making the classroom more girl-friendly by including teaching styles that catered to them." But while the gender gap has indeed narrowed, the attempt to make the classroom friendlier to girls made it unfriendly, if not openly hostile, to boys.

As a result of schools' turning away from competition and traditional expressions of masculinity, a visitor to almost any American lower-grade classroom over the past generation was apt to see the class busy at activities like painting, quilting, and journaling. If the visitor happened by during recess and observed the children at structured play activities, those activities were apt to be free-form games where no score was kept, no high-fives were permitted, and no individual player was hailed as a "star." Schools don't want to hurt the feelings of all those who don't excel, especially when boys are bigger and stronger than many of their female peers. Engaging in stereotypically male activities—especially war games, but also far milder chest-thumping ones—often draws severe chastisement. This has been particularly true since the Columbine massacre, as schools seek to identify and short-circuit students' aggressive tendencies.

School administrators have gone beyond curricular changes to achieve their aims. In 2002 the Seattle public school system required hundreds of middle-school students to participate in three days of sensitivity seminars at which they were repeatedly challenged to bring their feelings to the surface and share experiences when they hurt others. One student, interviewed in the *Seattle Times*, called the seminars a "psycho cry fest"—not an inappropriate description, considering that in some meetings up to half the students were weeping.

But according to John Rosemond and others, schools' attempts to "deprogram" gender can have the opposite effect on young boys. Teachers serve as parental surrogates, entrusted by parents to teach their children all day, and in today's educational environment, too many boys lose their bearings and act out in a destructive manner. For evidence of this counterintuitive reality, one need look no further than the sad plight of our inner cities, where male role models have long been absent, and boys grow up in households run by women. As Karl Zinsmeister has put it, "All those rap anthems about raping and torturing women come out of a world wholly devoid of male control."

More and more research indicates significant biological differences between the genders that have a profound effect on behavior. Researchers tell us, for instance, that by the sixth week after conception, a male embryo's blood contains at least three times as much testosterone as a girl's (anywhere from 250 to 500 nanograms per deciliter for boys versus 25 to 75 nanograms of testosterone for girls). As a boy's life progresses, additional infusions of testosterone are linked to increased propensities for risk taking and a willingness to fight. Nevertheless, explained Leon Podles, it remains impolitic to discuss notions of gender-identified traits, and countenancing them in a classroom setting has become "politically incorrect to the point of being a firing offense." Hence the "genderless classroom."

Politically incorrect or not, recognizing gender differences could prove critical if boys are to overcome the problems they currently face. In the June 2000 issue of the *American Enterprise*, Christina Hoff Sommers, the author of *Who Stole Feminism?* and *The War Against Boys*, wrote, "If, as the evidence strongly suggests, the characteristically different interests, preferences, and behaviors of males and females are expressions of innate, 'hardwired' biological differences, then their differences in emotional styles will be difficult or impossible to eliminate. But why should anyone make it his business to eliminate them?"

In Britain, where boys are also struggling academically compared to girls, some educators have hit upon the answer to Sommers's question: They shouldn't try to eliminate gender differences but instead should react to those differences. As Sommers recounts, a council of British headmasters devoted almost a decade to studying successful classroom programs for boys and concluded not only that the focus on students' self-esteem was hindering educational achievement but also that the emphasis on supposedly gender-neutral "creative" assignments was doing a disservice to male students. "Boys do not always see the intrinsic worth of 'Imagine you're a sock in a dustbin,'" the headmasters advised. "They want relevant work."

AN UGLY RECORD

Since the self-esteem movement made its mark in schools, America's students have not shown significant progress. Quite the contrary.

In recent generations, America's young have performed steadily worse on standardized tests. During the past two years, two separate analyses, one by Jay Greene, an education researcher, and one by the Business Roundtable in affiliation with Northeastern University, have suggested that the nation's official statistics severely undercount the number of high-school dropouts, and that the actual rate may be as high as 30 percent instead of the 11 percent quoted by the U.S. Department of Education.[1] Far too many of those dropouts are males, who may then go on to figure in two further sets of statistics—the unemployment rate and the prison population. The nonstop emphasis on feelings and self-worth has given us two groups of students, one consisting of those who do not feel appreciably better about themselves, and one consisting of those who perhaps feel a little *too* good about themselves and their rightful place in the universe. (In any case, few young people seem to have achieved that happy balance the self-esteem vanguard no doubt envisioned.) It is also clear that schools have done children no favor by essentially trying to extend the coddling "womb experience" throughout their educational years. Such students too often emerge woefully unprepared for the cold realities of postscholastic life. Like the broader SHAM phenomenon out of which it grew, the self-esteem movement not only has failed to deliver on its promises but, in at least some respects, has wrought the exact opposite of what was intended.

Maybe we need to rethink our emphasis on feeling good, before there's precious little left to feel good about.

11

PATIENT, HEAL THYSELF

> Modern health quacks are supersalesmen. They play on fear. They cater to hope. And once they have you, they'll keep you coming back for more.
>
> —*Stephen Barrett, MD, and William T. Jarvis, PhD, Quackwatch*

SCENE 1. On September 3, 2001, Larry King gave over his acclaimed CNN talk show to psychic and best-selling author Sylvia Browne "for the full hour," as King likes to say in touting A-list guests. Already celebrated among her disciples for reuniting the bereaved with long-lost relatives and diagnosing the unspoken upheaval in marriages, Browne lately had turned her attention to a more basic type of diagnosis: telling people what ails them. Her performance on King's show that night was classic. Undeterred by her lack of any formal credentials except a master's degree in English literature, Browne used medical terminology freely, and sometimes even correctly. She told one caller to "check your bilirubin," a hemoglobin by-product Browne misdefined as a liver enzyme. She recommended that another caller test herself for Epstein-Barr disease by analyzing her solid waste (even though the medical literature neither sanctions nor even mentions any such test). She used the words *embolism, hemorrhage, clot*, and *stroke* pretty much interchangeably, and at one point sounded as though she were prescribing the drug Tegretol, an anticonvulsant/painkiller with potentially life-threatening side effects, for a caller—something people bereft of medical licenses cannot, by law, do. Nonetheless, King seemed impressed, and viewers who got through no doubt felt truly fortunate, inasmuch as Browne usually charges $700 for telephone health readings.

SCENE 2. Debbie Benson's death in July 1997, at age fifty-five, punctuated a sixteen-month quest to avoid traditional medicine at literally any cost. The previous March, her first mammogram in almost a decade had revealed a small breast tumor. Though she agreed to a lumpectomy, Benson refused all conventional follow-up. Instead she consulted a succession of dubious healers who emphasized the medicinal power of positive thinking and prescribed oddball tinctures and salves. (One of them liked to check for the spread of cancer using a magnetized pendulum.) Even as Benson's condition deteriorated, the fringe practitioners to whom she'd entrusted her life continued to warn her away from conventional health care. When Benson's body began to shut down, her naturopath blamed not the questionable treatments, or even the rampant cancer, but the patient herself. Debbie, it seems, had "given up" and was no longer marshaling enough "positive energy" to beat back the rogue cells ravaging her body. Though diagnostic hindsight is unreliable, Benson's close friend of three decades, Ken Spiker, remains convinced that more aggressive mainstream treatment might have saved her life, could have prolonged it, and certainly would have eased Debbie's suffering at the end. "Her official diagnosis was cancer, but she was really a victim of quackery," Spiker told me.

If the first scene provides a quick snapshot of America's latter-day ardor for health-care "choice"—as we'll see, yet another illegitimate child of the self-help movement—the second one provides a vivid snapshot of the associated risks.

"FAITH HEALING FOR THE MASSES"

In a survey of thirty-one thousand U.S. adults released in May 2004 by the National Center for Complementary and Alternative Medicine (NCCAM), which operates under the aegis of the National Institutes of Health, 36 percent of respondents admitted to using alternative medicine in some form during the previous calendar year. When the various permutations of "therapeutic prayer" were added to the list of alt-med options, overall usage shot to 62 percent. A whopping 75 percent of respondents said they had turned to alternative medicine at some point in their lives. An earlier study on the subject, reported in November 1998 in the *Journal of the American Medical Association*, showed that Americans spent $27 billion out of pocket on unconventional therapies in 1997, and that between 1990 and 1997, alt-med use rose 47 percent. By the latter year, the total number of patient visits to all types of alt-med practitioners—at 629 million—easily eclipsed the 386 million visits to traditional primary-care physicians.

In what, specifically, are Americans investing this unblinking faith? Popular mind/body methods include:

THERAPEUTIC TOUCH. The theory here is that myriad conditions can be cured by correcting disruptions in the energy field that supposedly surrounds us. Therapists wave their hands over the patient without ever contacting skin. The catch: No such aura has ever been documented. Therapeutic touch is a favorite with nurses, who, as one knowledgeable observer puts it, "like to feel more personally involved in patient care and recovery." Practitioners typically charge $200 to $300 for the first visit and $125 to $150 for follow-ups. Incidentally, therapeutic touch is among the psychic phenomena covered under debunker James Randi's "One Million Dollar Paranormal Challenge," which offers the sum to anyone who can prove the existence of one of the disputed anomalies on Randi's list.

DISTANCE HEALING (*ALSO KNOWN AS* REMOTE HEALING *OR* REMOTE PRAYER). Patients agree to be prayed for by "experienced healers," usually clustered in far-flung healing communities like Taos, New Mexico, or Perth, Australia. Skeptics—which is to say, scientists—liken it to voodoo. The cost ranges from nothing (when done as "value added" to other alternative therapy) to several hundred dollars per session.

ART THERAPY, DANCE THERAPY, MEDITATION, CHANTING, *AND* GUIDED IMAGERY (*"NOW PICTURE YOUR BODY CASTING OFF THE TUMORS . . ."*). Sally Satel, the author of *PC, M.D.*, labels this category of prescriptives "Kumbayah medicine," a sly reference to the chantlike hippie anthem.

"Sure, some of it may make you feel better," Satel told me, "but so will lots of things. As therapies, they're no more medicinal than shopping or sex."

FENG SHUI. This fast-growing wing of alternative medicine would have you believe that improved health and other benefits can be had simply by rearranging the furniture. The American Feng Shui Institute teaches its followers how to "manipulate your surroundings such that you make an impact on your finances, health, and emotions." Devotees tout miracle cures for everything from Alzheimer's disease to weight problems. Feng shui is particularly popular in "enlightened" corporate settings.[1]

Note that none of these "methods" involves an actual device, drug, or other physical implement beyond what was originally present in the patient or his or her surroundings. "Could there be a more ingenious way of making money than by selling people a medicinal product that's intangible if not invisible?" asks Dr. Wallace Sampson, the editor of *Scientific Review of Alternative Medicine* and a former chairman of the National Council Against Health Fraud.

That's not to say there aren't legions of entrepreneurs trotting out catalogs full of New Agey products and practices designed to tap into today's unquenchable desire for self-management of health and well-being. Some of the favorites include:

MAGNET THERAPY. This hot fad purports to alleviate pain and enhance tissue vitality by attracting more blood to treated areas. Some athletes and Hollywood celebrities swear by it. Magnets for do-it-yourselfers retail for as little as $5; magnetic mattresses or car seats can cost upward of $1,000. Outpatient treatment runs $100 an hour and up. All this, even though University of Maryland researchers found in 2002 that magnets had no effect whatsoever on blood flow or pressure; the Maryland study echoed the findings of about a dozen previous small-scale trials. Such studies led California attorney general Bill Lockyer to file in 2002 a seven-figure lawsuit against Florida-based European Health Concepts, a major manufacturer of magnetic mattress pads and seat cushions, for making false claims about its products. The Sacramento Superior Court ultimately assessed $1.5 million in civil penalties against the company and ordered full restitution for the California consumers who purchased magnetic mattress pads and/or seat cushions from the company. Also in 2002, James Gary Davidson was convicted of criminal fraud for employing a fake treatment on terminally ill cancer patients. Posing as a doctor, Davidson ran makeshift cancer clinics in Mexico and Tennessee, ultimately pronouncing a number of his patients "cancer-free" after treating them with magnets. That did not stop them from dying. Davidson was sentenced to eighty-eight months in federal prison and ordered to pay $675,000 in restitution (a figure that testifies to the kind of money up for grabs in the world of alternative medicine).

MAGNETIZED WATER. The Internet is awash in companies selling magnetized water and the $60 cups in which to magnetize it. The extravagant promises made for the liquid encourage buyers to use it to treat liver, circulatory, and autoimmune diseases; gallstones and kidney stones; urinary infections; ulcers; allergies; diarrhea; rashes; arthritis; bursitis; tendinitis; sprains; strains; and sciatica. Oh yes, it can also stimulate extra special growth in plants.

DETOXIFICATION THERAPY. This therapy, one of the handful of new treatments that incorporate some facets of traditional medicine, assumes that our bodies have been ravaged by poisons in food and the environment. Though the concept may have merit in isolated cases—such as families who drink well water contaminated by industrial runoff—not a shred of evidence exists for universal contamination. Costs vary with the practitioner's favored method for extracting those toxins. A full sequence of intravenous chemical flushes can run between $3,000 and $5,000.

These and other products are featured at major exhibitions like Whole Life Expo or in megacirculation magazines like *Prevention*. They may be given the stamp of approval by big-name sponsors, like Andrew Weil, MD, who straddle the border between self-actualization and health care and wield tremendous clout in both. Some of the questionable methods have even found their way into the curriculum at such leading schools as the University of California at San Francisco's Center for Integrative Medicine.

This cross-pollination between traditional self-help and alternative medicine is seen most clearly in products that position themselves at the nexus of mind and body, and essentially promise to cure . . . well, just about everything. The One Brain System, developed by Three In One Concepts of Burbank, California, "is a new and unique approach to locate and correct stressors that may be causing dyslexia, fears, or anything that is limiting you from creating what you want for yourself," according to the company's Web site. Three In One president Gordon Stokes writes that by locating the experience that created the "emotional issue" and defusing it, you can rid your body of the limitations that stand in the way of many life goals. A product called Hemi-Sync promises to synchronize your brain waves in a way that will help you control your pain, boost your immune system, strengthen your circulation, combat autism, alleviate depression, sleep, wake again full of vigor and vim, lose weight, rid yourself of addictions, and so on.

"It's faith healing for the masses," Sampson told me. "It's a blend of New Age mysticism, cultlike schemes, and outright quackery masquerading as 'freedom of choice.'" Adds Dr. Stephen Barrett, the chairman of Quackwatch and a thirty-year crusader against medical quackery, "In this industry you have thousands of people working together to promote something where there's absolutely nothing there."

In addition to pseudotherapies, the alt-med craze has resulted in a proliferation of support groups for people connected by a common disease or physical complaint. A September 2000 report by a Canadian panel of health-care experts, entitled "An Overview of Self-Help Initiatives in Health Care," characterized the growth of support groups during the 1990s as "exponential" (adding that such groups inevitably produced a heightened interest in alternative medicine as a genre). In its February 2000 issue, *American Psychologist* estimated that health-care support groups now constitute roughly 40 percent of self-help's Recovery movement, with the other 60 percent consisting of the groups discussed in chapter 8 (which, as noted, tend to link those who share an *imagined* and/or psychological disease).

"In one sense the groups could be helpful, because they give people other people to talk to about their troubles," says Barrett. "My concern is that it can give people a way of coping with their illness that postpones other action. Comparing notes about cancer is not the same as being treated for cancer." *American Psychologist* observes that one of the primary functions of these groups is to provide a sense of stability; patients may emerge from their meetings with an illusion of good feelings that masks the silent progress of their disease. The Canadian report on medical self-help also describes "sharing" sessions for diabetes sufferers during which members swap stories about having cheated on their strict diets, and details how voicing such stories "gave a feeling of legitimacy to minor acts of noncompliance." Would their doctors really want such acts to gain legitimacy? Or, as Satel suggested with regard to alcoholism, is it better that they remain stigmatized?

Do we want people feeling better? Or *getting* better?

The downsides of health support (not unlike the downsides of SHAM as a whole) are seldom weighed, or even looked at, the Canadian report concludes: "A review of the support group literature reveals that almost all accounts relate only to successful group experiences. Although some evaluations of support groups have been conducted, most studies measure only the positive outcomes and tend to ignore negative effects."

We are reminded, again, of the rose-colored prism through which society tends to view self-help: By definition, it's a good thing. At worst, it's innocuous.

Not so with alternative medicine, whose problems really begin with its name. "There is no alternative medicine" was how Dr. Arnold Relman, onetime editor of the *New England Journal of Medicine*, put it in a landmark 1998 article for the *New Republic*. "There is only scientifically proven, evidence-based medicine supported by solid data, or [there is] unproven medicine, for which scientific evidence is lacking." The claims made for alt-med are anchored in a stew of pseudoscience, questionable testimonials, invented jargon ("geopathic stress"), and seductive buzzwords borrowed from self-help ("personal empowerment").

"They claim that science does not have all the answers, and that's true," Barrett told me. "But quackery has *no* answers. It caters to hope and preys on fear. It will take your money and break your heart."

What's more, the heartbreak isn't confined to the starry-eyed and medically naive. Debbie Benson, whose tragic story opened this chapter, was herself a registered nurse.

THE MEDICAL SHAM

The self-help movement cannot be directly blamed for alternative medicine, which has been with us since the dawn of orthodox medicine (and even has won a measure of respectability in some circles thanks primarily to acupuncture and chiropractic). But alternative medicine could hardly have been a more natural fit with self-actualization. SHAM catalyzed alt-med by establishing a climate wherein people not only felt "empowered" to "take charge of their lives" but also honestly believed that the cure to all things physical resided somewhere in the psyche and was under their conscious control—that the physical body operates at the behest of the will. "It's this postmodern notion that denies absolutes and objective reality, and puts it all up to the individual," says Sampson.

Believe it, achieve it.

The Canadian health-care panel that issued the September 2000 report on medical self-help made observations that apply just as well to a course of events throughout America and much of the free world. "During the 1970s," the panel stated in the report's introduction, "a strong self-help movement evolved which not only premised that it is reasonable for individuals to perform for themselves many of the tasks associated with health care, but that people with similar health conditions may be able to provide as much guidance and insight into how to live with certain health problems as can health professionals." The report went on to state that "these beliefs, *which challenge the exclusivity of knowledge and competency of professionals*, are basic to the self-help movement [emphasis added]."

It's a perceptive observation. By its nature, SHAM represents distrust of structure and orthodoxy. After all, the basic unit of social structure is the family, which, in Victimization, is the wellspring of so much adult malaise. Victimization thus urges its acolytes to throw off the shackles of oppressive, hierarchal thinking and to make their own decisions in their own self-interest. *You know what's best for you.* At the same time, we have Empowerment extolling the limitlessness of human potential, preaching that people can overcome anything if they simply believe in themselves and act on that belief.

Overall, SHAM strongly implies that people have been patronized and victimized by the herd mentality—this, even though the human-potential movement has its own orthodoxies that are just as dogmatic as anything in mainstream life. Much like early feminism, which told women, "It's OK to chart your own course—as long as you decide not to be a housewife"—SHAM preaches individual decision making and the pursuit of private truth but is openly contemptuous of the individual whose personal truth leads him to take the conventional path. Nowhere is this distrust of orthodoxy more dangerous than in the area of health care. Ken Spiker told me that Debbie Benson, his deceased friend, "lived in a Portland, Oregon, community which was a vestige of the counterculture." He emphasized her "deep, almost paranoid distrust of conventional medicine," adding that for Debbie, and for her like-minded cohorts, self-help represents "a wholesale rejection of conventional wisdom in favor of the primacy of personal feelings."

The alt-med mind-set thus promotes a bizarre, inverse credibility wherein the further something strays from mainstream approval, the more cachet it achieves among alt-med subscribers. Can a substance be administered in such minute/dilute dosages that (a) it cannot possibly have adverse side effects and yet (b) it magically realizes its full therapeutic action? The ability to believe simultaneously in (a) and (b) is what underlies the growing "field" of homeopathy. In just slightly oversimplified form, homeopathy employs trace dosages of substances (some of them toxic, like mercury or lead) to energize the body's immune system against diseases whose symptoms mimic an overdose of the curative substance. Similar pretzel logic guides cancer patients who "swear off chemotherapy because it's 'too toxic' but willingly swallow cyanide," says Dr. William Jarvis, the president of the National Council Against Health Fraud. (Cyanide is found in the alt-med anticancer agent lactrile.)

The relative handful of serious, formal inquiries into alternative medicine have produced damning results. In one eight-year retrospective study of 515 cancer patients conducted by a team of Scandinavian researchers and published in 2003 in the *European Journal of Cancer*, alt-med therapies as a class yielded higher mortality rates than those found among nonusers—79 percent versus 65 percent. Far from giving cancer patients new hope, researchers concluded, alternative medicine actually might worsen the prognosis, *even for patients simultaneously receiving conventional treatment*. In 1998 the University of California at San Diego looked at 172 childhood deaths from faith healing (in effect the same as distance healing) over a twenty-year period and concluded that 140 of the deaths were from conditions with a 90 percent survival rate when treated conventionally. Many other alt-med therapies are so lacking in protocols, controls, and any kind of consistent application, says Quackwatch's Barrett, that "there's just no way to reliably test them. You either believe it or you don't."

When confronted, alt-med proponents often fall back on the argument that such therapies don't lend themselves to clinical rigor or peer review in the first place. As Sally Satel says of the high priests of therapeutic touch, "They'll tell you, 'If you don't do it right, you can get a backup of energy—it flows back into the practitioner—so you won't see the expected results.' I mean, *really*." Other alt-med proponents claim that the tests are rigged. They allege a Machiavellian conspiracy on the part of the American Medical Association, the Food and Drug Administration, the American Cancer Society, and other institutional interests to keep the public sick and dependent.

Alt-med apologists can point to high-profile cases like the pharmaceutical giant Merck's 2004 recall of its top-selling arthritis drug, Vioxx. Merck summarily yanked the drug from pharmacy shelves after a new study revealed a disturbing pattern of sudden cardiac deaths among Vioxx users. More disturbing still were intimations, linked to Merck internal discussions, that the drugmaker had known for some time about the drug's cardiotoxicity but had tried to downplay the gravity: Vioxx had generated $2.5 billion in worldwide revenues in 2003. The story offered alt-med supporters proof positive that at the same time the medicine establishment was warning consumers away from "untested" therapies, it was selling them billions of dollars' worth of products and services it *already knew* could kill them. Dr. D. Edwards Smith, the president of the Maharishi College of Vedic Medicine in Lexington, Kentucky, which trains alt-med practitioners, told the *Lexington Herald-Leader*, "When you ask patients out there, they've sort of had it up to here with harmful drug side effects." Smith went on to say that he expected the Vioxx incident to be a boon for alt-med acceptance.

Still, even if malfeasance on Merck's part eventually is documented in court, such regrettable episodes hardly settle the score for alternative medicine's excesses and failures. And when it comes to rigging tests, the alt-med community has its own stable to clean. In December 2002 *Wired* magazine reported that advocates of remote healing had snagged $1.5 million in federal grant monies by massaging data they had submitted to the government, selecting only the results that supported their claims. In a sad postscript to the episode, Dr. Elizabeth Targ, the woman who so vigorously championed the bogus results, died of a brain tumor, despite a concerted prayer vigil by healers worldwide.

But if alternative medicine doesn't work, what keeps "satisfied customers" coming back? "For one thing, people use it for problems that are inherently time limited," Sally Satel told me. "In other words, whatever was wrong with them was going to get better by itself. Plus, there's always the placebo effect."

I asked the same question of Arthur Caplan, PhD, the director of the Center for Bioethics at the University of Pennsylvania and probably the nation's most respected bioethicist. "Some people go the alternative route because they feel they can't get their regular doctor's attention, so, for example, they'll see the chiropractor for everything," Caplan replied. "Now, the chiropractor's not going to cure their prostate. But he *talks* to them. He returns their calls. Heck, he's got *free parking*."

For not a few health-care consumers, this manifold need to feel empowered, considered, *nurtured*, overwhelms the desire to be kept healthy. A December 2000 study by the *Journal of Family Practice* tellingly suggested that alt-med users "prefer to deal with their own problems."

Whatever the reasons, alternative medicine's ubiquity marks a worrisome trend in self-diagnosis and health maintenance. Consider the danger it poses to cancer patients alone. They face salmonella infections from drinking raw milk and other unprocessed foods, electrolyte imbalance caused by coffee enemas, internal bleeding from deep body massage, and brain damage from whole-body hyperthermia; all of these have caused documented deaths. At clinics providing substandard care, intravenous infusions of various concoctions have caused septicemia and malnutrition; the gratuitous, irresponsible application of corrosive chemicals to the skin has caused horrific disfigurement. The Quackwatch Web site highlights the tragic case of Ruth Conrad, an Idaho woman who, like Debbie Benson, consulted a naturopath. In the course of seeking treatment for her sore shoulder, Conrad mentioned in passing that a bump on her nose was bothering her. The naturopath mistakenly diagnosed it as cancer and gave her an herbal salve to apply. Within days her face became painful and covered with ruddy streaks. The naturopath was delighted. "The lines are a good sign," he told her, "because they resemble a crab, and cancer is a crab." He told her to apply more of the salve.

Three years and seventeen operations later, traditional plastic surgeons and dermatologists finally managed to reconstruct what was left of Ruth Conrad's face.

A LICENSE TO KILL?

How, one might wonder, do alt-med practitioners manage not to run afoul of licensing boards or other regulatory bodies?

To begin with, alt-med gurus boast credentials that skate that fine line between mere silliness and provable fraud. Gary Young, who hawks his proprietary "raindrop therapy" through a multilevel company called Young Living Essential Oils, claims to have one of those notorious naturopathic degrees—from a college that's not accredited to issue conventional medical degrees. Authentic licenses aren't always that hard to come by. Steve Eichel, a psychologist in Philadelphia, once obtained five of them—for his cat. The documents came from some of the pillars of the hypnotherapy community, including the National Guild of Hypnotists and the American Board of Hypnotherapy.

Another effective way to skirt regulatory censure is to offer treatment for maladies that are themselves invented and for which, accordingly, no time-honored treatment protocols exist. Detoxification therapies frequently fall into this category, as do a long list of remedies for dubious emotional dysfunctions. "We all have aches and pains, or reactions to stress or hormones or the effects of aging," says Sally Satel. "Calling these normal ups and downs symptoms of some disease allows the quack to provide his illusory treatment. It's a huge scandal."

Stephen Barrett explains, "These folks have chapter-and-verse knowledge of FDA and FTC regulations and guidelines and work carefully around them." The upshot is that alt-med practitioners must climb out on some pretty long limbs before getting in trouble. "The large health-food stores and herbal interests have lobbied very effectively to block liability," Arthur Caplan told me.

This is where you might expect the federal government to step in, and it has—just on the wrong side. Far from protecting consumers, Washington has been complicit in the spread of unproven therapies, many of which bear the tacit imprimatur of NCCAM. One of twenty-seven specialized subagencies in the National Institutes of Health, NCCAM has its roots in the Office of Alternative Medicine, created in 1992 largely at the behest of Senator Tom Harkin of Iowa. As chairman of the subcommittee that allocated funding to NIH, Harkin, a longstanding alt-med cheerleader who credits megadoses of bee pollen for curing his allergies, earmarked $2 million in discretionary funds for the new agency. Six years later, despite an annual budget that had swelled to $19.5 million, the Office of Alternative Medicine had produced no scientifically valid evidence for any alt-med treatments—not even Harkin's beloved bee-pollen remedy. (The FTC, incidentally, later fined the primary pollen distributor $200,000 for making false claims.) The agency's scientific impotence should have shocked no one, critics argue, since it was a highly politicized affair run more by so-called Harkinites than by scientists. Nonetheless, in 1998 the Office of Alternative Medicine was elevated in status and rechristened NCCAM, receiving votes of confidence from Harkin and other Beltway heavy hitters like Senator Orrin Hatch of Utah and Congressman Dan Burton of Indiana. The new agency, which officially opened in February 1999, received an instant budget boost to $50 million. By FY2005, NCCAM's budget had reached a projected $121.5 million.

Federal "oversight" of alternative medicine is a striking study in conflict of interest. Dr. Sampson of the *Scientific Review of Alternative Medicine* points out that two members of the original NCCAM advisory board were later awarded an aggregate $9 million in research grants. Senator Hatch, who played a leading role in a 1994 law that permits so-called nutraceuticals to be marketed without prior evidence of safety or efficacy, has received six-figure campaign contributions from the supplements industry (which also paid nearly $2 million to a lobbying firm that employed Hatch's son). In 2000 President Bill Clinton empanelled the White House Commission on Complementary and Alternative Medicine Policy to assure that public policy "maximizes the benefits to Americans of complementary and alternative medicine"; Dr. Barrett's own investigations suggest that almost every member of that commission had a stake in the outcome. The commission's final report in March 2002 offered a sweeping endorsement of integrating CAM (complementary and alternative medicine) into America's medical, education, research, and insurance systems.

Still today, there is no mistaking the government bias in its support of alternative medicine. "I think there's very little skepticism left," Dr. Stephen E. Straus, director of NCCAM since 1999, told the *Scientist* magazine in May 2004, just as his organization released its report on alt-med use in the United States. "The reality is the scientific community by and large has been enormously supportive of this." In the release accompanying the 2004 report, Straus noted that with global estimates of alt-med usage hovering at about 80 percent, the United States "lags behind" the rest of the world. This was interesting, since in the same release, Straus conceded that the survey "does not look at safety or effectiveness." You have to wonder: If we don't even know whether this stuff does any good, how can it be said that we're "lagging behind"?

I wondered too, so I phoned Dr. Straus and asked.

He replied, somewhat obliquely, "We have an obligation to lead the way in innovative medical modalities."

"But shouldn't those modalities be proven safe and effective first?"

"That's what we're trying to do. Consumers are already spending billions of dollars. So you can leave them to their own devices, or you can say, 'We're going to look at it in the laboratory and maybe a decade or two from now we'll get back to asking whether that investment was wise or not.' "

"A decade or two? And how much money is spent in the interim? How many people do we leave to their own devices, as you put it, while we're doing our tests?"

"The amount of money as a percentage of all research is really quite small."

"If my math is correct, your total outlay since FY1992 is $717.4 million, most of that since 1999, when you were reorganized in your current form. It's a fact, isn't it, that to date you have not come up with research that validates a single CAM method you've tested?"

"We've provided important contributions to the existing body of knowledge of methods that show promise, and certainly we've helped dispel the aura around some methods that don't seem to work."

"So if I come out tomorrow with a statement that says that chanting 'I am well' while inhaling my special recipe for pesto sauce can cure, say, cancer, and I get some people in my neighborhood to buy in, I could conceivably get NIH to study it?"

Straus was not happy with the question, and he let me know it. He reminded me that NCCAM denies most grant applications and said he was tired of the "perception" that his office is "an easy mark" for research money.

"But," I pressed, "you make it clear that you study things based largely on whether or not consumers are using them. That might seem ass-backwards to some, especially with life and death at stake. Given the low odds of success, wouldn't NCCAM's current $121 million be better spent on an ad campaign warning people about the dangers of alternative medicine?"

"The studies show that alternative and complementary medicine is deeply entrenched. It offers a great deal of promise to people, as well as offering medical promise. For us to pooh-pooh it seems arrogant and unrealistic."

And 'round and 'round we went.

A decade from now, according to Wallace Sampson, Stephen Barrett, and other alt-med critics, the government's benign involvement in alternative medicine will have cost significantly more than $1 billion and probably will not have produced any functional guidelines for responsible usage.

Sampson offers a simple remedy: Defund NCCAM. "Its very existence," he says, "lends legitimacy to implausible methods. And it's an insult to standard, proven medicine."

COMING SOON TO A HOSPITAL NEAR YOU

Perhaps the most striking irony in modern health care is that many of the same major medical institutions that once went to such great lengths to discredit nonstandard treatments are now tripping over their crash carts in their rush to embrace CAM therapies. "We're all channeling East Indian healers along with doing gallbladder removal," says Arthur Caplan of the University of Pennsylvania, who has no illusions about what's behind the trend. "I wish it were as noble as 'I want to be respectful to Chinese healing arts.' But it's more 'Gee, people are spending a *fortune* on this stuff. We could bring it inside, do this plus the regular stuff we do, and bill 'em for all of it!'" With stunning candor, he adds, "I have seen in my own school [the attitude that] if this stuff wasn't billable, we wouldn't be doing it. You are *not* going to convince me that most of the doctors who see the aromatherapy office down the hall say, 'Good, yeah, this really works.' They know they're just capturing customers."

All of which suggests a cloudy prognosis for health-care consumers. "You have the books, the Internet, the infomercials, the multilevel marketing," says Barrett. "You have it in hospitals now. You have all these channels for the charlatans to communicate misinformation."

It must be remembered that the "wellness" market has become a major target for self-help impresarios like Tony Robbins and Dr. Phil. If, as Caplan argues, even hospital administrators are getting sucked into the world of alternative medicine simply because they see the financial possibilities, it's hard not to think that the same incentive applies when motivational speakers begin selling vitamins, nutrition bars, "nutraceuticals," antiaging devices, and assorted other products that are supposed to maintain good health and vigor. The fact that self-help gurus with no medical credentials have styled themselves experts on how to maintain good health should be enough to give one pause when considering various nontraditional medical options.

With Americans enduring an onslaught of medical misinformation, the oldest consumer-protection advice is still the best advice, says Sampson: "Use common sense. Be an educated consumer. Do your homework. Don't rely on testimonials from friends, because there may be a multilevel marketing thing going on. When it comes to health care, it really is a caveat emptor world out there."

Or maybe just keep in mind that CAM rhymes with SHAM.

CONCLUSION

A SHAM SOCIETY

This is the beginning of a civil rights movement.

—The late senator Paul Wellstone, in his keynote address to two hundred representatives of "America's community of alcoholics and addicts in recovery," at the Faces and Voices of Recovery Summit, St. Paul, Minnesota, October 2001

Over the past thirty years, American society has largely remade itself in SHAM's bipolar image. The movement has gone from personal to political, individual to collective. It may be impossible to reckon the full cost of this (d)evolution, taking into account both money actually spent and revenue lost to decreased productivity and other problems. But without question, SHAM's overall societal impact resides in the *trillions* of dollars. Though the self-help industry raked in "just" $8.56 billion in direct revenues in 2003, we'd do well to remember, for example, a Special Report to Congress on Alcohol and Health issued in June 2000, which estimated the broader costs of alcoholism alone at $185 billion—per year. Other estimates run even higher. Clearly the nation's nagging substance-abuse problem, which we will explore further, reflects shortcomings in the nation's approach to solving substance abuse. Just as clearly, those shortcomings have everything to do with the abiding influence of self-help and Recovery in the structure of those programs.

In the end, then, far more problematic than Dr. Phil's latest book, Tony Robbins's Life Balance Pack, some expensive corporate junket to a faraway wilderness retreat, or an inspirational lecture by a "contrepreneur" is what has been wrought, widescale, by SHAM's social ascendancy and the increasing public buy-in.

The mainstreaming of SHAM dogma did not occur by design. No

government spokesperson ever called a press conference to announce, "We've decided to reorganize the State Department according to what Dr. Phil says in *Life Strategies*" or "If we want human services to work better, we need to consider what John Gray tells us in *Mars and Venus in the Bedroom*."[1] Nor can SHAM alone be blamed for all of the issues facing modern society. But it is a major factor in numerous societal problems. And even when it's just one of several contributing factors, SHAM's influence on its cofactors cannot be overlooked. To cite one obvious example, political correctness, which has played havoc with so many areas of American life, owes much to both the culture of blame, spawned by Victimization theory, and the self-esteem movement, which grew out of Empowerment.

In that regard, SHAM has become like the iceberg beneath the waterline: mostly unnoticed, but always there, and capable of exerting a life-changing effect on all who travel those seas.

SHAM dogma probably has begun to sound pretty familiar by now to any reader who works at even a midsize company. You may recognize it in your office protocols and regulations. Or your boss might be one of those true believers who invests thousands of dollars to have high-priced lecturers come motivate the staff, even though there's no real evidence that such motivation helps employees or the company's bottom line. If you have children in school, no doubt you've seen signs of today's emphasis on self-esteem in the work they bring home, though you may not see evidence of the school's emphasis on much else. Perhaps you're one of those whose family, marriage, or other relationship has been damaged by SHAM's disdain for "codependency," and by its exhortations to put your own happiness first, coupled with its insistence on allaying any guilt people might feel about their own questionable behavior.

We have even seen how SHAM crept into "hard" realms like medicine and health care. It's disturbing enough that some patients are deferring if not forgoing proven medical treatment to pursue fanciful (or downright fraudulent) alternative "cures." Worse, scientific disciplines themselves have felt the pressure to incorporate elements of actualization and have yielded to it; the University of Pennsylvania's Arthur

Caplan told us as much about his own, much-respected university hospital. Even an august body like the World Health Organization now defines health as "a state of complete physical, mental and social well being, not merely the absence of disease or infirmity." Funds that should be earmarked for no-nonsense health programs and disease prevention are sometimes diverted to softer, "wellness-based" models that fund everything from after-school play programs to research on loneliness.

Meanwhile, public health officials have invested millions in "outreach programs" for drug abusers at the urging of advocates like Nancy Krieger, an epidemiologist at the Harvard School of Public Health. Describing women of color who contract HIV from dirty needles and unprotected sex, Krieger wrote: "In response to daily assaults of racial prejudice and denial of dignity, women may turn to readily available mind-altering substances for relief. Seeking sanctuary from racial hatred through sexual connection as a way to enhance self-esteem also may offer rewards so compelling that condom use becomes less of a priority." This language of Victimization helped win approval for a seven-figure outreach program for addicts.

A textbook example of SHAM's ability to turn things topsy-turvy can be found in the field of mental health, where a legitimate interest in supporting the independence of the mentally ill has also given birth to a radical form of patient advocacy. At a presentation to the National Alliance for the Mentally Ill in 1996, Dale Walsh, the vice president of Riverbend Community Mental Health, came front and center with such revisionism. He spoke of how some among the mentally ill have taken to using the term "psychiatric inmates" to "make clear their dissatisfaction" with the "power inequities" of their treatment, and how, in California and elsewhere, backlash against that "patriarchal system" had caused the mentally ill to refer to themselves as "consumers" or even "clients" of the system. The use of such terminology, said Walsh, captured their newfound "sense of empowerment and the place they feel they occupy within the hierarchy" of mental-health treatment. Of his own mental-illness history, Walsh said he used to think "there was something wrong with me," while lamenting the fact that traditionally "people who have been labeled as mentally ill have been considered to have poor judgment." Walsh wrapped up by asserting that modern-day consumers "who use the mental-health system" must "play a significant role in the shaping of the services, policies, and research" that affect them as part of "taking back power from the system." Another mental-health activist, Selina Glater of Sanctuary Psychiatric Centers, has written that "empowerment," in a mental-health setting, is about "clearly stating what it is you need in order to feel whole again." Inmates running the asylum indeed.

Such bold rhetoric invites skepticism on many grounds, the most obvious, perhaps, being the implication that just because people *want* power, they're entitled to it, regardless of circumstances. But the most compelling flaw in arguments like those made by Walsh and Glater might be their assumption that people who know there's something wrong with them are ipso facto the best ones to decide how they can be cured. The notion date backs, of course, to 1935, when a wire-rope salesman and a rectal surgeon convinced America that their new organization, Alcoholics Anonymous, had the answers to treating addictive behavior. Let's take one final look, then, at alcoholism and its impact on a nation that, for seventy years, has put its faith in solutions for which little evidence exists.

During the research phase of this book, I was struck by the words of Henry Kranzler, a psychiatrist at the University of Connecticut and a champion of new pharmacologic approaches to treating alcoholism, who gave an interview to *Psychology Today* in 1994: "There's tremendous excitement, a watershed feeling, as if something is just beginning to happen. We're really beginning to understand this condition, to develop promising medications and psycho-social interventions." *Something is just beginning to happen. We're really beginning to understand this condition.* This, six decades after the inception of Alcoholics Anonymous! Unfortunately, AA has consistently opposed attempts to assess its core beliefs and methodologies. So invested is the organization in its own socio-spiritual approach that it has issued repeated critical statements on chemical interventions, like the drug topiramate, that appear to show promise.

Should it surprise anyone that alcohol abuse in America has been *rising*, not falling? The number of adults who either consume too much alcohol or have an outright dependency on it rose from 13.8 million in 1992 to 17.6 million in 2002, according to the National Epidemiologic Survey on Alcohol and Related Conditions (NESARC). The direct social costs of alcohol abuse are extraordinary. Figures differ somewhat depending on the source and the agenda, but U.S. surgeon general Dr. Richard Carmona says that each year alcoholism claims one hundred thousand American lives in various ways. Some forty thousand die from alcohol's biochemical actions in the body. The substance works its mischief on every major system, particularly targeting the liver, heart, pancreas, kidneys, and arteries, and laying waste to important receptors in the brain. Those who evade the physiological damage itself may succumb to other tragic events incident to alcohol abuse.

In April 2004 Carmona cited a Massachusetts General Hospital report showing that of the 108 million annual visits to U.S. emergency rooms, 7.6 million are alcohol related. Chillingly, that ratio is *three times* the previous estimate. Up to one-fourth of all hospital admissions are believed to be alcohol related in some way. According to the National Highway Traffic Safety Administration, automobile accidents are the leading cause of death for Americans ages thirty-four and under—and 41 percent of those accidents involve alcohol. In 2002, all told, 17,419 Americans died in alcohol-related traffic mishaps. Alcohol also is implicated in one-third of all suicides; for teens, the grim stat is 46 percent. About half of all people who die in house fires are found at autopsy to have had significant amounts of alcohol in their systems.

Despite the effort and money expended on treating the problem—largely, to date, under the twelve-step model and derivative "talky" approaches—health-care expenditures stemming directly from alcohol abuse soared from $18.8 billion in 1992 to $26.3 billion in 1998. The latter year, alcoholism had a total economic impact, including lost worker productivity, of $184.6 billion. Throw in costs related to drug abuse (treated frequently through Narcotics Anonymous, Cocaine Anonymous, and like programs), and the figure soars to $276 billion—a sum exactly equal to the total customer assets on deposit at J. P. Morgan

Private Bank, one of the world's leading wealth-management institutions. Here's another way to put that number in perspective: $935 for every man, woman, and child in America. Year after year after year.

Corporate America, of course, must eat much of that lost productivity. And America as a whole must factor that lost productivity into its battle to remain competitive in an increasingly ferocious global marketplace, against other nations who take a less "enlightened" view of workers who abuse alcohol.

We also have SHAM to thank for the fact that alcoholism is regarded as a full-fledged disease. This forces companies or their insurers to assume billions of dollars in treatment costs and to look the other way when marginal employees relapse time and again. Firing workers for substance abuse, without taking every possible step to help rehabilitate them and reintegrate them into the corporate culture, can open a company to seven-figure civil lawsuits as well as other governmental sanctions. This also puts companies in the damned-if-you-do, damned-if-you-don't position of having to employ ticking time bombs who—as a direct result of their alcoholism (or drug addiction)—may wreak havoc on society at large. Exxon learned this firsthand when it hired "recovered alcoholic" Joseph Hazelwood to captain the *Exxon Valdez*. One night in March 1989, after having a few, Hazelwood left the oil tanker in a subordinate's hands. It ran aground. The result was one of the worst ecological disasters on record, which involved Exxon in a $2 billion cleanup and opened the company to a $900 million settlement of federal and state claims, as well as a $4.5 billion fine. Following the incident, when Exxon quite sensibly decided to bar those with substance-abuse problems from captaining its ships, affected workers sued, accusing the company of violating their rights under the Americans with Disabilities Act.

An estimated 19.4 million Americans suffer from alcohol or drug abuse, says NESARC. Further, according to Hazelden, a nonprofit agency that offers addiction services and data, the typical substance abuser incurs twice the health-care costs of a nonaddicted employee, is three times more likely to report for work late, and is five times more likely to file a worker's compensation claim. He or she is more likely to steal from his or her employer and be involved in, or cause, workplace accidents. As Joseph Hazelwood demonstrates, the addicted worker's subpar performance may compromise the safety, productivity, and morale of fellow workers, as well as endanger the health and well-being of citizens outside the company. An ingenious online tool called the "Alcohol Cost Calculator for Business" (www.alcoholcostcalculator.org/business/calc.php), maintained by the George Washington University Medical Center, reveals that a typical midsized construction firm with 1,000 employees will likely have on its payroll 101 problem drinkers who each year miss 892 days due to injury or illness and cost the company an extra $265,762 in health-care costs and $152,009 in lost productivity. And thanks to SHAM and its fallout, corporate America is often powerless to do anything about this until such a worker crosses a line that no one wants to see crossed.

Ask yourself: If the various SHAM doctrines can exert so much influence in fields dominated by well-credentialed professionals who are expected to depend on science and hard research to guide them, what happens when they infiltrate other areas of American life in which they have far fewer obstacles to overcome?

THE SHAM EFFECT

Although a complete accounting of all areas in which SHAM has shown itself defies compilation, consider a few examples that point to the magnitude of the phenomenon. If SHAM is the iceberg beneath the waterline, what follows represents just its shiny tip.

US VS. THEM FACTIONALISM AND THE RISE OF BADASSE

In America today, the first thing people do is unite under a common banner of victimhood.

The second thing they do is hire an attorney.

We tend to criticize the lawyers for this, and it's true that lawyers exploit the system in devastating ways. They're the force multipliers, taking the evidence for an existing malady and applying it in just about any situation. They have also worked tirelessly to block tort reforms that would curtail their ability to win multimillion-dollar awards from juries. But lawyers did not create the climate wherein people seek to collect millions for slipping on a wet floor or burning themselves with hot coffee—or in which juries buy in. Lawyers did not invent the madness. (Are we no longer responsible for knowing that wet floors are slippery?)

The costs of negligence lawsuits have been chronicled chapter and verse, and lawmakers finally are managing some legislative relief (over the ongoing objections of the powerful American Trial Lawyers Association, the American Bar Association, and other fraternal groups). But few recognize the hidden costs to society, in particular the chilling effect these lawsuits, as a class, have on innovation and—irony of ironies—safety.

In a 1991 article for the *American Legion* magazine, "The High Cost of Product Safety," I wrote of the aviation industry's earliest attempts to develop equipment that might alert pilots to the atmospheric peril known as wind shear, which can send a jet hurtling earthward as efficiently as a Patriot missile. Thankfully, such warning equipment is now standard on commercial jets, and wind-shear-related incidents have plummeted to almost nothing since 1985. But implementation was stalled for years by developers' concerns about the huge negligence awards that would surely result if the detection equipment ever failed. (Everything fails eventually.) To many research-and-development executives, it didn't seem worth the risk. No matter how much good the product would have done or how much initial revenue it might have generated, some companies saw it as a path to certain ruin. Other products that needed inventing entailed far less liability exposure.

As *20/20*'s John Stossel explains in his excellent book *Give Me a Break*, "Tort lawyers attack the very people we need most in order to be safe: innovators, companies that make safety devices, hospitals, drug makers, paramedics, those who stand on the front line between life and death. The lawsuits *threaten* the people who make us safer." Stossel describes how, during the 1980s, trial lawyers made a mint by suing vaccine manufacturers for neurological damage those vaccines supposedly caused in children. "It's impossible to know whether these problems were caused by the vaccines," Stossel writes. "Some kids get terribly sick after vaccinations, but in any group of millions of kids, some will get sick. And the FDA had approved the vaccines." Still, the onslaught of litigation savaged the industry. Whereas once America had twenty-five companies doing this vital research, says Stossel, now there were five. He quite reasonably asks, "In an era of AIDS, anthrax, SARS, and who knows what bioweapon might come next . . . [a]re we safer with five vaccine makers instead of 25?"

Lawyers and lawsuits play an essential role here, as Stossel documents, but step back for a moment and consider the consumer mindset that spawns them: *My kid is sick. Someone is to blame. Hey, he got vaccinated last week. I will blame THEM.*

Years ago there was a popular bumper sticker that read SHIT HAPPENS. It's a lowbrow way of communicating the sentiment, but it embodies the (perverse) optimism that got us through the day, once upon a time. *Shit happens*. Life is life. Deal with it and move on. Because of SHAM and allied influences, however, Americans now operate under a quite different bumper-sticker mentality, one that forms the acronym *BADASSE—Blame All Disappointments And Setbacks on Someone Else.* Whatever goes wrong, we must run through the entire cycle of causation until we find someone else to blame. Ideally, someone else with deep pockets. Like, say, corporate America.

Clearly, some corporations have been guilty of selling unsafe products or otherwise harming consumers, as in the case of the Ford Pinto, the Dalkon Shield, or Firestone's Wilderness-series tires. But too often litigants pin the blame on corporations even when all the evidence indicates that the companies were doing nothing to willfully harm people and that they couldn't possibly have prevented the chain of events that led to tragedy. The fact that people would even think to sue in such cases—and expect to find jurors who will sympathize—is a direct result of BADASSE.

In the mid-1990s I profiled attorney William Lerach for a long magazine piece. Lerach's specialty was the so-called strike suit, which he would file against high-tech companies that had experienced precipitous drops in their stock prices. These class-action suits accused management of fomenting unwarranted public optimism, and thus seducing investors, with full knowledge of a coming reversal. (He was so identified with this type of litigation that executives called being served in such an action "getting Lerached.") Lerach would file his suits based on something he found in a company's published materials or in public statements by executives that appeared to hint at rosier results than the company delivered. Some of these statements took the form of those blustery, *we're-gonna-knock-'em-dead!* rallying cries executives always issue when trying to boost morale among the troops.

In these post-Enron, post-Martha days, there's natural sympathy for any attempt to hold companies accountable for false promises made to investors. But overall, even though evidence existed that in *a few* cases, *a few* executives Lerach sued may have acted willfully, his strike suits had a frightening influence on the scientific culture. To a man or woman, everyone I interviewed on the technology side told me the same story: When you're working at the cutting edge, you can't really promise results. You can *hope*—you can sketch for people your grand visions of the wondrous things this new technology *might* do, someday—but you can't promise anything. That is the nature of the bargain in vanguard research: a few spectacular successes, lots of heartbreaking failures. Everyone, they said, knew this and accepted it.

Not Lerach and the people he represented. If investors lost money, *someone* had to be blamed.

For a period starting in the late 1980s and extending into the 1990s, Lerach's lawsuit machine ran with startling efficiency and horsepower. Most of the cases never saw the inside of a courtroom; merely seeing his name on a complaint would often induce top management to settle. Lerach's considerable legal skills surely played a factor in this, but more important, his targets simply recognized that, no matter the evidence, too many jurors might be sympathetic to the plight of investors who lost money. As T. J. Rodgers, CEO of Cypress Semiconductor Corporation, told me then, if you're not IBM or Hewlett-Packard, "you can't gamble on what a jury might do. There are too many people today who buy into what he's selling; the blockbuster jury award is too prevalent. So you pay your tribute."

They paid, and paid, and paid again. At the time I wrote my story, Lerach claimed to have recovered $5 billion on behalf of his class-action clients.

Well, one might think, at least that money was coming out of the coffers of large corporations. But damage awards rarely come solely out of a company's profits. They come from insurance companies or reinsurance companies, which lay off the tariff to others and/or raise premiums. Or they are passed on to the consumer in the form of higher prices on the company's goods and services. Moreover, punitive verdicts and the attendant bad publicity drive down stock prices, which hurts millions of investors, few if any of whom had knowledge of, or responsibility for, the company's misdeeds. Corporate America operates on the principle of homeostasis: As much as possible, the company will maintain a steady state of operations and profitability. If the company must pay $10 million to Joe Smith, that $10 million must be made up elsewhere. Or, worst case, the company goes under. That may throw thousands of people out of work, most or all of whom, again, bear not a shred of blame for whatever the company did wrong, or was *accused* of doing wrong. Many people, therefore, bore the burden of the $5 billion that William Lerach wrung out of corporations.

Lerach's "success" exacted other hidden costs. That $5 billion could have funded additional R&D, for instance. Furthermore, entire exciting-yet-speculative projects, like the wind-shear device, were scrapped because executives and the venture capitalists they relied on couldn't figure out how to whip up investor enthusiasm without risking an encounter with the likes of Lerach. "There's no doubt that there is risk aversion being built into the system," Rodgers told me. "And in high tech, risk aversion is no good."

Here, then, we see the Law of Unintended Consequences: Companies must provide relief to those who supposedly have been wronged, but in the process of providing restitution, they must put many other people at risk. We see the same effect, for example, when a small number of families who have suffered unfortunate experiences in child care band together and successfully sue or get legislation passed to address the problems. This *should* be good for society; it *should* make life safer. In practice, it does something else unintended: It makes child care not worth the trouble for many potential providers, largely by mandating cumbersome, intrusive paperwork or making liability insurance unaffordable. This gives families fewer choices in child care. It also prices some families out of the market entirely, resulting in more latchkey kids, with all the dangers of same. Is that good for America?

Between 1986 and 1994 I coached Little League baseball, and during that time parents took a laissez-faire attitude toward the inherent, mostly minor risks of Little League. Our league thrived, as did leagues across America. More recently, there has been an inexplicable series of incidents, totaling under a half dozen, in which children hit in the chest with baseballs during games went into cardiac arrhythmia and died. As a result, leagues have had to purchase extra protective gear and more expensive liability insurance. This sounds like a good thing, until you consider leagues in the poorest neighborhoods, which can't afford to make the accommodations. One might assume that those kids are "safer" anyway, because they now have zero risk of being killed by a pitched baseball. Not so. Some will continue to play on sandlots and street corners, probably without any equipment at all. And what of the ones who give up baseball entirely when the league folds? What are they now doing with their free time, in those poor neighborhoods, many of which are high-crime areas?

So: We take draconian steps to prevent the loss of a few lives. We end up putting thousands in peril. These are among the many hidden costs and unintended consequences of SHAM.

A CLIMATE OF UNDUE FAITH IN WHAT WE KNOW—OR THINK WE KNOW—ABOUT WHY PEOPLE DO WHAT THEY DO

Simply put, the growing visibility and acceptance of SHAM dogma helped legitimize psychobabble. It also popularized the idea that mental-health experts know exponentially more about the mind, and its functions, and the root causes of its *mal*functions, than anyone truly does. As self-help books began dominating best-seller lists, as the John Grays lectured America from their pulpits on *The Oprah Winfrey Show*—where they posited their outlandish, self-serving regimens as "fact"—the marginal psychospew that had once been ripe for spoofing acquired an aura of credibility. Heady with their newfound clout and status as social oracles, many psychologists and psychiatrists sought to expand their horizons by peddling their expertise. Meanwhile, others in society, notably lawyers and prosecutors, began to see their potential utility. It wasn't long before psychologists became part of an unholy alliance in America's courtrooms.

In *Whores of the Court: The Fraud of Psychiatric Testimony and the Rape of American Justice*, Margaret Hagen, a psychologist, courageously admits that the booming business of expert testimony not only wastes resources but also yields dangerous verdicts by injecting fanciful psychological theories into life-and-death settings. Hagen portrays modern psychiatry as a "junk science," overly influenced by faddists, that has picked disorders out of a hat in order to ascribe blame where it doesn't exist or allay blame where it does. Though Hagen does not indict the self-help movement by name, she describes much the same historical phenomenon and makes reference to the catalog of dubious dysfunctions it has introduced to American jurisprudence: battered-wife syndrome, recovered-memory syndrome, intermittent-explosive disorder, urban-psychosis disorder, and post-traumatic stress syndrome.[2] All are promoted by growing legions of hired guns whose expertise, essentially, is in nothing but SHAM.

Writes Hagen, "When we admit into our courts as experts those whose main claim to professional expertise is their admittedly anti-scientific intuition guided by a psycho-political mythology with intellectual foundations akin to tea leaf reading, the concept of expert opinion becomes a farce." She argues persuasively that (not unlike Dr. Laura) clinical psychologists render authoritative conclusions based on the flimsiest anecdotal evidence and the briefest exposure to clinical subjects and their problems.

Fellow psychologist William Winslade agrees. "We ask the expert in this area to rescue us from the troublesome task of judging our fellow citizens and their actions," Winslade told me. "He has obligingly provided us with his own confusion in an appealing 'expert' way, with 'special' language and 'special' tests to validate his 'special' knowledge."

Such mumbo jumbo, spoken as fact, skews the legal process, sometimes resulting in the acquittal of the guilty and the conviction of the innocent. The infamous child-molestation trials of seven teachers at the McMartin Preschool rested on imagined abuse and wild theories about how such abuse would subtly express itself in the behavior of child victims who appeared normal. The trial cost California $15 million, stretched seven years from initial accusations to final verdicts, and devastated almost everyone involved.

Similar attenuations in trial procedure can be seen throughout the criminal-justice system, thanks in no small part to the proliferation of he said/she said expert testimony. Even when they involved serious crimes, jury trials once lasted an average of two or three days. Nowadays a trial may stretch on for two or three extra days just to accommodate the roster of psychiatric witnesses brought in by both prosecution and defense "to whack the ball back and forth across the net at each other," as Paul Pfingst, a longtime prosecutor, puts it. In murder cases, an average of one year now elapses between the arrest of the accused and the final courtroom disposition of the accused. No single factor gets all the blame here. But this "psychological component" cannot be discounted.

Capital murder cases easily can take *two* years from arrest to disposition. The costs are staggering. One study of the Texas court system revealed that death-penalty cases cost $2.3 million *over and above* what Texas spends for other murder trials. In New York, between 1995 and

2002, defense expenditures alone totaled $68.4 million for the 702 individuals involved in cases that might (but didn't always) end up warranting a capital charge. A not insignificant part of that sum goes toward psychiatric witnesses whose testimony may be flawed, moot, or even fraudulent.[3] And the kicker: *More than two-thirds of death-penalty cases are overturned* when brought before higher state or federal courts on appeal, according to a 2000 study by Columbia University Law School. *All that posturing by all those "experts," for nothing.*

As Hagen points out, the problem of "expert psychological testimony" isn't limited to murder cases. Parents will lose their children, people will lose their jobs, companies will lose a substantial percentage of their profits—all based on an expert's subjective appraisal of whether or not someone's behavior manifests one of the imaginative "diseases" SHAM introduced into the lexicon. Judge Jeffrey Boles of Indiana is one of a growing number of jurists who has begged others in his profession *not* to allow the courtroom "to become a laboratory for social experimentation . . . based on weak or unproven theories."

"It's completely out of hand," Pfingst told me with a sigh. "The defense gets his guy to talk about why the defendant is really a victim, too, and I get my guy to talk about why he's a monster. Then the defense gets another guy to talk about why the things my guy said don't apply, because of such-and-such a circumstance. We talk about sanity and insanity, but *that's* what's insane. . . . The facts of the case get lost in all the deflection of blame. The law is supposed to address what somebody did. *Why* he did it is secondary." *The facts get lost. Deflection of blame.* Sound familiar?

"I hate the whole concept of the 'expert witness' in my profession," Michael Hurd told me. "The idea of going in there and claiming knowledge of things you have no knowledge of . . . We only know what we know. And a lot of psychology so far is just theory."

A few years ago, this growing concern over "mental experts" induced New Mexico state senator Duncan Scott to propose whimsical legislation covering the state's licensing guidelines for psychiatrists and psychologists. "When a psychologist or psychiatrist testifies during a defendant's competency hearing," Scott's bill read, "the psychologist or psychiatrist shall wear a cone-shaped hat that is not less than two feet tall. The surface of the hat shall be imprinted with stars and lightning bolts. . . . [He] shall be required to don a white beard that is not less than 18 inches in length, and shall punctuate crucial elements of his testimony by stabbing the air with a wand [and] the bailiff shall dim the courtroom lights and administer two strikes to a Chinese gong." The state senate approved the bill, though it was later struck down by the New Mexico house of representatives. A pity, really.

THE FEMINIZATION OF SOCIETY

In a movement filled with contradictions, here's one of the most astonishing: On the one hand, SHAM clearly upholds women as a more enlightened gender and has been embraced by them in large numbers. (It's not men out there snapping up all those books by Dr. Phil and John Gray.) On the other hand, SHAM just as clearly implies that women (a) feel instead of think, (b) prefer mediocrity to excellence, and (c) would rather submit than prevail.

However women rationalize their fondness for self-help, the fact is, SHAM is an inherently feminizing movement, by all the traditional benchmarks of what it means to be feminine. This is true to such a degree that one begins to suspect its overtures to men are mostly for show. On its surface, for example, *Men Are from Mars* purports to teach the genders to peacefully coexist. But a closer reading suggests that its author, John Gray, expected most of his readers to be female and therefore wrote the book as a kind of shop manual to teach them to "tame," or at least comprehend, their Cro-Magnon lovers.

SHAM's feminized thinking has had a dramatic effect on society. It begins in the schools, as we saw in chapter 10. Christina Hoff Sommers, a resident scholar at the American Enterprise Institute, writes that self-styled reformers "have succeeded in expunging many activities that boys enjoy: dodge ball, cops and robbers, reading or listening to stories about battles and war heroes." In their place, she continues, reformers have installed such benign activities as "quilting, games without scores, and stories about brave girls and boys who learned to cry." Sommers recounts the tale of the day-care center in North Carolina that was censured by the State Division of Child Development for allowing boys to play with "two-inch green Army men." The agency evidently felt that left unchecked, such impulses cause all boys to turn into Eric Harris and Dylan Klebold—when, in reality, the opposite may be closer to the truth. Boys have been playing with toy guns and soldiers, and before that toy cowboys and Indians, pretty much since toys existed. But it is only in recent years—since the advent of "sensitivity," "self-esteem," and "getting in touch with your feelings"—that America has seen so many boys and young men acting out in horrific ways. Is it fair to draw a straight line of psychological causation that connects the two? No. But the coincidence is hard to ignore. More to the point, as many psychologists and other experts have argued, attempts to "deprogram" gender and make little boys "nicer" can actually backfire.

SHAM-inspired feminization isn't just happening in schools. Aggression, everywhere, in almost every form, is considered impolitic. A stern, tough-talking president is portrayed as reckless, "macho"; a presidential candidate who displays an unguarded moment of intensity becomes nonviable as a political entity overnight. (What would today's media make of Harry Truman or Teddy Roosevelt?) The introduction of large numbers of women into traditionally male roles—police and prison work, to name just two—came in part because women were finally afforded opportunities they had long been denied. But also, the psychologists and sociologists law-enforcement agencies hired as consultants advised them that an influx of women could soften realms that had been dominated by men for too long.

Women are, in fact, more likely to find a nonviolent resolution to tense situations. A 1987 study of the New York City Police Department found that female officers were substantially less inclined than their male counterparts to discharge a firearm. The most exhaustive look at the subject was undertaken between 1995 and 2000 by the International Association of Chiefs of Police, which analyzed all available reports of American cops' use of force while on duty. Of the 129,963 instances studied, women, then comprising more than 11 percent of the total American police force, were involved just 7.8 percent of the time.

But for one thing, the knee-jerk assumption that nonviolence is always preferable to violence—itself a product of the "progressive" thinking of SHAM and related movements—is open to question. More to the point, the eagerness to involve women in traditionally male realms, buttressed by all those statistics on women's superior skills at "conflict resolution," speaks volumes about what SHAM really thinks of men and masculinity. One finds a fairly overt statement of the ethic in a hallmark opinion piece on the subject, coauthored by a male Los Angeles legislator, that appeared in the *Los Angeles Times* in late 2000. In the essay, County Supervisor Zev Yaroslavsky wrote that the "city of Los Angeles has an opportunity to fundamentally change the culture of the LAPD" through "the hiring of more women." Yaroslavsky concluded that more females should be added to the force "not only because of the skills women bring to the job but because women also bring out the best in their male colleagues." Such intensely patronizing attitudes toward men fairly scream the same premise that lurks behind all those quilting and journal-writing programs that have taken hold in schools: how wondrous life would be if all boys could just learn to be girls!

It took 9/11 to reassert the legitimacy of aggression in American society, to move the nation past "feeling your pain" and into notions of inflicting it, when appropriate. Months later, when reporters asked Secretary of Defense Donald Rumsfeld why U.S. forces were dropping 500-pound bombs in Afghanistan, he unblinkingly replied, "They're being used on al-Qaeda and Taliban troops to try to kill them."

It's the mark of SHAM's imprint on society that such a commonsense answer would have sounded untenably harsh and impolitic before the wake-up call of 9/11.

THE RISE OF THE DEMAGOGUE . . . IN A NATION OF LEMMINGS

It is not hard to see how feelings of Victimization would make groups of people who share in a common form of oppression exquisitely susceptible to the demagogue: the politician or political activist who vows to level the playing field and win proper redress for his constituency. The demagogue consolidates his power by fanning the flames of your impotence. He plays to the paranoia of those who feel downtrodden and persecuted, which SHAM counsels just about everyone to feel in one sense or another.

SHAM, though, has done worse than merely make Americans latch on to the demagogues who purport to speak for them. It has encouraged and facilitated a lemming culture, a political system full of constituents who, having surrendered themselves to their favorite higher power, now follow blindly and unquestioningly. And so, no matter how outrageous the platforms these politicians advance, no matter what scandals they may become embroiled in, their followers—who, remember, long ago gave up thinking for themselves—swear continued allegiance, make excuses for them, and attempt the most improbable logical gymnastics in order to rationalize the demagogue's behavior. How else to explain a Marion Barry? You may recall that Barry served as mayor of Washington, DC, for a dozen years—until his videotaped hotel crack-fest landed him in federal prison in late 1990. After his release, the good people of Washington elected him as a councilman, then made him their mayor again in 1994; that last mayoral term proved unsuccessful, but in 2004 the ever-resilient Barry was elected once again as a city councilman.

One also has to feel the "check your brains at the door" approach to political faith bears some responsibility for the bitter ad hominem tenor that characterizes today's political discourse, as well as the philosophical absolutism that grips the followers of the two main parties. Republicans can't find anything bad to say about fellow Republicans, or anything good to say about Democrats. Democrats can't find anything bad to say about fellow Democrats, or anything good to say about Republicans. Watch *Hardball* or *Hannity & Colmes* sometime. No one gives an inch.

"At a certain point," says pundit and *This Week* anchor George Stephanopoulos, "people are committing to the label, not what it means." For example, his old boss, Bill Clinton, basically switched parties before his second term, proposing a welter of reforms that co-opted the Republican agenda, while disavowing some key facets of traditional liberalism. No one jumped ship, and Clinton won reelection handily. "He was the party standard-bearer," Stephanopoulos told me. "That's all that mattered."

Demagoguery tends to be victim-specific. Jesse Jackson and Al Sharpton speak for blacks, Patricia Ireland and Gloria Steinem hype women's issues, John D'Emilio presents himself as the voice of homosexuality. Most elected politicians are expert at incorporating aspects of demagoguery into their standard patter, cleverly pandering to this or that "disenfranchised" group while they're in front of the group itself, cleverly backing away from those remarks when they're in front of a competing group. (This balancing act has become tougher, since SHAM has created so many more classes of hopelessness.)

Today, the great danger of a careless demagogic outreach to a perceived set of politically expedient victims is that it ends up as a horribly expensive, maddeningly imprecise piece of legislation. The Americans with Disabilities Act (1990) was championed by lawmakers of both parties, who framed it as an attempt to do right by a class of unfortunate citizens that had been too long ignored. But as the ADA took shape, it became clear that it would ignore almost no one. Its proponents and their working committees were so afraid of offending or excluding the voting blocs they had courted that they left the language of the bill as vague as possible. The information sheet accompanying the act described it as "a landmark federal legislation that opens up services and employment opportunities to the 43 million Americans with disabilities." In 1990 the U.S. population stood at just under 249 million. That means a law designed to help victims of "disabilities" would end up covering one in six Americans. Subsequent cases brought under the law have resulted in challenges that—experts predicted at the time—could have expanded the ADA's purview to as many as 160 million.[4]

That's nearly *two-thirds* of America's citizens. Is everyone disabled?

Though the ADA has brought about many useful reforms for the people who truly needed accommodation, it has also resulted in a fair amount of opportunistic lunacy, much of which can be traced back to the overly broad vocabulary of Victimization used by vote-seeking demagogues:

- A university fires a professor for sexually harassing students. He sues, claiming he has a "sexual disability."
- A cop in North Carolina refuses to work the night shift, saying she has a "shift-work sleep disorder."
- A woman who dislikes working alongside a number of older male coworkers sues, alleging that lingering childhood trauma over sexual abuse inflicted by her father and his cronies made her paranoid about working among men of his generation.

All in all, the law stands as a prime lesson in what happens when sloppy demagoguery meets over-the-top application of Victimization theory.

Demagogic overtures to SHAM-bred audiences have a natural tendency to oversimplify the message. "Political message points today aren't overly nuanced," one top political consultant told me. "You'll support a war or you won't. You favor affirmative action or you don't. There's none of this 'Depending on the course of events in such-and-such . . .' That's nuance, and nuance doesn't sell." Let's be clear here: Vulnerability to a simplistic message has little to do with intelligence per se, but rather stems from what one might call conditioned impatience. A constituency accustomed to twelve straightforward steps, or the facile bullet points inspired by SHAM in general, has no tolerance for esoteric rants or multiple shades of gray. The kind of audience that's ripe for demagoguery expects the same monosyllabic clarity from politicians that it gets from a Dr. Phil, or finds in any of Stephen Covey's hallowed *7 Habits*. During his sometimes embarrassing late-1970s stint as U.S. ambassador to the United Nations, Andrew Young told an interviewer that American jails held "thousands of political prisoners." Certainly racism figured in the incarceration of some young African Americans, especially then. But that's not how Young—the nation's formal emissary to the world's best hope for mutual understanding—chose to say it. He appealed to a paranoid, simplistic view of the American social divide. Andrew Young used the bullet points. That was demagoguery at its best, or worst.

SHAM, translated into demagoguery, puts even more pressure on all politicians to reduce the most complex topics to simpleminded sloganeering. Health care, global terrorism, and welfare reform must be distilled to the geopolitical equivalent of "Get real!" This is not helpful in a nation trying to sort through issues that defy a quick fix.

But what the demagogue mostly stresses is "Get yours!" Demagoguery boldfaces the culture of us versus them that simmers in so many Americans after years of immersion in Victimization theory. There is your side, or there is my side. There is no middle ground that provides a safe haven in this roiling sea of disparate cliques, with its masses of helpless, angry people looking for a lifeline that canny politicos are only too happy to throw.

And throw, and throw. The rise of the demagogue has created a self-perpetuating class of forever-victims. There was a time when almost all Americans viewed victimhood and oppression as a temporary, transitional status. American values, with their profound sympathy for the underdog, have always favored victim assistance, in part because it was assumed that affected individuals sooner or later found their way back to solid ground. But the emergence of SHAM dogma created a permanent class of victims who keep voting the demagogue, or demagogic party, that reinforces and rewards their victimhood. It's a never-ending cycle.

This same cycle rewards poll-based governance, with politicians making crucial decisions based less on what they think is right and more on how their actions might play to politically attractive blocs. In the end, America gets the political leadership it deserves. As Wendy Kaminer writes in *I'm Dysfunctional, You're Dysfunctional*, "This cynicism, this willingness of people who feel victimized and out of control to believe anything or nothing, trust everyone and no one, hardly makes for responsible political leadership."

In light of the SHAM worldview that presupposes widespread helplessness and the necessity of remedial intervention from on high, I think again of what the esteemed historian Stephen Ambrose once told me about the way Americans used to look at government: "It wouldn't have occurred to you to think of your station in life in the context of government policy. For better or worse, it was your life, and you owned it." That has changed in recent decades. The blame for this cannot be pinned on SHAM alone, of course. But there's little question that Victimization's early notions of masses of people trapped by their deep-seated shortcomings helped solidify the view of government-as-surrogate-parent. Washington's job was to ameliorate any gross differences between the "lucky" and "unlucky" children in the great family of man.

It should surprise no one, then, that politicians increasingly are reaching out to the ready-made victims' groups—alcoholics, drug addicts, ex-cons, and the like. This was explicitly the case at the Faces and Voices of Recovery Summit 2001, chaired by Senator Paul Wellstone and intended to give substance abusers a louder voice in society.

The real question seems to be: What took so long?

THE NEED TO BELIEVE

Should you ever have occasion to use the master bathroom in my house, one of the first things you'll notice is a small framed plaque that reads I DON'T JUST BELIEVE IN MIRACLES . . . I COUNT ON THEM.

I admit to being an accomplice to the plaque's presence. I hung it for my wife, who professes to believe in miracles and, yes, probably counts on them, no less so because she's been married to me for three decades and still awaits my rehabilitation.

These days, as we've seen, my wife has tens of millions of cobelievers in salvation via mechanisms that can't be seen, touched, felt, or even explained in any cogent sense. Of course, I'm no longer talking about religious phenomena here—though in a way I am. Surely parallels exist between religion and today's SHAM. Surely people expect the same transformative magic from self-help that they once would have expected only from divine intervention. Surely the self-help movement's evangelical outreach equals, if not exceeds, that of many organized faiths. And surely there are hordes of Americans whose loyalty to Phil McGraw or Tony Robbins bespeaks the same fanaticism that a half century ago might have been found only in places of worship, or maybe at witchcraft covens. You think I overstate? Remember that Marianne Williamson calls her signature program "a course in miracles."

As with so many troubling trends, the Self-Help and Actualization Movement took shape around the core of a good idea. After all, what could be so wrong with showing people "how they can use the power of their bodies and minds to make their lives better," as my former employer Rodale put it? Nothing—on the face of it. But self-help hasn't lived up to its self-billing, or even its name. In fact, almost by definition, the most successful self-help guru will *not* help people, or at least will never alleviate their growing dependency on him. If his customers continue to have the problems that brought them to him—or if he can send them home with new ones—they will run to buy the next book in the series, or line up to buy tickets when the guru's seminar comes to town, reverting to the wide-eyed children they once were, only flocking now to a different kind of circus. That would be bad enough if the problem was limited to those wide-eyed millions who file into bookstores and seminar halls. But as we've also seen, none of us today is immune.

There's a tendency to heap most of the criticism on Victimization, but in the end Empowerment is just as flawed, just as silly, and maybe even more diabolical. If Victimization teaches us to deny our faults, Empowerment teaches us to revel in them. A New Jersey group, the Overweight Association of America, proclaims in a press release that fat people are sick and tired of being harassed over their appearance and overall physical condition. That is all well and good, but the group goes on to say that its members are happy with the way they are, that they see fat as "a positive" in their lives, as well as part of their collective self-image. They have no plans to change and the world had better learn to take them as they are.[5]

Maybe they shouldn't be exploited or used as props, as was the case on Dr. Phil's TV show. But should they be selling obesity as a merit badge? Is it a good thing to feel that empowered about a proven risk factor in so many life-threatening medical conditions? Should society really take them as they are, without complaint, when they cause so many added costs for employers and society as a whole? Should their families look the other way while they continue to self-destruct? Is *that* what we mean by Empowerment?

In SHAM's distorted view of life, each of us is his or her own special-interest group. This has contributed to the splintering of society into endlessly smaller segments and subsegments, each divided from others by the "nichiest" of concerns, each pursuing its own private-label happiness.

Ironically, it may be *there*—the pursuit of happiness, "reaching for the stars"—where SHAM has most led us astray, as individuals and a nation.

For one thing, the actualization worldview rests on a logical foundation that would never pass inspection. Today's champions of uncompromising positive thought portray their endeavor as the rising tide that lifts all boats—a society-wide metamorphosis that's supposed to enable America en masse to reach new levels of fulfillment and prosperity. That is plainly impossible. Barring a wholesale change in the way the free market (in the broadest sense) operates, we can't all be chiefs. In any competitive closed system, there must be a loser for every winner. By definition, then, self-help *cannot work for everyone*, and the more competitive the realm, the more this is so. Two wonderfully optimistic women who both desire the same man or the same job cannot both succeed. So yes, in an abstract sense, if it works—*if* it works—self-help could conceivably help some of us achieve our goals. But not all of us. Certainly not all the time.

Mass-market self-help is a contradiction in terms. I have been to sales seminars where the overeager trainer implied to 250 real-estate professionals from the same company that *all* of them could be the firm's number one salesperson next year. One of them will be. The other 249 will not. No matter what self-help promises, it is simply reality that in life only a certain number of people can achieve the kind of success that many more strive for. True, we have no way of knowing which of us will achieve that success, so there's some value in saying "why not me?" But the straight-line progression that the current brand of self-help draws between effort and result—"do this, get that, be happy"—is spurious and misleading. Though we don't know *who* will win, we do know that the vast majority of people *will lose*. (And we don't really know if winning whatever it is we're out to win will make us happy—do we? Not till we get there. And sometimes not till much later.)

Today's overly optimistic brand of self-help prevents its followers from concentrating on what's realistically achievable for them; in fact, it teaches them to take umbrage at the very notion of realism: *Who are you to tell me what I can and can't do? What I should and shouldn't aspire to!* Legitimate mental-health experts will tell you that you have to be able to try your best while also knowing *and accepting* that the higher you aim, the greater the odds that you will fail. Not all such counsel or criticism is intended to "rob you of your dreams" per se, especially when that counsel comes from multiple people who know something about what it is you're out to achieve for yourself. In most cases they're just trying to save you from a life of frustration, humiliation, and defeat, while also encouraging you to focus your energies where they'll likely do you the most good. "There are a lot of young people today," jokes one expert I interviewed, "who really need somebody to rob them of their dreams."

Kidding aside, there's a serious message here: Rising expectations are not always a good thing and can even backfire. In fact, that is one obvious interpretation of a small study released (mostly to a media yawn) in October 2003. The study, based on a random telephone survey of 1,015 households, concluded that 5 percent of the country's adult population—some nine million people—feel so much daily stress that they can no longer cope. Fully half of those surveyed said they were fans of *The Oprah Winfrey Show*. The study therefore assumed a relationship between stress and watching Oprah. Now, even if the study is statistically valid, the mere fact that Oprah viewers may feel more stress than nonviewers does not mean that Oprah *causes* the stress. Perhaps her show simply attracts people with high levels of existing stress. But one can't help wondering if Oprah's can-do message is having an effect she did not foresee: To wit, if you make people believe they have full control over their lives, and then their lives don't get better (or even get worse), how could that *not* throw their synapses into turmoil? Thinking in such terms, one begins to see the importance of realism and being shielded from false hope; one begins to see the potential downside of being uplifted.

Imagine a world in which all of us went about our days constantly taking the pulse of our personal fulfillment. On the basis of that exercise, let us suppose that in every case we "choose happiness," as a popular bumper sticker puts it. Sounds reasonable enough. But happiness and fulfillment are probably not what the mother of three sick toddlers is feeling as she divides her afternoon between changing foul diapers and sopping up puke laced with SpaghettiOs. Should she pass on that experience, walk out the door, and spend her afternoon dallying with Russell Crowe?

I can hardly claim ownership of the sentiment, but it occurs to me that happiness is less a moment-to-moment condition than a long-term undertaking, a series of choices that eventually produces lasting peace of mind. Here again, it is not an orderly, straight-line progression. To put that more specifically—and this is what really rankles many young people—happiness is something you must be willing to sacrifice on a short-term basis so that you may one day have it on a long-term basis. During your younger years you may choose many times to be *un*happy and *un*fulfilled, like that mother of the sick toddlers, knowing, or at least hoping, that in the long run you'll come out the better for it. Surely your children will.

The mother/child construct is just one example. There are many instances in life when the "choose happiness" mantra makes little sense and will only result in chaos, if not devastation. Sometimes, paradoxically, in order to keep yourself on the Road to Happy, you must choose Sad. Regrettably, it can be almost impossible to know, in the moment, *when* those transient sacrifices are needed in order to "buy" future benefits. The mother with the sick toddlers has a pretty good idea: She has to stay home and take care of her kids, no matter what she'd rather be doing.

What about the person who's presently stuck in a stable but less-than-exciting job? Or the newlywed whose marriage is getting him down? Those are harder calls that cannot be mediated by the simple-minded, black-and-white language of self-help in any of its forms. "Americans have this notion that if we only do certain things, we can be happy all the time; we *should* be happy all the time," says David Blankenhorn. "That's just not so. It's not real life. We need to reach a level of acceptance of what real life is about."

After all the reams of data I have studied for this book, after all the interviews and years of research, when I try to encapsulate SHAM in my mind, I can't help thinking of a woman I know who's been buying self-help books for twenty years and has never made a meaningful change in her life. She sings the ennobling mantras from memory, she's got the vaunted self-talk down pat—but her life remains the same. In short, she remains who she is—and who she is, I might add, is a lovely human being. Still, she has been led to believe that there's something wrong with her, that she is failing to achieve the mission God (or at least Dr. Phil) intended for her. To my read, she is constantly asking herself if she's "happy enough," instead of simply kicking back and experiencing the many smaller joys along the way. She passes them by, unseeing, her eyes focused on the elusive pot of gold at the end of an always-receding rainbow.

We all want so badly to believe in miracles.

That's what makes us vulnerable.

And that's what makes them rich.

NOTES

INTRODUCTION: HOPELESSLY HOOKED ON HELP

1. On their hilarious cable TV program *Bullshit*, confirmed skeptics Penn and Teller made this point succinctly. Referring to self-styled guru Hale Dwoskin and his so-called Sedona Method, which promises to solve a cornucopia of problems for its followers, they remarked, "If the problem is that you have $295 too much, he can help you."

CHAPTER 1. HOW WE GOT HERE—WHEREVER *HERE* IS

1. You, on the other hand—again, depending on the state in which you live—have the right to simply stand in front of your car with a baseball bat and tell your banker to get lost. At that point he may choose to go to court and take the next step, which would be engaging armed marshals to visit you with a court order. This is why repo men often come in the dead of night, when you're presumably asleep.

2. Harris did not invent this way of looking at human behavioral function, which was rooted in the "transactional analysis" theories of his mentor, Eric Berne (*Games People Play*). But in terms of *mood*, Harris's effect on the course of SHAM, and society, vastly outweighed Berne's.

3. Self-help gurus from the Victimization camp did not, of course, invent the idea of projecting onto others the blame for all of one's major failings. Blame shifting figures in some of the key passages in the Bible, beginning with a little bit of interplay between God and Eve in the Garden of Eden. In Genesis 3:13, when He asks Eve to explain that nasty apple business, she

replies, "The serpent beguiled me, and I did eat." (Several millennia later this morphed into the rather snappier trademark line of comedian Flip Wilson's Geraldine character: "The devil made me do it!") But not until the 1960s, with the meteoric ascendancy of self-help publishing as a category, did this idea coalesce into a true *philosophical system* targeting the average Jane or Joe.

4. Sample est motivational patter: "Don't you realize you're acting like a dumb motherfucker and your whole life up to now has been nothing but meaningless bullshit?!" Erhard, who was born with the rather less exotic name Richard Paul Rosenberg, cleverly picked the name est for its two levels of meaning: It was an acronym for Erhard Seminar Training as well as Latin for "is."

CHAPTER 2. FALSE PROPHETS, FALSE PROFITS

1. An acquaintance of mine jokes: Can *Chicken Soup for the Ax Murderer's Soul* be far behind?

2. Her doctoral dissertation was titled "Effects of Insulin on 3-0 Methyl-glucose Transport in Isolated Rat Adipocytes." In other words, the usual background for relationship counselors.

3. Deryk's legal surname is Schlessinger, not Bishop. This is a practice Dr. Laura strongly discourages among her listeners.

4. One wonders how this might play out geopolitically, given the many disparate (and probably unresolvable) views of heaven and its entry requirements. "We have seen bin Laden's view of godliness," says Robert Ellwood, "and it is not a comforting one."

5. Check out, for example, the cover photo on her *Financial Guidebook*.

CHAPTER 3. DR. PHIL MCGRAW: ABSOLUTE POWER

1. For the record, beef prices in some commodities markets actually had dropped by even greater percentages the week before these remarks were made. And beef markets recovered a few weeks after the show. Those facts were only haphazardly reported at the time, however.

CHAPTER 4. TONY ROBBINS: LEAPS (AND BOUNDS) OF FAITH

1. Both men are colorful characters with fascinating backgrounds. Grinder was a Green Beret whose facility for languages at one point made him useful as

an "operative for a well-known U.S. intelligence agency," to quote his official bio. And in 1986 Bandler—who also, apparently, did some covert work for the CIA—was arrested and tried for the murder of Corine Christensen, the ex-girlfriend of Bandler's friend John Marino. It was a bizarre case involving cocaine and Christensen's work as a professional dominatrix, among other things. A jury acquitted him.

2. Though I'm sure Robbins did not intend it this way, even the name—Dreamlife—projects that same hollow quality, that sense of unreality, that surrounds Robbins and SHAM as a whole.

CHAPTER 5. "YA GOTTA WANT IT!"

1. Interestingly, this is no longer the case in sports itself. Players routinely skip games to tend to family matters.

2. Unfortunately, some coaches take this approach because their own egos are so inextricably tied to the success or failure of their teams that they simply can't bear the thought of losing.

3. This is a common way of depicting performance throughout the sales world. The home-improvement firm for which I worked during the 1970s expressed our sales numbers as batting averages: total dollar sales volume divided by total number of customer visits.

CHAPTER 7. KILLER PERFORMANCES: THE RISE OF THE *CON*TREPRENEUR

1. Hackers have emerged in droves from the underground and now wear the pinstriped raiment of the network-security expert. A case in point is "Dark Tangent," who founded Def Con. Today, using his less colorful given name—Jeff Moss—he commands large per diems in exchange for teaching companies how to keep the Dark Tangents *out*. A second reformed hacker, Christian Valor—yes, that *is* his true name—once admitted to topping $90,000 in annual consulting fees; he boasted that his collection of grungy T-shirts had given way to Armani. But eclipsing them all is the fabled Kevin Mitnick. The best-known computer criminal of all time has gone mainstream with a consultant venture he calls Defensive Thinking.

2. Some of that six hundred thousand consists of repeat offenders being released for a second or third time, so, in effect, each year's six hundred thousand

is not a discrete amount. Because of the way the figures are compiled, some of those six hundred thousand have already been counted at least once in the thirty million.

CHAPTER 8. YOU ARE ALL DISEASED

1. In recent years, a scandal rocked the Catholic Church when it became clear that a disturbing number of its clergy had been involved in sexual-abuse cases. Clearly the Church has not done right by an alarming percentage of those who trusted it; most shocking were the documented cases in which Church officials protected or covered up for priests whom they knew to have committed sexual abuse.

2. Other attempted definitions of the term *codependency* read as oblique, New Agey pabulum. Typical is this, from a Web site headlined "What is codependency?": "Boundaries are personal human property lines. Every human is a Stand Alone Model. Certain conditioning through guilt can wrongly convince us that we are not." Even a leading medical dictionary describes codependency as "a relational pattern in which a person attempts to derive a sense of purpose through relationships with others." It has been pointed out that the definitions put forth for codependency could describe most people whose lives are built around empathy and self-sacrifice, which are qualities we once admired in ourselves and others. The world of codependency also includes many subordinate labels that twelve-steppers apply to members of malfunctioning family units. Two of the best-known are *enabler* (a person who covers for the dysfunctional family member or otherwise tries to make everything all right) and *scapegoat* (a person who comes to believe he or she is the source of the family's problems). I once received a list of sardonic "children's book titles that didn't make the cut." One of them was *Daddy Drinks Because You Cry*. That is classic scapegoat thinking.

3. In contrast, the psychologist/"masculist" Warren Farrell (*The Myth of Male Power*, 1993) in some interviews has sounded as if he revels defiantly in his more misogynistic outlooks.

4. This study was presented at a conference held by the International Doctors in Alcoholics Anonymous, which bills itself as "a group of approximately 4500 recovering health care professionals of doctorate level who help one another achieve and maintain sobriety from addictions."

5. Bill W. himself succumbed to emphysema in January 1971, after at least twenty years spent trying to quit smoking. Apparently Bill's higher power had no power over cigarettes.

6. The cultlike devotion among Recovery groups has even resulted in internecine squabbling. For instance, a fairly wide gulf separates those trying to conquer heroin addiction via methadone use and those trying to conquer it via twelve-step programs. Though they're working to resolve their differences, the reality is that each group routinely competes with the other for new funding, grants, and publicity. Since each thinks the other is philosophically and procedurally misguided, each group also acts as if it begrudges the other its success stories.

7. For the purposes of the study, both alcoholism and substance abuse are considered psychatric disorders, along with mood disorders and anxiety disorders. Also, it's important to understand that the groups are not necessarily distinct from one another, so you can't simply add the numbers to get a total picture of the problem. As NIAAA's Ann Bradley explained to me, some depressed people are also in the anxiety group, and vice versa. Some alcoholics are also drug abusers but have no mood-disorder or phobic symptoms, while presumably at least some people are in *all four* groups: both alcohol and drug abusers, as well as suffering from both depression and anxiety. However you slice it, it's a sad commentary.

8. Founded in 1976, SLAA is the oldest and largest of the various major sex-addiction organizations, with more than twelve hundred affiliated groups worldwide. Another of the larger groups in this category, Sex Addicts Anonymous, publishes a newsletter called the *Plain Brown Rapper*.

9. Experts credit Dr. Benjamin Rush, a Revolutionary War–era physician, with first floating the disease model of alcoholism in 1784. Among the other things Rush believed were physical diseases: dishonesty, all mental illness, and having black skin.

CHAPTER 9. LOOKING FOR LOVE . . . ON ALL THE WRONG BASES?

1. Also, even more than most SHAM gurus, Gray has a penchant for stating his "profound" points in circular terms. The very first line of *Mars and Venus in the Bedroom* is a classic example: "One of the special rewards for learning and applying advanced bedroom skills is that sex gets better and

better." But wouldn't that be the whole point of "applying advanced bedroom skills"?

2. Data from two other major studies—the National Health and Social Life Survey (1992) and the American Sex Survey compiled by ABC News's *Primetime Live* (2004)—suggest that even if men and women once were sharply divided in their sexual habits, that gap is closing. For example, in the ABC News poll, though gender differences in the lifetime total of sex partners were clear at their outer limits (one man admitted to four hundred encounters, four times the highest figure for any woman), the "average" number of partners—between five and ten—was reported by 26 percent of men and 29 percent of women.

3. The seven sisters are *Better Homes & Gardens, Family Circle, Good Housekeeping, Ladies' Home Journal, McCall's, Redbook*, and *Woman's Day*. In their halcyon days, these seven magazines had a combined circulation of 45 million. *Ladies' Home Journal* still runs "Can This Marriage Be Saved?" though many industry insiders consider it more campy than relevant.

4. Schlessinger had a point here, but that's a separate issue from the substance of this woman's call, and whether Schlessinger handled it properly.

5. The service offered by the dating sites is not self-help in the classic tradition; subscribers are not so much "working on themselves" as looking for someone who's a good fit for the self they already have. It must be said, however, that the dating sites have their own problems, exemplified in the "we know best" paternalism of Neil Clark Warren and his eHarmony.com, which chooses its customers' prospective dates for them based on Warren's much-ballyhooed "29 points of compatibility." It's interesting that so many people nowadays would think the path to personal fulfillment lies in surrendering control of one's options to others.

6. And it doesn't help that society has grown ever more suspicious of over-the-top displays of romantic ardor. A latter-day Cyrano who stood outside his lover's window spouting intimate verse probably would run afoul of stalking laws in many jurisdictions.

CHAPTER 10. I'M OK, YOU'RE . . . HOW DO YOU SPELL *OK* AGAIN?

1. The change involved a different way of doing the count. With minor variations from state to state, the official count involves comparing the

number of students who began twelfth grade with the number of students who actually graduate—a methodology that, of course, ignores all of the students who never even make it to twelfth grade.

CHAPTER 11. PATIENT, HEAL THYSELF

1. I learned this firsthand when I was an employee at Rodale, where we were mandated to observe feng shui's strictures.

CONCLUSION: A SHAM SOCIETY

1. Even this could change, however, if SHAM gurus have any say in the matter. Some have extended their activity into the political arena. Case in point: After writing eight of SHAM's airiest, most introspectively spiritual books, Marianne Williamson decided to fix America. The result was *Healing the Soul of America: Reclaiming Our Voices as Spiritual Citizens*. In this ninth book, which has served as a springboard for lectures and workshops, Williamson weighs in on politics, violent crime, America's global role, the perils of capitalism ("Our national conscience is barely alive as we slither like snakes across a desert floor to any hole where money lies"—this, from a millionaire many times over), and sundry topics great and small. Her antidote for these problems is "holistic politics," even if she has trouble explaining exactly what actions that might entail. In interviews about the book, Williamson has shown a propensity for sweeping statements that almost invite belly laughs. She assured one interviewer that the world's problems can be easily solved—"all that we lack is the intention, the will, and the mass commitment." That's a bit like saying that such-and-such disease can be easily conquered—all we need is the money, the diagnosis, and the cure.

Though she expects her followers to cast out the demonic oligarchy that rules America, she is curiously pacifistic in her view of world affairs. In her book as well as public appearances, she has issued a clarion call for Golden Rule–based diplomacy: "If you give to a person," she has said, "the form of good that you receive in return may or may not be the form that you had in mind and your attachment to the form of the result is in fact part of what you want to heal. When you understand spiritual law, then you realize that everything you give, good or bad, will in fact come back to you tenfold and that's just the way it is."

Sounds good, Marianne. Now go tell it to bin Laden.

2. Psychologists generally agree that extended exposure to truly horrific circumstances can have tragic lasting effects, but post-traumatic stress syndrome has been misapplied to almost any situation in which someone has a bad day.

3. Fraud occasionally occurs because defense witnesses know who's paying the tab and what they're expected to say on the stand.

4. The most notable case was *Sutton v. United Airlines*, which challenged the airline's vision restrictions.

5. As is usually the case in diagnosing self-help's effects, it is probably a slight oversimplification to attribute their stance entirely to Empowerment. Elements of late-stage Victimization may be in play here as well, since these people probably feel "trapped" in their bodies and that their obesity is "not their fault."

AUTHOR'S NOTE

Probing the Self-Help and Actualization Movement and its impact on American society is not unlike pressing your finger along the surface of a thawing, cracking lake: Each fissure you follow seems only to lead to more fissures.

Like many writers embarking on a major work, I began this book with a naive sense of its scope. I soon found that everywhere I "pressed," no matter how gently, yielded new thematic fissures that led me off in new directions. Eventually I realized that this project would compel me to take a comprehensive look at American mores, the broad landscape of human aspiration, and countless related themes, each with its own complexities and ambiguities, each in turn trailing off to yet another set of subthemes. (And sometimes, to major themes I hadn't previously considered. Alternative medicine is in this category.) Early on, when I described *SHAM*'s concept to a former student who now works in daily journalism, she remarked, "It sounds more like a work of anthropology." How right she was.

All of which is a long way of saying something simple: This book could not possibly address every question that occurred to every reader about self-help and its underpinnings. For the preternaturally curious, it may even have provoked as many questions as it answered. That's because *SHAM* tackles any number of subjects and cultural factors whose underlying truths are presently unknown, if not unknowable. For starters, there is the little matter of free will, which was debated in Aristotle's time, is debated now, and in all likelihood will be under heated debate, somewhere, in those final moments before the human race slips into oblivion. Does free will exist at all? Or does our outward behavior merely answer the call of roiling internal forces that make our "choices" for us? Are we predestined, or at least predisposed, to do what we do? If we don't know the truth about such matters, we cannot know the absolute answers to the questions put forth in this book.

That is, in fact, the primary complaint I would lodge against the gurus themselves: They don't know the unknowable either, yet so many of them act as if they alone, among all of mankind, have ironclad solutions to problems that have stymied us since, well, since there was a mankind. (Another example: Just how alike are men and women, under the skin?) Your personal feelings on these subjects no doubt had a direct bearing on the way you interpreted this book. I encourage you to draw the conclusions that make sense for you and the way you live your life. If we seem to have arrived at different endpoints, so be it. That is, after all, what the pursuit of "self" is really about, or should be—isn't it?

But if this book achieves nothing else, my most fervent hope is that it provokes some thought about the things you always took as "givens"—like the knee-jerk assumption that self-esteem is good for you in every case.

A few procedural notes. Though the bulk of the research and writing of *SHAM* took place over the past eighteen months, one could say that this book has been a work in progress for the past twenty years—or my entire career in journalism. Many sources who originally were consulted on other, seemingly unrelated topics ended up shaping key parts of my thinking on self-help. I have interviewed many of my sources multiple times during that span, and have watched their own positions on self-help evolve as the movement slowly refined or redefined itself. In one or two cases, I've watched as sources were effectively conscripted into the movement and became unwitting gurus, of a sort, in their own right. They shall remain nameless, though the alert reader can probably take a good stab at who's who.

I would like to thank my editor, Jed Donahue, for being the irredeemable pain in the ass that he was throughout the editing phase of this process. Time and again he forced me to dig deeper, find one more source, unearth better evidence than I'd given him to begin with. Don't almost all writers say something like that about their editors? Yes. But if you didn't live through the editing of this book, you can't appreciate how sincere I am in saying it about

Jed. I would also like to thank my agent, Scott Hoffman, for his major contributions to the concept of this book.

Finally, it occurs to me that there's a second way in which self-help is like a thawing lake: In both cases, once you fall in, you're in danger of never coming up again.

Steve Salerno
March 2005

INDEX

ABOUT THE AUTHOR

For the past two decades, **STEVE SALERNO** has been a freelance feature writer, essayist, and investigative reporter, writing on business, sports, and politics and their wider social ramifications. His articles have appeared in *Harper's, The New York Times Magazine, Esquire, Playboy, Reader's Digest,* the *Wall Street Journal,* the *Washington Post,* the *Los Angeles Times, Good Housekeeping*, and *Sports Illustrated*, among other publications. He has also served as editor in chief of the *American Legion* magazine and as editor of the books program associated with *Men's Health* magazine, a division of Rodale. In addition, Salerno has been a visiting professor of journalism/nonfiction writing at three different colleges. An accomplished musician, he lives in Pennsylvania.